Migrant Youth, Transnational Families, and the State

Care and Contested Interests

Lauren Heidbrink

PENN

UNIVERSITY OF PENNSYLVANIA PRESS

PHILADELPHIA

Published by
University of Pennsylvania Press
Philadelphia, Pennsylvania 19104-4112
www.upenn.edu/pennpress

Printed in the United States of America
on acid-free paper

10 9 8 7 6 5 4 3 2 1

A Cataloging-in-Publication Record is available from the Library of Congress
ISBN 978-0-8122-4604-9

For WPA

CONTENTS

CHAPTER 1

Children on the Move

In November 1999, a fishing boat rescued a five-year-old boy clinging to a small raft in the waters south of Florida. His mother and stepfather died while traveling from Cuba to the United States when their vessel capsized. A fisherman took young Elian Gonzalez to the home of his great-uncle living in a Cuban enclave of Miami. For the next seven months, a transnational battle between family members, U.S. immigration enforcement, and Cuban authorities ensued, each claiming to serve Elian's "best interests." Family members in the United States claimed that a life of stability embodied by regular schooling, family, and Disney World was best for Elian—not political turmoil under dictator Fidel Castro, which spurred his treacherous maritime journey. Yet Elian's father and stepmother insisted he belonged with his biological parent in a nurturing home and in a supportive community. While the U.S. Immigration and Naturalization Service (INS) considers Cuban nationals a unique category of political refugee, Elian's alien presence revolved around his status as a dependent minor, who under U.S. immigration law could not independently stand before the law. Declining a congressional offer for political asylum, Elian's father, still residing in Cuba, requested Elian's immediate return. Despite a political asylum application filed on his behalf by his uncle, Elian was ultimately repatriated to Cuba, though only after an armed raid by immigration officers "freed" Elian from the captivity of his extended family members in Miami. Images of a masked law enforcement agent aiming a semiautomatic rifle at Elian and his uncle filled the front pages of international newspapers. The "unaccompanied" migrant child entered the U.S. public imaginary with tremendous force, as if Elian were the first child to arrive alone on U.S. shores.

The figure of the "unaccompanied alien child"—an individual under age eighteen who has no lawful immigration status in the United States and who has no parent or legal guardian to provide care and custody—challenges dominant Western conceptualizations of child dependence and passivity, explicitly through these children's unauthorized and independent presence in the United States and implicitly in the ways they move through multiple geographic and institutional sites. Unaccompanied children are economic, political, and social migrants who arrive both lawfully and unlawfully and originate from nearly every country around the globe. They face similar challenges to those of other populations of migrants who confront language barriers, intergenerational conflict, cultural assimilation, and limited access to resources, but what remains unique are the ways the law and institutions frame children seemingly without parents or kinship ties. Independent, or unattached, migrant children bereft of family or kinship networks therefore threaten the notion of how children can and should act. Their unauthorized presence and exercise of "independent" agency threaten the state's reliance on the nuclear family as the site for producing future citizens. Thus, migrant children become a problem to be solved.

In response to their independent presence, the state provides care for youth including food, shelter, and medical attention; yet simultaneously, due to their unauthorized entry, state institutions initiate deportation proceedings against unaccompanied youth. Deportation (often framed erroneously as "repatriation") itself could be seen as a form of care in which the state seeks to reunify children with their families or their country of origin; however, as I will elaborate, in practice, the law may separate children from their families who remain in the United States. In stark contrast to domestic child welfare protocols, there are very few safeguards at the state and the federal levels governing the repatriation or deportation of children, minimal resources invested to confirm the risks of abuse or neglect of even the availability of care on arrival, nor is there basic knowledge about how children are received in the short and long term by governments, communities, or families.[1] More commonly, there is little known about children who are returned to their countries of origin. Some families manage to claim their children on arrival or at shelters for deportees. Some research participants from Guatemala, El Salvador, and Honduras report being abandoned on the tarmac, detained in local jails until a family member could pay a fine or a bribe to secure their release, or, in one extreme case, institutionalized in an asylum for children until a family member located the child three weeks later. In short, with only minor differences, migrant children are removed from the state just as their adult counterparts are, but they face additional risks because of their minor status.

As such, youth encounter the state as both paternal protector and punishing regulator. The policies and practices of the state in response to the presence of unaccompanied children reveal how the state operates through an ideal of a unified entity yet splinters into a multipronged labyrinth with potentially conflicting objectives for solving the "problem of migrant youth." By interrogating child welfare initiatives and legal interventions, this book argues that state practices enforced by nongovernmental organizations and the forms of legal relief available to migrant children trap the unaccompanied child at the intersection of the family and the state by denying or restricting their social agency. I detail how youth distinguish among state and nonstate actors staking varied claims on their behalf and contend that children are active and creative subjects engaged in constant negotiation with state power. While those in power, be it the state, nongovernmental organizations (NGOs), or parents, may assign meaning to their social agency, youth may acquiesce, push back, and, at times, evade normative positioning in their everyday interactions. This ethnography of youth migration traces the ways youth understand and express their social agency in highly restrictive spaces, such as immigration detention. Amid contentious national debates on immigration and security, this ethnography argues that the state's criminalization of immigrants and bureaucratization of care challenge the historic reputation of the United States as a place of refuge for the most vulnerable—children.

Child Migration: A New Phenomenon?

Although children have migrated throughout history, migration studies remains a predominantly presentist endeavor, focusing on historical migration trends only enough to situate existing changes in population-level movements. The presumption that mass migration is a new phenomenon that places childhood itself at risk is unfounded.[2] Historically, government programs have facilitated and even actively encouraged the movement of children. The seventeenth and eighteenth centuries in the United States were marked by an influx of migrants, from Africa, Asia, Europe, and Latin America. African child slaves and children kidnapped from the streets of London alike were forced into indentured servitude in the United States (Bailyn 1986: 302–12); both groups fundamentally altered labor practices of local children working on plantations. At the time, the migrant child, just as the migrant

adult, became a vital unit of labor necessary for economic growth in predominantly agricultural regions. Ship captains and plantation owners
viewed children as vital cargo or units of labor, not distinguishing them as
more vulnerable than adults to harsh labor conditions as we do today (Fass
2005: 939; Haefeli and Sweeny 2003). Similarly Native American children
suffered physical displacement from their homes on reservations due to
institutionalizations of disease and war. In effect, migrant children and
Native American children were expendable and allowed to suffer, just as
their adult counterparts were, not warranting special treatment or intervention. Disruption was inescapable in the lives of many children during
this period.

From the 1850s to the early twentieth century, the U.S. government
orchestrated the transfer of children, mostly teenagers, from overcrowded
orphanages in northeastern America to live on small, family-owned and
-run farms in western states. Many of these children had biological parents
who were unable to care for them due to poverty; some parents enlisted orphanages as temporary shelters for their children during particularly difficult times, later claiming them from institutional care to return home.
Government programs removed some of these children from institutional
care and sent them west via train with the justification of an anticipated
"better life" with their adoptive families. Beyond its perceived altruism, the
state was invested in the perseverance of the nuclear family, removing children from orphanages near their families and often placing them with predominantly childless couples. In this context, the state investment was the
child's "well-being," but ultimately a means of ensuring the "proper" place
of the child within the family. The orphan train riders also became an essential source of labor to struggling farmers and, critics argue, a national
strategy for population redistribution (Patrick, Sheets, and Trickel 1990).

Nara Milanich (2004) provides a detailed account of how Chilean courts
in the nineteenth century mediated disputes over the care and custody of
predominantly illegitimate, orphaned, and poor children, who had been
"sent out to be reared." According to Milanich (2004: 312), the unremark-
ableness of this phenomenon stems from the normality of child circulation
between multiple households, care providers, and, at times, the street. Such
cultural and historical variations in the roles of institutions in the care of
children persist in the contemporary context (e.g., Fonseca 1986; Leinaweaver
2007, 2008). For example, following a 7.0 magnitude earthquake in Haiti in
January 2010, the international community misinterpreted children living

in orphanages as orphaned by both parents. Several children were misclassi-fied as available for international adoption or as "unaccompanied children," evacuated to the United States, and placed under the care of the Office of Refugee Resettlement (ORR), despite having intact families who desired to maintain custody of their children.

Yet, not all child migration was forced; for some, migration actually held allure and promise. In seventeenth-century Britain, urban areas were "magnets to young people drawn by dreams of employment, excitement and entertainment" (Coldrey 1999: 32–33). The early eighteenth century brought millions of immigrant families from Europe to the United States in pursuit of change and prosperity, while the later eighteenth and nine-teenth centuries brought migration of predominantly Africans and Amer-indians. Paula Fass (2005: 940) reminds us that, although families willingly migrated to the United States during this era, "migration had highly varied consequences for children with some becoming successful beneficiaries of the migration, while others became its victims, and that many of the differ-ences were sharply etched along racial lines." It was not until the end of the nineteenth century that both antislavery movements and organizations against abusive factory conditions for children gained purchase among middle-class Americans, forcing a shift in sensibilities toward childhood. This nineteenth-century sensibility, cloaked in discussions of culture, race, and religion, continue to pervade in child protection interventions, which rely on a particular, privileged ideal of childhood still valued in the West (Fass 2005: 939).

Since World War II, the United States has admitted thousands of chil-dren in ad hoc programs or under the auspices of refugee resettlement pro-grams. Such programs range from the 1940 evacuation of British children; Operation Peter Pan, which evacuated over 14,000 Cuban children follow-ing Fidel Castro's 1959 coup (Rumbaut 1994); and Operation Babylift, which evacuated over 2,500 Vietnamese children during the Vietnam War, placing them in American adoption agencies (Ressler, Boothby, and Steinbock 1988: 142). Each of these examples illustrates how orchestrated rescues of children align with strategic government interventions in politically charged contexts of war and political conflict. The state maintains a political investment in the protection of certain children, while others remain ignored or marginalized. Why, for example, was the United States justified in intervening in the lives of British children, while Guatemalan children during genocide did not benefit from formal resettlement programs? Is it acceptable or beneficial to monitor children from other countries only when it is in the geopolitical or economic interests of the state?

Only in the past thirty years have U.S. legislators acknowledged children as migrants to the United States outside established refugee resettlement programs.[3] Between the mid-1950s and the 1990s Asian and Latin American migration, both authorized and clandestine, significantly increased to the United States. Among these groups were children migrating without adults whom authorities regarded with suspicion. Challenging assumptions that the natural state of childhood is stable, dependent, and innocent, the figure of the migrant child has become one to be feared and cast as Other. Pejorative labels, such as "parachute children" (children who migrate to a new country to live alone or with a caregiver while their parents remain in their home country), "anchor children" (children of Vietnamese refugees following the Vietnam War), and "anchor babies" (who by virtue of birthright citizenship in the United States become a future means for their families to secure legal status in the United States), evidence the politicization of the migrant child. Such terms not only dehumanize the migrant child but also condemn parents' reproductive choices as benefit seeking. The persistent use of derogatory terms in the media and legislature has only emboldened conservative efforts to repeal the Fourteenth Amendment of the U.S. Constitution, which grants birthright citizenship to individuals born in the United States (Lacey 2011). Immigration policy analyst Angela Maria Kelley analogizes, "But to say that you want to change the Constitution because of this feels like killing a fly with an Uzi" (Medina 2011). In the past decade, the stakes of the lawful and unlawful presence of the migrant child in particular have intensified.

A "New" Social Problem

There is an overwhelming belief among state actors and NGOs that children are increasingly on the move—migrating both with families and alone. Immigration and Customs Enforcement (ICE, formerly INS), ORR, and advocates alike contend that the rates of children migrating to the United States have risen since 2000, yet these claims are difficult to substantiate. Very little is known about flows of children across borders. Quantitative data are scarce for a number of reasons. The movement of children is often folded into the migration statistics of adults or left out entirely; conflicting definitions of the type and motivations for child migration problematize any systematic account of migratory flows; and specialist literatures on refugees, trafficking, and fostering, for example, stand in contrast to migration literature, which consolidates variation in order to trace large-scale demographic trends over time and space.

Until recently, the U.S. government has not maintained a centralized or even coordinated effort among the various government agencies and departments involved in the care and custody of migrant children to track the inflow of unauthorized migrant children, accompanied or unaccompanied. In their 2006 report *Seeking Asylum Alone*, Jacqueline Bhabha and Susan Schmidt make a valiant effort to gather government statistics on the volume of unaccompanied child migration to the United States.[4] They found a significant lack of communication and coordination between the four government departments and fifteen agencies involved with migrating children, resulting in incomplete, convoluted, and at times misleading and contradictory data regarding the scope of child migration (Bhabha and Schmidt 2006; see Figure 1). It was not until the reorganization of the Department of Homeland Security and the transfer of care from INS to ORR in 2003 that a more systematic, though still problematically incomplete, mechanism was developed for tracking the migratory flows of children into the United States.[5]

While statistics on the flow of children across U.S. borders remain largely untraced, legal experts estimate that over 500,000 immigrant children enter the United States each year (Seugling 2005: 863). Central American experts have estimated over 45,000 Central American children immigrate to the United States each year.[6] Estimates from the Department of Justice indicate 101,952 unaccompanied children apprehended in 2007, with four of every five children from Mexico.[7] However, many children evade apprehension and pass clandestinely into the United States, joining the more than 11.9 million unauthorized immigrants currently residing in the United States (Passel and Cohn 2009). Other child migrants may successfully pass through official points of entry with fraudulent documents or without inspection. Still other migrant children enter the United States with valid documents but overstay their tourist or student visas, shifting their status from student or tourist to unaccompanied alien minor once their visas expire.

Of the 100,000 unaccompanied minors apprehended yearly, approximately 6,000 to 8,000 enter the care of the ORR. From 2007 to 2011, the number of children in ORR care fluctuated from 800 to 1,500 daily. In 2012, there was a notable increase in the number of children identified as unaccompanied

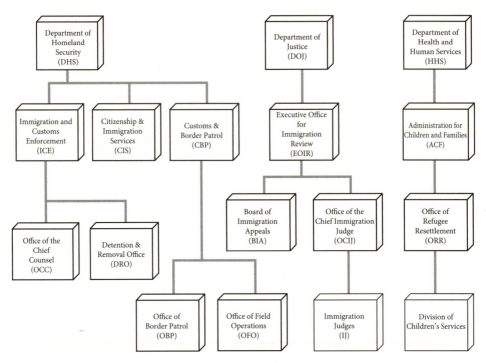

Figure 1. U.S. government organization chart. A network of federal government departments government agencies, and myriad nongovernmental organizations are involved in the care and custody of apprehended unaccompanied children.

and transferred to ORR custody, with estimates reaching 16,000 children annually. Even amid improved record keeping, this relatively small number of total migrant children is largely guesswork for a number of reasons. First, ICE may reclassify some unaccompanied children as accompanied and release them to family members or detain entire families together in family detention centers as a more "humane" way to keep families together in retrofitted county jails.[8] Second, ICE or Border Patrol may not identify unaccompanied children as minors. Some youths lie about their age or some law enforcement do not believe their minor status, continuing to categorize them as adults subject to expedited removal from the United States, instead of benefiting from some of the specialized provisions of detention of children. Third, unaccompanied Mexican and Canadian minors are removed from the United States within seventy-two hours to their countries of origin without a hearing before an immigration judge as a result of the Contiguous

Territories Agreement between Canada, the United States, and Mexico.[9] Some Mexican youths do enter ORR facilities, but at much lower rates than their actual rates of migration. Fourth, some unauthorized youths in the juvenile justice system may be transferred to ICE and then ORR custody after serving their sentences rather than being released to their intact families who live locally.

Since the transfer of the responsibilities from the INS to ORR in 2003, there are more reliable statistics but only for the small fraction of children who have been apprehended. Of the migrant children in ORR custody, approximately 85 percent come from Central America, primarily Honduras, Guatemala, and El Salvador. Of these, consistently 20 percent are between ages zero and fourteen and 80 percent between fifteen and eighteen. Between 74 and 77 percent are male and 23 to 26 percent are female. Table 1 shows the countries of citizenship of unaccompanied children in ORR custody since the program's inception.

The absence of reliable or coordinated statistics is emblematic of the ways children have been overlooked in immigration; either considered as miniature adults or folded into family migration statistics. In other words, children are not worthy of being counted or of specialized treatment or care. Instead of acknowledging this critical deficit and recognizing children as contributors to migratory decisions and as migrants themselves, state dis-

Table 1: Country of Origin of Unaccompanied Children in ORR Custody (percent, fiscal years 2004–2011)

	FY04	FY05	FY06	FY07	FY08	FY09*	FY10	FY11
	N=6471	N=8015	N=8160	N=8227	N=7211	N=6074	N=8207	N=6855
Honduras	30.0	35.0	28.0	29.0	30.8		17	20
Guatemala	20.0	23.0	26.0	29.0	27.4		26	36
El Salvador	26.0	24.0	31.0	27.0	23.4		29	25
Mexico	10.0	6.0	7.0	9.0	10.6		20	12
Ecuador	2.0	2.0	1.0	1.4	3.2		4	3
Nicaragua	0.8	0.9	1.0	1.1	0.8			
Brazil	3.0	3.0	1.0	0.8	0.5			
China	2.0	1.0	1.0	0.6	0.6			
Other	6.2	5.1	4.0	3.2	2.7		5	

Source: Office of Refugee Resettlement
N=total number of unaccompanied alien children in ORR custody.
* Fiscal year 2009 percentages based on country of origin were unavailable.

courses frame child migration as a burgeoning social phenomenon worldwide. Some legislators have advocated for a growing body of laws and system
of care for this growing "social problem" of unauthorized child migration,
as a U.S. representative framed it during my interview with her. The "surge"
or "flood" of child migrants forcing open the proverbial American gates is
an image not unlike one of European migrants at the turn of the twentieth
century or of contemporary flows of adult migrants. An attorney with the
American Bar Association observed, "My sense is that it is not so much that
the numbers are mushrooming, but now our legal system is seeing immigrant children for the first time. They [the children] are here and we have to
deal with it. The law is just late to the game but perceives child migrants as a
new problem, when it really isn't." Children have been migrating for centuries both inside and outside of state-run programs, but not until the late
1990s and early 2000s has there been a critical shift in the "visibility" of
migrant children, through which the state has begun to assign specific significance to their presence. Recognizing that with globalization come increased flows of information and commodities across time and space, child
migration should come as little surprise; yet, it unsettles entrenched notions
of childhood, race, legality, and agency in society and in the law in remarkable ways. This ethnography examines the contradictory nature of how and
when children are seen and of which children remain invisible.

     Following the September 11, 2001, attacks on the World Trade Center,
the U.S. Congress passed the Homeland Security Act of 2002. The act would
prove to be the largest reorganization of federal government agencies since
the 1947 National Security Act, which created the Central Intelligence Agency
(CIA) and the National Security Council and shifted the military under the
secretary of defense. As part of the newly declared "war on terror," the Homeland Security Act also consolidated antiterrorism initiatives, border security, and immigration enforcement under a single "homeland security czar."
The renamed Immigration and Customs Enforcement came under the auspices of Department of Homeland Security (DHS). In March 2003, care and
custody of unaccompanied children was transferred from ICE to the Office
of Refugee Resettlement, a division of the Department of Health and Human Services (HHS). While ORR's expertise in the intersection of child
welfare and refugee populations has shaped the policies and procedures for
the care of unaccompanied children, this program was the first in which
ORR had to collaborate with ICE on a regular basis due to the unauthorized
presence of unaccompanied "alien" children. There has certainly been greater

attention to the care of children at the facilities, in terms of their educational programming, recreation, access to mental health services, and health care; yet hastily crafted legislation has left significant deficits in guidance in the ways ORR should collaborate with ICE. ORR continually struggles to negotiate the best interests of the child, which often stands at odds with ICE's mandate to remove unauthorized migrants and to respond to threats against the homeland.[10]

The diverging state agendas come into regular conflict in a range of areas that I will discuss in greater depth, such as guidelines for legal custody, age determination procedures, placement and transfer practices, family reunification policies, and most fundamentally in the classification of which children are accompanied or unaccompanied. As a result, the transition from ICE to ORR has led to an institutional bias in favor of law enforcement in which the security and safety concerns of the nation continue to outweigh the child welfare concerns of this population. For example, since 2003, we see an institutional trend within ORR toward heightened surveillance gaining momentum. ORR initially reviewed and phased out twenty-eight contracts with secure detention facilities (juvenile jails), placing only a fraction of children in these secure facilities in contrast to the 34 percent INS placement rates; yet, in the past four years, a number of staff-secure and secure facilities[11] have opened in response to the perceived demand for detainment of unauthorized children who have some juvenile justice involvement.

There is an inescapable tension between an increasing preoccupation with the universalization of childhood—a space characterized by play and innocence, by the absence of responsibility and "adult" knowledge, and by less physical and emotional maturity—and the differential geopolitical interests that underlie the uneven treatment of domestic versus migrant children in the contemporary context. The "child savers" movement of the 1820s until the 1920s and the subsequent settlement house movement fostered the creation of a romanticized ideal of childhood in the United States (see Chapter 3). Reformers sought to socialize newly arrived migrant children into productive members of society through compulsory education, public health initiatives, the construction of playgrounds, and the establishment of the juvenile court. Over time, this privileged notion of childhood has become embedded in multinational treaties and conventions, such as the United Nations Convention on the Rights of the Child (CRC); financial and development agreements though the International Monetary Fund and the World Bank; and specialized agencies, such as the International Labour Organization, that guide child labor laws and practices worldwide (see, e.g., Boyden 1990). Yet in the U.S. context this notion is only selectively applied and enforced. The consolidation and production of a universalized childhood stands in the face of how, when, and to whom that image applies. In a national landscape of racial profiling, particularly of African American and Latino males, a judicial process that tries children as adults, with an increased reliance on incarceration of people of color and immigrants, the application of a universalized ideal of childhood is hypocritical at best and racist in its worst forms. Unaccompanied migrant children traverse these contradictory "modes of being" in which facility staff attempt to foster opportunities for education, play, and socialization amid an absence of freedom in detention (De Genova and Peutz 2010: 14).

Seeking Consent

This ethnography focuses on a largely invisible population of unauthorized migrant children in highly restrictive and largely inaccessible spaces, such as immigration detention, border stations, immigration and family courts, and underground communities.[12] While there are inherent challenges to conducting research with unauthorized or "underground" communities, negotiating access to detention facilities for migrant children proved the greatest obstacle. While news reporters have been granted access to ORR facilities on a case-by-case basis, there are very few independent researchers who have been granted access to conduct long-term qualitative studies within ORR facilities and even fewer with children themselves. There are some who have provided in-depth insight from their vantage point with NGOs engaged in the national coordination of services for unaccompanied children, identifying trends in the treatment of children across facilities (Duncan 2002; Uehling 2008) or as former ORR supervisors (Ensor and Gozdziak 2010). Several attorneys have written critically about challenges in representing unaccompanied children in both immigration and family court (Georgopoulos 2005; Nugent 2005, Somers, Herrera, and Rodriguez 2010). Given the dearth of information and access, a 2007 report from the Office of the Inspector General identified the increased need for transparency within ORR and for oversight of facilities in order to ensure the appropriate care of migrant children. Organizations such as the Women's Refugee Commission (formerly Women's Commission for Refugee Women and Children) have responded with research on evaluating the treatment of children and the efficacy of ORR programs and policies, conducting interviews of a wide range of actors involved in the lives of unaccompanied children held in ORR facilities (Women's Commission for Refugee Women and Children 2002; Women's Refugee Commission 2009). The extensive work of Jacqueline Bhabha and Susan Schmidt (2006) approaches the phenomenon of child migration in terms of the legal obstacles children confront in seeking political asylum in a post-911 era in the United Kingdom, United States, and Australia. Their important work speaks to the challenges of securing reliable information and the lack of cooperation among the diverse government agencies and departments. These reports have praised the dramatic improvements ORR has made in the care of migrant children since inheriting the program from the INS in 2003, though highlighting many of the concerning trends in the placement and transfer of children from ICE to ORR custody and between ORR facilities. The irony, as one advocate remarked, is "As much as we [advocates] criticize ORR, we are still saying that putting kids in their custody is what we want. On the one hand, we are finding all of these problems and abuses, but on the other we say, 'Keep putting kids in your custody because it is better than ICE.' It is all a little crazy." My request for access to the detention facilities directly benefited from the timing of these reports and public calls for transparency and supervision. Since then, the window has closed and several researchers have been denied access.

In each of the abovementioned studies, the dearth of access to children in the facilities stems, in part, from the logistical challenges of securing permission amid the bureaucratization of care and in a politicized national context of immigration reform, but also from the perceived extreme vulnerability of migrant children and their need for protection from abuse and exploitation. In order to conduct research, I secured permission not only from my university's institutional review board and two of the organizations' research review committees but also from the thirteen other individuals and organizations who laid claim to speak for the best interests of the child. Although the director of the ORR Division of Children's Services is the legal guardian of all detained "unaccompanied alien children" in the United States, other state and nonstate actors recognized themselves as integrally involved in the care and custody of unaccompanied children. Despite their lack of legal standing to grant or deny consent on behalf of detained children, they were very protective of this population of children, wary of those who might capitalize on their vulnerability—be they traffickers, smugglers, an abusive parent, an inquisitive reporter, or a researcher. Interestingly, never was seeking parental consent a concern or a suggestion from any of the boards, committees, agencies, organizations, or individuals.

The legal organizations representing detained children were most preoccupied with the truth-seeking aspect of the research. What if children disclose information that contradicted their legal claims? What if children lie? What if ICE subpoenas my records and uses my notes against children in their legal petitions? These concerns are founded on past violations of children's due process rights in which ICE used a child's ORR records as evidence of a child's inconsistent or unreliable testimony in immigration court. In Texas, lawyers experienced ICE enlisting children as bait to entice their unauthorized parents when attempting to take custody of their child. In contrast, ICE and my university's research review board for this research were principally concerned with the illegality of unaccompanied children as "an indicator of their greater disposition toward criminal activity" and the special measures I would take to report threats of potential criminal activity, as well as my ethical responsibility to report crimes committed. These concerns stem from public discourses on unauthorized migration, which conflate "illegality" with criminality and are bolstered by a shift in federal policies toward the criminalization of unauthorized migrants. Particularly in the backlash following 2006 efforts for comprehensive immigration reform, the politicization of unauthorized immigration brought real traction to the board's concerns, though most advocates and facility staff working with children strongly disagreed with this perception. The two-year process of permission seeking highlights the often conflicting and always tense relationship between the state, law enforcement, nongovernmental subcontractors, family members, and the often excluded migrant children themselves in decisions about the best interests and legal rights of unaccompanied children.

These very disparate concerns—on the one hand, the criminal potential; on the other, the victim—gestures toward the potential malleability of the image of the unaccompanied child—at once a child and an "alien" in a highly politicized context of racism and xenophobia in the United States. I take seriously the concern of one administrator who warned early on, "Be careful what you find and what you write. They will use it against the very child that we seek to protect." The malleability of the image of the migrant child—the victim, the delinquent, the "illegal," the gangbanger, the terrorist—makes me acutely aware of the ethical responsibility I assume in writing about the experiences of migrant children. I have seen firsthand how information about specific children becomes distorted to serve a particular organization or agency's political or institutional agenda. The impact on the child and his or her family is devastating. For this reason, I have been highly selective in the narratives of individual children I write about in these pages. I have maintained the integrity of the narratives of youth, using their words whenever possible, and of the ways they understand and navigate their everyday lives.[13] The narratives balance the unique and diverse experiences of youth migrants with the themes and trends identified during an initial survey of participants in the study.

While in the past decade, the migration of unaccompanied children as a social phenomenon has become increasingly visible, what remains obscured are the perspectives of children on the growing layers of bureaucracy developed to protect or to prosecute them. My ethnographic research attempts to carve out a space in which children's voices might enter the discussion in a way that accurately reflects their understandings of the law, institutional interventions, and their own best interests while taking precautions to guard against the manipulation of their experiences.

Exposing the Snapshot: Social Agency

Migration studies is not a discipline with a set of well-defined methodological procedures but a topic of great interest to scholars of sociology, geography, anthropology, political science, history, and law (Brettell 2003). As such, myriad approaches to children and migration have merged under the rubric of "migration studies." Most avoid the complexities of migration as a dynamic process, in which people circulate through time and space with great flexibility and uncertainty (Ong 1999: 10), instead locating the child in social and legal categories of the family, by which they infer the conditions of children from those of the household. Interestingly, the family in migration studies is defined by the presence of dependent children, yet few studies take children as serious contributors to household decision-making processes.

Woven throughout migration literature and immigration law is the presumption that adults are the decision makers and providers for children. The social position of the child as inferior or somehow exclusively dependent stands in marked contrast to the integral roles children often assume in familial decision-making processes as well as the decisions they make as individual social actors. From my research with child migrants and their families, it is clear that the decision to migrate is often a collective one. Children contribute to the discussion on whether to migrate, the destination, and the timing of migration. Children may spark adult migration through a change in the number of household members due to birth, death, adoption, fostering, the departure of older children, or a change in the needs of household members, such as education or illness (McKendrick 2001: 464; Young 2004: 471). Children may be the reason for postponing migration, waiting until they are older, or they may catalyze migration, given a desire for improved living conditions or education (Boyle, Halfacree, and Robinson 1998: 119; Rossi 1980: 178; Tyrrell 2011). At times, adults pursue additional opportunities or resources for their children, such as access to education, health care, or future employment opportunities (South and Crowder 1997). Children may shape migration decisions in terms of the completion of their school year and program of study or in the violence or instability they experience in their everyday lives (e.g., pressure to join a gang). In spite of this rich variation, discussions of household migration largely subsume child migration, in which children are just one of a myriad of factors shaping family migration decisions. Even as they may provide a family with central motives for migration, they remain liminal figures in most interpretations of migration practices.

In this ethnography, I argue that an analysis of the social agency of children and youth is critical to uncovering the shortcomings and dangers of current conceptualizations of child migration. "Social agency," a term used by social scientists, refers to the actions and choices that individuals (and nonhumans in some cases) often make of their own free will. Shaped by upbringing, cultural beliefs and norms, and social status, among other factors, social agency may be conscious, intentional actions or unconscious, involuntary behaviors. I depart from historical, moral framings of agency as exclusively individualized and self-determined by attending to the ways agency may assume historical and collective dimensions. Even in the contexts of extreme isolation—detention and deportability—conversations with youth and their families repeatedly revealed that youth make small and large choices as actors embedded in kinship networks and informed by their cultural context.

Early in my research, I was struck by the ways policymakers, government bureaucrats, detention facility staff, and legal advocates each conceptualized social agency in their descriptions of the conditions spurring, context of, and reasons for migration and how these narratives did not reconcile with my interactions with migrants in the United States and Central America with whom I had worked since the late 1990s. Amid emerging anxieties about childhood and migration, powerful discourses in the media and legal and advocacy spheres have emerged—discourses that either embrace dependency and victimhood (read as a lack of agency) as defining features of child migrants or fold child migrants into the pervasive criminalization of immigrants (read as transgressive agency). On the one hand, civil society has staked a claim in the research of child migration in order to respond to a perceived increase in occurrences of children made vulnerable by their exposure to the "street" (Becerra and Chi 1992; Nann 1982). The pervasive belief among civil society is that the sheer presence of an unaccompanied child marks his or her acute risk of abuse, trafficking, harsh labor arrangements, and sexual exploitation. Discourses of trauma and exploitation frame children as inherently vulnerable, and thus reliant on the interventions of well-meaning (adult) professionals to guide their psychic and physical development into adulthood and to ensure their long-term legal permanency in the United States.

Legal advocates and scholars have also taken interest in child migration, questioning how the law contends with the "illegal" and "unaccompanied" presence of migrant children, as in the notable case of Elian Gonzalez. In particular, attorneys must navigate convoluted and ethically murky terrain that routinely places them in positions of power over children and their narratives. They must balance their professional commitment to zealously advocate on behalf of the child with recognition that the complex experiences of migrant children do not easily fit into the few forms of immigration legal relief available to them. A seasoned immigration attorney characterized the predicament as "having no reliable signage. If I move to the right, I risk having [my client] returned to a place he has left at risk to his life. If I move to the left, I risk exaggerating a truth that I know to be incomplete at best. So, I forge straight ahead but wonder if I'm helping to build more dead ends for these kids by not putting the full story out there. The risks for [my client] are too great and the benefits for others too uncertain." Attorneys must grapple with how to distill a child's narrative into the requisite eligibility criteria without reifying the child victim into the law.

Claims of victimhood and vulnerability carry significant risks. In the humanitarian and legal arenas, a child's victimhood becomes problematically synonymous with the child's social, economic, and political rights as detailed in the UN Convention on the Rights of the Child (CRC). The absence or violation of those rights constitutes a child's vulnerability. Pervasively, advocates fail to recognize the fraught history of the drafting and ratification of the CRC, which embodies Western social, cultural, and legal norms of childhood and ignores cultural or historical variation. While inherent victim-hood justifies protection, care, and legal advocacy in the name of a child's best interests, it also diverts advocates from inquiring how children view their own best interests (Ensor and Gozdziak 2010). Denying the social agency of children by advocating for their rights rather than their wants discounts social and kinship dimensions of migration and ignores divergent cultural meanings. In claiming rights on behalf of vulnerable children, advocates struggle to solicit adequately their desires, perspectives, choices, and decisions and to recognize the very social agency that led them to the United States.

In contrast to humanitarian or legal advocacy realms that view children's social agency as either violated or biologically undeveloped, law enforcement criminalizes a child's social agency as either delinquency or indistinguishable from adult "criminal aliens." In the law enforcement regime, a child's social agency has led to a social and legal transgression of the law that requires punishment and rehabilitation. The production of the legal category of the "unaccompanied alien child" and the institutionalization of children in federal custody is a product of the overlapping enforcement regimes encapsulated by the wars on drugs, immigrants, and terror. The past fifteen years have seen record levels of U.S. government funding of immigration enforcement ($18 billion in 2012); the militarization and technologization of the U.S.-Mexico border; the fluid collaboration between local law enforcement and federal immigration authorities; and an infusion of U.S. funding, technology, and training to Mexican authorities to thwart migration through Mexico. The stakes in the detention of migrants have intensified.

Relying on modes of behavioral pathology or biological and developmental models of childhood rooted in universalized and romanticized ideals of childhood glosses over the complexity and variation in experiences of migrant children. In order to penetrate the powerful discourses, an analysis of the social agency of children allows for a transcendence of the clashing binaries of dependency or independence, natural or pathological, delinquent or victim, positive or negative that are the basis of institutional policies, professional practices, and legal frameworks. A contextualization of the ways children and youth navigate structural constraints and express agency may begin to deconstruct the oversimplifications that underpin the institutional interventions and legal frameworks that shape migrant children's everyday lives. With such an exploration, we may begin to understand how children comprehend and express social agency rather than the ways those in power assign meaning to it. These often diverging, moralized meanings attributed by "stakeholders" to a migrant's social agency routinely come into conflict in courts of law, institutional practices, and on the bodies of children.

Unaccompanied children as a juridical category justifying institutional and legal intervention discounts the significant variation in experience, context, and social relatedness of children across cultures. "Always embedded in broader structure, child agency, like adult agency, is inevitably partial and conditioned by multiple factors" (Coe et al. 2011: 9). Categorically ignored, the agency of migrant children and youth is conditioned by their upbringing with notable differences across culture, age, gender, family position, sources of caregiving, and social obligations. Financial and social indebtedness, language, emotionality, and household economy may encourage, deny, or make relevant or irrelevant child agency (Coe et al. 2011: 15–16). A child's agency may be contextualized by his or her experiences of (dis)empowerment, access to knowledge and information, employment or labor, and exposure to trauma or violence. Children maintain individualized capacities for innovation, creativity, strength, and resilience that may shape their ability and willingness to express agency either actively or passively.

The burgeoning field of new childhood studies recognizes children and youth as actors in their own right and whose worldviews are worthy of inquiry. Scholars have argued that youth are both "makers and breakers" engaged in dynamic social processes of making and being made (Honwana and de Boeck 2005; Maira 2009). In this vein, I engage youth less as agents in process of "becoming," instead focusing on their "being." Youth negotiate complex networks of actors and institutions that may aid them in evading deportation, earning income, and contributing to household economies in the United States and in their home countries. Considering only the structural forces on youths' lives and reducing childhood and youth into periods of transition or molding threaten to negate their contributions as social actors. Youth challenge, resist, or shape the law and institutional practices. Youth may understand the law differently than adults and their experiences may differ across time and space, and through an examination of their everyday interactions and confrontations with institutional networks and legal systems, youth shape the very laws that govern their everyday lives. Through my research, I came to realize that migrant youth reflexively understand social agency, not as an act of one's own free will but as a responsibility, a form of belonging, or a mode of being. Thus, an analysis of agency and rights becomes central in the narratives of migrant youth in the ways they cross physical, social, and metaphoric borders and reside in overlapping spaces of impossibility—be it social invisibility, illegality, or independence.

Methods

Research methods employed in the study of youth often adopt either "adult" scripts for understanding youth or "child" scripts for understanding a child's perspective on adult domains. Yet, as social actors, youth negotiate and develop ways of understanding conflict, the law, and justice all their own. As Samantha Punch (2002: 337) cautions, anthropologists should employ "research participant-centered" methods rather than "child-centered" approaches (see also A. Best 2007). Instead of segregating youth from other social actors, developing a particular set of methods exclusively for youth is not only patronizing, Punch warns, but negates their competencies. Taking heed, I adapted methods based on research contexts, not on assumptions of the capacity or character of migrant youth as a category of persons.

This three-year ethnography is based on fieldwork with four principal groups. First, I conducted research in three federal detention facilities (euphemistically called "shelters") for unaccompanied children in Texas and Illinois and in four federal foster care programs in Texas, Michigan, and Pennsylvania (periods 2006–2009). At the facilities and foster care programs, I observed children in their everyday activities: at intake, class, mealtime, recreation, medical appointments, house meetings, legal appointments with their attorneys, at court hearings with immigration judges, and with foster families and peers. I conducted a survey over multiple, one-on-one interviews with eighty-two detained and nondetained children, tracing demographic data, detailed family histories, migration journeys, and the expectations reported by all migrant youths entering the facility regardless of country of origin. The survey provided a distributional analysis of the population of children entering the facility, the variations in experiences, and a baseline from which I tracked change over time. I compared the narrative structures of surveyed youth and identified key terms to track throughout my research. I conducted interviews in Spanish, Portuguese, or English and enlisted a Mandarin interpreter as needed. All translations from Spanish and Portuguese are my own.

Since the completion of this research, I have visited five additional facilities in Arizona, Texas, and Illinois and maintained communication with individual children and staff of fourteen facilities and seven foster care programs in Arizona, California, Florida, Michigan, New York, Texas, Virginia, Utah, and Washington, D.C.

Second, I conducted one-on-one structured and semistructured interviews with nearly 250 "stakeholders"—individuals engaged in the apprehension and detention of migrant children, including government bureaucrats, nongovernmental facility staff, attorneys, guardians ad litem, judges, members of Congress, community leaders, Border Patrol agents, ICE agents, consular officials, foster families, teachers, researchers, and policymakers

Table 2: Country of Origin, Gender, and Location of Children Participating in Study

Country of origin	Total	Male	Female	Texas facility	Midwest facility	Midwest secure facility	Non-apprehended
Mexico	21	16	5	1	13	6	1
Honduras	14	9	5	4	5	3	2
Guatemala	12	12		5	2	3	2
El Salvador	13	11	2	2	7	1	3
China	5	2	3		5		
India	2	2			2		
Ecuador	2	1	1		1		1
Somalia	2	2			1		1
Brazil	1		1		1		
Guinea	1	1			1		
Indonesia	1		1		1		
Liberia	1	1				1	
Macedonia	1	1			1		
Nicaragua	1	1					1
Nigeria	1	1			1		
Pakistan	1		1		1		
Russia	1		1		1		
United Kingdom	1	1			1		
Disputed	1	1			1		
Total	82	62	20	12	45	14	11

across multiple sites, including in El Salvador and Mexico.[14] Many of these individuals were eager to engage in thoughtful reflection on their work with migrant children and the structural challenges they face in serving this population. Many stakeholders (facility staff, legal service providers, voluntary agencies, guardians ad litem, policy researchers) are funded almost exclusively by ORR, which significantly and financially dissuades public critiques or lawsuits regarding the care and custody of children. Confidential interviews for a study approved by ORR provided simultaneous anonymity yet institutional blessing for stakeholders' candid observations.

I collected and analyzed the various types of institutional paperwork produced by governmental and nongovernmental "stakeholders" tracking the presence of unaccompanied youth in federal custody in the United States, including custody transfer forms between ICE, ORR, detention centers, and families; immigration applications and rulings; and fingerprint and photographic records—each asserting the lawful or unlawful status of the youth's tenuous presence in the United States. I analyzed the marks of the state through genres of writing and practices connecting youth to the state. This focus on institutional paperwork and shifts in the law and legal practices provides a critical space in the analysis of youth agency as it provides an avenue through which to consider how youth are shaped by and shape institutions they encounter. While the law is often assumed to be impermeable, youth as social actors dynamically interact and engage with the law and legal practices. By focusing on the persistence of certain legal notions of youth over time amid specific moments of legal change, I examine how the law simultaneously reflects change and continuity in the space of youth, even as it shapes their daily lives (James and James 2004).

Third, I maintained regular communication with children released from detention who remained in California, Washington, D.C., Maryland, Texas, Illinois, and New York and with unauthorized children who evaded apprehension altogether. Tracing the social and familial networks of migrant youth was particularly challenging given the transnational and mobile character of children's lives. Many of the youths circulated between households in multiple living arrangements, requiring creative methods and fluidity inherent in a multisited project. At other times, I was astounded by what appeared, at first glance, to be pure chance of encountering the same youths in multiple locations or once again in immigration detention. While I expected children detained in one location to be released in other localities, I did not anticipate the remarkable extent of mobility of nondetained children or children following their release from federal custody. Children moved quite frequently between households, jobs, cities, and even countries. Their transnational social networks and their nimble ability to foster new social ties facilitated their movement to improved living arrangements or employment opportunities. The sedentary demands of childhood customary in the West rarely applied to the children and youth with whom I worked.

Given the variations in experience and social and legal trajectories, my interactions with youths and their families varied over time and space. Some youths would maintain weekly phone or Skype contact with me for extended periods of time, while others would come in and out of communication with me, and I would receive a text message after three or four months of no contact. For many youths following their release, I served as a cultural interlocutor, assisting them in securing copies of documents from ORR, enrolling in school, and facilitating legal referrals, or navigating health care needs. In the days and weeks following their release, many youths and their parents would call me daily to ask questions, seek translation assistance, or simply say hello. My phone number was passed to family members, friends, and neighbors, identifying me as "a person who helps." I continue to receive phone calls from Georgia, Maryland, and Indiana with requests for assistance. Many youths with whom I worked moved multiple times, changed phone numbers routinely, or lacked the financial resources to charge their prepaid cellular phones. Tracking down updated contact information proved extremely difficult, so I relied on the youth keeping me informed of changes in residence. Because of the geographic distribution and mobility of many youth, I was restricted to only occasional in-person visits with youth and their families in Washington, D.C., Maryland, Texas, and New York. For released and nondetained youth living in the Midwest, communication was much more predictable and regular. I attended school events, family picnics, soccer games, religious celebrations, doctor's appointments, meetings with attorneys, and court hearings. Unable to "leave the field," I continue to communicate with several youths, now ranging from twenty-one to twenty-six years, as they secure legal status, enter college, get married, and start families.

Fourth, I conducted interviews with members of the Guatemalan and an communities in Maryland and Illinois with whom I have worked for over a decade, and I spent several months in El Salvador (2007) with children deported from the United States and with the families of unaccompanied children who remain in the United States.[15] With convoluted and ambiguous directions from detained youths, I located some families in El Salvador in an effort to understand not only the specificities of the local situations and networks of these youth, but also the national context that informs both the motivations for migration and the state and home communities' reception of repatriated youth. I encountered several youths who had migrated and had since returned or been deported to El Salvador. Their experiences on return added depth I had not anticipated. I met with several governmental and nongovernmental actors who provided assistance to returned migrant youth, as well as two research institutions that were coordinating efforts on migration both into and out of El Salvador. Many of the migrant youth I encountered in El Salvador were Nicaraguan children who had come to El Salvador in search of work or Salvadoran children who had recently returned from Mexico and the United States, often planning their next trip. Since the completion of this project, I have initiated a study with deported youth in the highlands of Guatemala. Their experiences of deportability and removal have added dimensions of experience and complexity to this work.

While a multisited ethnography was an imperative given the mobility of both detained and nondetained youth, there are inherent limitations to ethnography as a methodology, particularly for researching a structurally decentralized federal custodial system.[16] A multisited ethnography proved critical for a number of reasons. I sought to explore the differing sensibilities and anxieties about unaccompanied children between the "border" and the "interior"; the varying personalities and capabilities between subcontracted voluntary agencies; the conservative Fifth Circuit Court versus a more moderate Seventh Circuit Court; the localized tensions between state-run Children and Family Services and the federal Office of Refugee Resettlement; and the local court jurisdictions' receptiveness to the Specialized Immigrant Juvenile (SIJ) status—a hybrid form of relief that requires a dependency finding in state court to pursue federal immigration relief. SIJ is a step in immigration law toward identification of unaccompanied minors by permitting unauthorized children to stand before the law as primary petitioners in cases of abuse, neglect, or abandonment. In spite of these variations, trends emerged across three countries and five states where I conducted research. These trends are further refined by my subsequent communication and visits with staff and children at an additional twenty-six programs and facilities from my applied work as a guardian ad litem.[17]

As I map out the actors, organizations, state and federal institutions, and international governments and organizations involved with unaccompanied children in the United States, the sheer number is dizzying. The overlapping and at time conflicting responsibilities and interests consistently trap children and their families in untenable situations with few alternatives and marginal opportunities to voice their desires and concerns. Forced to navigate this "Kafka-esque" network, as Bhabha and Schmidt (2006) describe, that espouses a simultaneous desire to care for and to remove them, unaccompanied children, as I argue, exercise their agency as social actors to challenge, shape, and reformulate the very laws that define them.

Anxieties of Power

There is a critical power imbalance that pervades research of marginalized populations by Western, privileged researchers. These differentials are only magnified when engaging in participatory research around children's lives, especially in the context of their detention. Research with migrant children and youth in federal immigration facilities, a quintessential "captured population," presents a number of complex ethical and methodological considerations. My university's Institutional Research Review Board and the American Anthropological Association Code of Ethics provided the ethical guidelines that directed my research. Researchers working in "vulnerable populations" or correctional settings (e.g., prisons, parole, probation, juvenile justice, and so on) assisted me in anticipating and attending to critical issues of (dis)empowerment, choice, and consent in this project (Fisher et al. 2002; Haggerty 2004; Levine et al. 2004; Waldram 2009). I found myself drawing on my previous work in Guatemala, Argentina, Angola, and the United States with survivors of war, genocide, and torture. On the basis of these professional experiences, I was particularly attentive to the profound and prolonged impact of trauma on people's lives and how institutional practices can exacerbate symptoms and even retraumatize people.

I attempted to be mindful of the multilayered power imbalance between myself (an adult middle-class citizen) and the children (unauthorized, often impoverished legal minors). Methodologically, I tried to create spaces of privacy and feelings of confidence during our meetings. When interviewing children, we met one on one in a private room. While we were unable to escape the gaze of surveillance cameras throughout the facilities, we did experience a level of privacy children were not permitted at any other time during their detention. I explained to youth that I did not work for the government, facilities, attorneys, or consulates. I had no benefit to give them. I could not influence their legal or custody cases in any way. I simply explained that I was writing a book about youth, their experiences of migration, and their lives in the United States. I told them I wanted to learn about why they came, about what they hoped to find, and about their everyday lives both in detention and beyond. By writing about their thoughts, perspectives, and experiences, I hoped my book might educate the public and perhaps improve the laws, practices, and policies for the treatment of migrant children who came to the United States in the future. For detained youth, I explicitly sought consent multiple times throughout their participation in the study—at initial meetings, every three months of detention, on release, and following their removal from the United States. Most children welcomed the opportunity to escape the everyday monotony of detention and to spend time talking about their lives. Some children who were reserved or quiet in class and group activities overwhelmed me with their willingness to speak at great length and with candor. It seemed they had been storing up conversations over time that only erupted when provided the space and time to speak. One youth told me, "No one here [at the facility] has talked to me like this before. They are all too busy to talk." Indeed, always-harried staff had very little time to be present for children because of their heavy caseloads. Time to talk was a luxury I uniquely possessed as a researcher.

During my research at the facilities, I engaged with youth on a regular basis. I attempted to occupy a space beyond the everyday expectations children had of staff and various "stakeholders" they encountered on a daily basis in the facilities. Contingent on the flows and needs of children, I tried to circulate with them in their everyday lives—sitting among the children in the classrooms, doing homework alongside them, sharing lunch at tables apart from the staff, standing in line to be perpetually counted and surveilled, and engaging in recreational activities. From my perception, the children's interactions with "stakeholders" were fundamentally different. They fulfilled a specific purpose—completing a questionnaire with facility staff identifying potential "sponsors" for release; responding to an intake assessment with legal service providers determining their eligibility for legal relief; cataloging medical or psychological concerns with a clinician at intake; or requesting a continuance or legal determination with an immigration judge in court. For fear of overwhelming children with additional inquiries, I tried to place as few constraints as possible on our informal interviews, open-ended conversations, and daily interactions. I hope they too felt our dialogue was structurally different.

Spontaneous conversations—at mealtimes, during free time, the rare outing, or on the soccer pitch beyond earshot of staff—proved qualitatively more informative than one-on-one interviews. Amid an influx and exit of children, knowledge circulated in the facility in impressive ways. Particular youth, often those who remained in custody longest, became sophisticated power brokers. They revealed to new arrivals which staff to trust or distrust; which youth to align with or guard against; which stakeholders to discuss past histories or current concerns with or not; what to disclose or conceal in court; how to orchestrate unauthorized phone calls with boyfriends or girl-friends; and where to hide from the surveillance cameras either to share an intimate moment with another youth or to seek retribution for interpersonal conflicts.

Sergio, a fifteen-year-old youth who migrated to the United States with his mother at age seven and who was detained for over nine months during my research, was a critical interlocutor for me. Able to navigate English and Spanish fluently, Sergio had a keen understanding of the institutional logic, staff dynamics, American culture, and the social and political contexts from which children came. Gregarious and knowledgeable, Sergio listened attentively to others. He let them vent their frustrations with family members who were reluctant to "sponsor" them out of detention. He counseled youth soliciting his legal and relationship advice. He imparted to them his knowledge about life in America beyond the confines of detention. He had seen, as one youth articulated as the source of her intrigue in his stories, "*el otro lado*" (the other side). To my reassurance, Sergio communicated explicitly to other youth that I was "*alguien de confianza*" (a trusted person). He let them know that the information shared with me would not be divulged to others. I made an explicit methodological choice to interview staff at the initiation and completion of my research in the facilities to create clearer boundaries during my interactions with children. This was made transparent to staff at the outset so as not to compromise their comfort or candor in our conversations and formal interviews.

Even with Sergio's confidence in my silence, in a handful of cases, children refused to meet with me. I was grateful that they felt empowered to do so. In some instances, I suspected that children were being guarded and, in some cases, even untruthful. The factual accuracy of their statements did not matter to me, though it proved intriguing. I became interested in why some youth would conceal or tell only partial truths. Was it a sense of obligation to protect their families from disclosing the truth to an outsider? Was it fear or coercion from smugglers or traffickers? Was it suspicion of the facilities and government authorities? Was it a survival skill that assisted some youth who lived in the streets? Or was it because I, essentially, at least to them, was no different from their detainers? These refusals and misgivings reminded me that, despite my efforts to establish trust and confidence, my position of privilege was insurmountable.

For children who had been institutionalized, either in the juvenile justice system or in several ORR facilities, initial conversations followed a "script," one that appeared told and retold to various stakeholders, likely in differing variations. They had learned to be suspicious and guarded, attempting to decipher the "right answer" to my questions. When I first met Emilio, a seventeen-year-old whom authorities had bounced between four federal and juvenile facilities for nearly two years, he recounted his life's narrative with little affect, relative ease, and impeccable chronology. Mindful to include only the pertinent individuals and events, he neatly (re)told of his past traumas, the reasons for his incarceration, and his desire to make better choices. Only after eight months following his release, over our monthly coffee at the local Pancake House, did he begin to break from his script with subtle shifts in vocabulary, changes in narrative structure, and divergent stories. Elements of his narrative from our initial meetings fell out of our conversations, while other facets of his experiences unfolded.

For some children, the inescapable reality that I would return home to my family at the end of the day could only be overcome by meeting them following their release from detention. Julio, sixteen, had been detained in three facilities over fourteen months. At the outset of our first interview, he asked: "Why is my life important to you?" and "Can what I tell you cause me harm?" Savvy to the multiple and shifting meanings of confidentiality, Julio tested my sincerity and his ability to trust me. I was one in a long line of professionals, primarily women, asking him to describe his life. I do not believe that the distinction for Julio sank in until I met with him at his father's home in New York. We were eating *pupusas*, following my return from visiting his mother and siblings in El Salvador, when Julio joked, "You must be a socialist like my dad if you traveled all the way to see my family." When I asked what he meant, he replied, "You care about me and my family and my future." He said that neither the facility staff nor the attorney in Texas ever called him to see how he was faring with his father whom he had not seen in eight years. Facility staff routinely reported that ORR does not permit staff to maintain communication with children following their release from detention. My relationship with Julio shifted over time and space. It was only on his release from detention and over a year's time that he grew to trust me. And while I maintained that I had no power or influence over Julio's legal status, I helped him navigate the local school system that refused him admittance because of unauthorized status. Helping Julio and his father manage the legal and social particularities of their community in small ways communicated, I felt, my enduring receptiveness to learning from him. I believe my approach helped to enable him either to accept or to refuse my presence over time.

I tried to engage both detained and nondetained youth as ethnographers of their own lives, employing methods of journaling, game playing, kinship mapping, auto-ethnographies, and storytelling projects.[18] Youth as ethnographers helps to deflate perceptions of youth as incomplete social subjects and as potentially dangerous and delinquent. Furthermore, these activities served as a constant reminder of what I could learn from and with children rather than about them (Freire 1970; Tilton 2010: 11). The methodological strategies I enlisted helped me understand how the state enters into the domestic sphere in the everyday and how children actively shape and navigate their environments. By engaging youth directly in the research and examining the practices of youth migrants, not just the structures that attempt to direct and confine migration, I was better able to analyze the dynamic and complex nature of child mobility. I could better recognize child participation in local, national, and transnational processes (Bourdieu 1977; Ortner 1984). Each of the subsequent chapters opens with an excerpt from these activities, framing the thematic content of each chapter through the voices of youth themselves. The pieces were also chosen to remind us of the profound human stakes of how the law, institutions, and we as individuals respond to youth as people deserving of respect.

The Chapters Ahead

Chapter 2 begins with the examination a pivotal historical moment within immigration law—the 1997 Flores Settlement Agreement—and the ways it specifically shapes political and institutional discussions of the social agency of unaccompanied children. Competing perspectives of law enforcement and legal advocates force to the surface a critical question: are unaccompanied children humanitarian refugees or unauthorized aliens? The competing discourses of victimization and delinquency create a false binary that does not account for the multiplicity of experiences and narratives of unaccompanied children. Unaccompanied migrant children cannot be characterized as a monolith category; rather, they represent a diverse cross-section of migrants whom legal and governmental institutions homogenize by virtue of their unauthorized presence and the absence (whether perceived, real, or constructed) of their parents. This homogenization derives in part from juridical indolence and a lack of political will but also rests quite comfortably in social constructions of childhood and of deviancy among youth of color. Neither approach allows space for thoughtful consideration of a child's agency or the cultural significance of the decision to leave the home country or the need to do so. Untangling the multiple ways in which the state and social discourses entrap youth between law enforcement and care sheds light on public imaginations of youth; Chapter 2 challenges these problematic conceptions of youth as either dangerously susceptible to delinquency or as victims due to their malleability and status as not-yet adults.

Acknowledging children as important social actors is a critical step; yet to conceptualize children and adults as equivalent social actors is also problematic in that it downplays the disparity in power between children and adults. Adults and children do participate in distinct power hierarchies that also shape their everyday lives. Discussions of delinquency provide a clear example of the court's differential recognition of youths' ability to enact violence (delinquency) versus their ability to speak on their own behalf; the courts recognize the agency of youth as both legally and morally responsible for their transgressive behaviors, thus necessitating harsh punishments (Coutin 2000; Terrio 2004: 10; Terrio 2009). In such instances, the youth temporarily is granted the full agency of an adult, in spite of his or her limited power in many daily circumstances. In the adjudication of cases, judges view youth agency as approximating that of adults, not as a separate type or quality of agency identifiable as belonging to youth. However, the court's recognition of a youth's ability to speak remains confined to certain contexts and only when adults with disproportionate power consider it appropriate or fitting to their agendas (Neale 2002: 458). Thus, the youth's access to "adult" capabilities shifts and slides depending on the court's will, which often seems to arbitrarily assign rights as well as to rescind them. None of these shifts actually account for the youth's experience of agency or (dis)empowerment in his daily life or what sorts of rights are available to him.

A careful theorization of unauthorized child migration necessitates situating migration and illegality in the social, historical, and political context in which the law produces migrant "illegality" (De Genova 2002: 419). Chapter 3 locates the analysis of child migration within a broader field of historical knowledge in terms of the circulation of people but also within the often-absent context of immigration law. Early American law did not recognize children as individual rights holders independent of their parents. Treated as property, "children were parental, or more specifically paternal, assets who were under the direct and extensive control of their fathers" (Thronson 2002: 982). A shift occurred with the late nineteenth-century reformist discourse that "viewed children not so much as individual property . . . but as a form of social investment in which custody produced . . . social duties on the part of each parent, the performance of which the state could supervise" (Fineman 1988: 737). It was during this time that the still-prevalent legal principle of "best interest of the child" emerged, rooted in the presumption that children were inherently weak, dependent, and vulnerable. In 2001, the development of special legislation for unaccompanied children marked another historical shift in American law in which, for the first time, immigration law recognized the migrant child as potentially independent of his or her family despite decades of court records replete with such cases. Chapter 3 details the evolving relationship between the state, the family, and immigrant children, examining the relevant laws and judicial cases that have shaped the ways the state enters into or mediates domestic life of unaccompanied children and their families.

Chapter 4 traces the journey of one youth from his home in Guatemala to an Illinois courtroom and his simultaneous experiences of disempowerment and agency. The chapter details the ways he navigates a complex network of actors and institutions in pursuit of safety and security for himself and for his sister and the ways the law affords him some rights by virtue of his being a child while restricting other rights due to his independent presence in the United States. His narrative reveals how he negotiates the imposition of the law on his everyday life. Perceived as unruly, delinquent, and somehow dangerous to society and the nation-state, he embodies the intersection of the law's attempts to contain and to reintegrate those existing outside of the law. At the same time, he is not merely a passive recipient of the law; he actively shapes legal discourses on migration in his everyday negotiations of institutional and community networks.

In Chapter 5, I enter federal detention centers for detained unaccompanied migrant children to examine the complex, everyday negotiations between the federal government, NGOs, and youth. These subcontracted, nongovernmental facilities are a direct response to the incarceration of immigrant children prior to 2003 under the INS, creating a less restrictive environment for children while they await family reunification, foster care, or deportation. I examine the institutional practices of the facility staff in simultaneously caring for and detaining migrant youth and the ways these practices produce migrant children as a category of persons. The facilities embody the competing frameworks of care and law enforcement through the increasing bureaucratization of care and containment amid minimal transparency and oversight. Yet youth resist the facility staff's socialization programs, which attempt to "rehabilitate" youth into a specific image of a child that reflects socioeconomic and culturally specific American norms. The dynamics of a child's agency are defined in a context of social interactions that emphasize reciprocity of individuals and structures while recognizing asymmetrical distributions of power between the facility's staff and detained children. I focus on both the context in which youth interact with other social actors and institutions and the forms these interactions assume. Chapter 5 reflects on perceptions of institutional practices from "below" (Griffiths 2002), questioning how youth make sense of and shape legal and institutional practices.[19]

One of the few benevolent aspects of immigration law is that children may be released from "shelters" into federal foster care, group homes, or with sponsors who may or may not be family members. Chapter 6 turns to institutional policies and procedures that determine the conditions of release and the viability of certain kinship ties. In tandem with the law, institutional policies reformulate kinship ties both in the United States and abroad. I trace the lives of unaccompanied children on their release from immigration detention, examining the ways children reconcile their aspirations in the United States with their roles as children and providers for their transnational kinship networks. Departing from the study of highly visible youth cultures marked by deviance from social norms, Chapter 6 considers everyday life as a theoretical framework that will allow for, as Veena Das and Pamela Reynolds argue, an examination of the ways children enact cultural belonging and express discord "repeatedly and undramatically" (2003:

1). To these ends, this book argues that children are not merely passive recipients of the law and institutional practices but actively shape legal discourses on migration and kinship in their everyday negotiations of institutional and community networks. By failing to recognize the legal personhood and social agency of unaccompanied children, the state undermines the rights of children and compromises their pursuit of justice.

A Note on Terminology

Illegal Alien

While the term "illegal alien" appears throughout the U.S. Code, it is not explicitly defined. However, "alien" is defined as "any person not a citizen or national of the United States."[20] The popular usage of "illegal alien" has become increasingly politicized as someone who willfully trespasses on national sovereignty. Among the migration and human rights networks, "no human is illegal" has become a rallying cry against the derogatory connotations of the term, often associated with criminality or along specific racial lines. In the United States, rhetoric has begun to define the debate on immigration—dehumanizing the "illegal" or the "alien" as one without due process and without rights. Such politicization resulted in the Associated Press changing its stylebook to end its usage of the term "illegal alien." The Associated Press, followed by the *Los Angeles Times* and *USA Today*, now distinguishes that actions are illegal and people are undocumented.

In legal terms, the boundary between citizen and illegal is porous. Under some conditions, such as Temporary Protected Status (TPS) or certain types of visas, individuals can transform their illegal status to legal, just as individuals with legal status in the United States can lose that status through committing certain crimes. Unaccompanied children can lose their eligibility for the Special Immigrant Juvenile (SIJ) status simply by turning eighteen.[21] Kitty Calavita (1998: 531) adds that not only does the law create illegality, but, in the case of Spanish immigration law, actively "regularizes and 'irregularizes' people, by making it all but impossible to retain legal status over time . . . the boundaries between legal and illegal populations are porous and in constant flux, as people routinely move in and out of legal status." As such, illegal alienage is not a preconditioned set of rules and regulations but is culturally informed, derived, and constructed. For these reasons,

I enlist the term "unauthorized migrant," which is a more neutral term that recognizes both the integrity of individual migrants and the fluctuation of their legal status in the United States.

Unaccompanied Alien Children

The U.S. legal code defines "unaccompanied alien children" (UAC) as those under age eighteen who have no lawful immigration status in the United States and are without a parent or legal guardian in the United States who is available to provide care and physical custody (6 U.S.C. §279(g)(2)).

The juridical category of the unaccompanied child and those who assign it to specific children are particularly problematic. With the 2003 transition of the care and custody of unaccompanied children from the INS to the ORR came several points of conflict, which my research details. One such tension derives from the determination and classification of a child as accompanied or unaccompanied at the point of apprehension. ICE (formerly INS) maintains exclusive power to determine if a parent or legal guardian accompanies a child or if the child is alone in the United States; yet, this practice is teeming with contradictions. Advocates have accused ICE of misclassifying children, determining them as accompanied in order to deport them quickly with family members or to prolong detention of those suspected of criminal activities. In other instances, advocates claim that ICE misclassifies children as unaccompanied to avoid the expense of family detention (shifting the expense for children from ICE to ORR) and unnecessarily separating a child from his or her family. For example, ICE may detain or deport a biological parent traveling with his or her children, leaving a child unaccompanied and in the care of ORR when, at the point of apprehension, the child was accompanied. During the period of my research in ORR facilities, there were two cases in which ICE classified children as unaccompanied in what appeared to be an effort to bait their unauthorized parents, apprehending the parents when they come forward. There were also several cases in which ICE forcibly separated children from parents or customary caregivers because the parent was accused of a crime and detained separately or because the parent had a mandatory order of deportation for a previous unauthorized entry. Furthermore, if ICE lacks the bed space in family facilities, a child may be reclassified as "unaccompanied," separated from his or her parents who remained in adult detention, and transferred to an ORR facility. In three cases, immigration enforcement authorities separated and deported an elder sibling or parent leaving a child deemed unaccompanied.

Although many children outside their country of origin are without their parents or legal guardians, they may be accompanied by customary care providers, extended family, family friends, or community members, or they may be entrusted to smugglers throughout the duration of their journey. Many of the unaccompanied children with whom I worked, in fact, had parents or immediate family members who have resided in the United States for many years. Some parents, due to their own unlawful status in the United States, are apprehensive about coming forward to claim their child from federal authorities. Parents must provide information regarding their status, employment, housing, and finances when seeking custody of their child. Despite the legal or illegal presence of their parents in the United States, ORR reinforces ICE classifications of unaccompanied status if ORR determines that a parent is unfit for family reunification. This "suitability" may be determined by a pending deportation order issued for the parent, a parent's own criminal history, or even the inability of a parent to meet the family reunification criteria for housing, employment, financial support, or child-care arrangements, much of which is informed by middle-class social norms for parenting and caregiving.

Both ICE and ORR may (re)classify children at multiple points in their apprehension, detention, and release, in spite of the physical presence of parents or family members in the United States. Even with a notice classifying a child as an "unaccompanied alien child," some asylum offices systematically ignore this classification once a child is reunited with his or her parent, determining a failure of jurisdiction to adjudicate the child's asylum petition because the child is "accompanied." While legal advocates contend this is a misreading of the federal statutes, the practice is gaining prevalence particularly in areas with large concentrations of immigrants—namely, New York, New Jersey, and California. Thus, the term "unaccompanied alien child" is not a preconditioned state but constantly vacillates based on culturally informed notions of care and kinship and on the fiscal and political interests of law enforcement. Internationally, the more prevalent term is "separated children," which, in many ways, more accurately reflects the temporary or contingent nature of travel or living arrangements of many children. In my research, I recognize this problematic and shifting definition, but choose to enlist the juridical term "unaccompanied child" because it is a critical intersection between migrant youth, their families, and U.S. law. The legal category, constructed though it may be, becomes a useful site of inquiry into the ways the law attempts to identify and to shape the capabilities and rights of children and their relationships to extended kinship networks both in the United States and abroad.

Children and Youth

Immigration law defines a "child" as an unmarried person under twenty-one (a minor) who fits into one of the following categories: (1) a child born to parents who are married to each other (born in wedlock); (2) a stepchild if the marriage creating the step-relationship took place before the child reached eighteen; (3) a child born out of wedlock (the parents were not married at the time the child was born); (4) an adopted child if the child was adopted before age sixteen and has lived with the adoptive parent(s) in their legal custody for at least two years; (5) an orphan under sixteen when an adoptive or prospective adoptive parent files a visa petition on his or her behalf, who has been adopted abroad by a U.S. citizen, or is coming to the United States for adoption by a U.S. citizen; or (6) a child adopted who is under eighteen and the natural sibling of an orphan or adopted child under sixteen, if adopted with or after the sibling. In effect, a child is defined specifically by the child's relationship to his or her parents and may forfeit certain forms of legal relief based on the child's own marital status or the age at which a parent petitions for the state's recognition of his or her legal status as a child.

Scholars have shown the legal and social categories of a child and childhood to be highly problematic; U.S. immigration law is no different. For example, in immigration law, a "child" summons attributes of dependency on the actions and relationship of his or her parents; while in the country of origin, the same "child" may maintain his or her own household, work independently, and even have his or her own family—attributes often associated with adults in the U.S. context.

To call someone a child, or a minor, is to summon specific attributes of age, dependency, agency, citizenship, rights, and responsibilities in a socially and historically informed context. For unaccompanied children, there are often-conflicting ways in which the state, political parties, NGOs, courts, households, and children themselves identify childhood and the ways the law or institutional actors specifically mobilize discourses on childhood or youth to achieve certain political ends. Because unaccompanied children explicitly and implicitly challenge the constructed legal and social category of "child," I often interchange the term "youth" to reflect the specific social and legal positioning of young adult migrants with whom I collaborated. I contextualize how migrant youth intersect with, inform, and at times resist the social, legal, and political landscapes that make and unmake citizenship and how these landscapes may also simultaneously contradict migrant youth's experiences as subjects of the state.

CHAPTER 2

====

Criminal Alien or Humanitarian Refugee?

INTERLUDE

"Sueños Rotos" (Broken Dreams)

Sometimes, we young people get together to talk about our unrealized dreams. It is easy at times for others to assume why we are here.

The answer is easy: for a better tomorrow. Nobody understands that even though we are young, we have the necessary maturity to confront reality. Here is a country with so many opportunities for everyone but I find myself along a road with no exit—I have only thoughts of my loved ones and of the possibility of moving forward. Yet, my worst enemy is always by my side. I am Latino and an immigrant.

Today I find myself locked up by the laws of the USA as a criminal wearing a prison uniform. I live like a criminal with sadness in my heart. I look at American kids going to school and think, I too am an American child. I should go to school. Is being Latino so different? Is coming here for our family such a bad thing? Is this so difficult to understand?

You will never understand that for my family, I am capable of so much more.

—Mario, fifteen-year-old Salvadoran youth

The Refugee Act of 1980 recognized the needs of refugee children who are unaccompanied, creating special legal provisions for their acceptance into the United States via formal refugee resettlement processes. The act established and funded specialized programs through the Department of Health and Human Services Office of Refugee Resettlement (DHHS-ORR) for minors who are identified as refugees prior to entry in the United States. The State Department identifies refugee children living in UN refugee camps who do not have a parent or legal guardian. On arrival in the United States, refugee children are placed in ORR's Unaccompanied Refugee Minor (URM) program and resettled by refugee resettlement agencies, similar to refugee adults. However, the Refugee Act of 1980 did not include "unaccompanied alien children," as they are neither recognized prior to entry nor do they maintain legal status in the United States as their refugee counterparts do. The specialized provisions and procedures for refugee children excluded unauthorized migrant children despite their shared experiences of war, violence, and deprivation in many of the same countries of origin. "Unaccompanied alien children" can be reclassified as "unaccompanied refugee minors" and enter the URM programs if they are granted a qualifying legal status, such as political asylum or specialized visas. In the early 1980s the rates of reclassification were quite low because a child must first be granted political asylum or prove that he or she was trafficked into the United States. Given the absence of court-appointed legal counsel, no recognition of persecution on account of being a child, and no specialized procedures distinguishing children from adults, such feats were rare. With key revisions to legislation for abused, abandoned, and neglected children in the 1990s and on trafficking in the early 2000s, these rates have risen somewhat, though they are still quite low. Instead, the state continued to fold unaccompanied alien children into the unauthorized adult population under the care and custody of the INS, subject to expedited deportation and prolonged detention.

For nearly twenty years advocates vied for a transfer of care and custody of unaccompanied, unauthorized children from the INS to the ORR analogous to that of unaccompanied refugee children. Advocates highlighted the irreconcilable conflict of interest in which the INS simultaneously served as guardian, jailer, and prosecutor of unaccompanied children. While the INS was responsible for housing, feeding, and providing medical care for detained children, it was also charged with "the departure from the United

States of all removable aliens," including the children entrusted to its care (U.S. DHS/ICE 2003). Prior to 2003, the INS held one-third of unaccompanied children in secure facilities, which were subcontracted bed space in existing state and county juvenile detention facilities. Although the INS claimed that unaccompanied children were housed in separate cells, in practice unauthorized children were commingled with juvenile offenders, some of whom had committed violent crimes. There were limited opportunities for education, access to interpreters, and recreation in these facilities (Duncan 2002). While in INS custody, children lacking the requisite documents to remain in the United States were detained for extended periods, sometimes up to two years while awaiting a ruling on their immigration cases.

During this time, a principal cleavage crystalized between legal advocates and immigration enforcement that persists in more recent discussions of the treatment of unaccompanied children—are unaccompanied children humanitarian refugees or criminal aliens? In this chapter, I elaborate the development and current status of the competing humanitarian and law enforcement regimes and the ways these imaginaries continue to shape the interventions of advocates, government bureaucrats, and nongovernmental staff involved in the lives of both detained and nondetained migrant children. I identify three overlapping sensibilities—the illegal alien, the criminal, and the enemy within—that contribute to a punitive approach to child migrants. To illustrate, I trace the circulation of a youth, Mario, from his home in El Salvador to immigration detention in the United States to his uncle's home in Maryland. Classified as an "unaccompanied alien minor," Mario faces critical legal decisions that shape not only his fate but also his family's. The blunt tool of the law compels Mario along prefigured trajectories intended either to protect him as a vulnerable child or to expel him as a criminal alien. I analyze two key legal cases, *Flores v. Reno* and *Plyler v. Doe*, which shaped the ways unauthorized children both in and outside of the context of detention are viewed as legal subjects and the rights afforded to them. The activism of DREAMers,[1] unauthorized youth who are the contemporary beneficiaries of *Plyler v. Doe*, highlights the failure to recognize the social agency of children and youth within the law and institutional practices. The law is not a disembodied, independent force, but is culturally constructed by the legislature, media, law enforcement, legal advocates, and helping professionals. While children are not traditionally considered contributors to the law and legal discourses that determine their fate, the narrative of Mario and the political organizing of DREAMers prove otherwise.

"But These Are Not *Our* Children"

Prior to a meeting at a Border Patrol station along the Texas-Mexico border in which I sought to discuss the agents' experiences apprehending migrant children, a station commander played a video that showed "inside the work of the Border Patrol." Reminiscent of the reality television show *COPS*, the fifteen-minute video opened with blasting music with a deep bass as quick images of uniformed Border Patrol and ICE officers flashed across the small television in the three-room station. A white Border Patrol vehicle pursued a van at high speed along a deserted highway, resulting in a violent crash as the driver lost control of the van; officers contended with a raging grass fire; youths firebombed officers as they arrested an unauthorized migrant. At the video's end, the station commander explained, "This is what we must contend with. We are not dealing with nice little kids."

In the law enforcement regime, the migrant child is folded into the pervasive rhetoric of the "illegal alien" who must be apprehended, controlled, and removed from the state. This social sensibility taps into anxieties about an *invasion* or *flood* of "illegal aliens," requiring repression and containment of unaccompanied children in the same ways that their adult counterparts do (Chavez 2001; Rodriguez 1997). Relying on the state's authority to regulate inclusion or exclusion of subjects, the migrant youth is an ungovernable subject—an outlaw. As Esther Madriz (1997) observes, the figure of the outlaw "brings together members of society in a common conviction, to direct their disapproval against those who are outside the social boundaries. Fear is a very important component in the creation of outlaws: we should fear them because they are dangerous, or evil, or just threatening to 'us'" (96; see also Durkheim 1982). Despite limited evidence supporting its efficacy, the detention of unauthorized migrants is an increasingly pervasive state strategy enlisted to control and remove the "contagion" or "criminal" as well as to deter and to deincentivize future unauthorized migratory flows.

As there is minimal distinction between children and adults in immigration law, there is little difficulty in identifying unauthorized immigrants exclusively in terms of illegality, rather than distinguishing any markers of difference along lines of age, gender, race, or ethnicity or any specific need for rights. While children are often held in an immutable category of innocence, the law enforcement approach toward unauthorized migrants prioritizes their "alien" status over their status as children. The fear that drives the creation and proliferation of the migrant as "outlaw" fails to recognize that illegal alienage is not a preconditioned set of rules and regulations or inherent traits as law enforcement suggests but is culturally informed, derived, and constructed.

The illegality and criminality of migrant youth are not innate social or legal qualities of unaccompanied children: "the line between alien and citizen is soft" (Ngai 2004: 6). As Mae Ngai (2004) argues, "illegal alienage is not a natural or fixed condition but the product of positive law; it is contingent and at times unstable. The line between legal and illegal status can be crossed in both directions" (6). Various forms of legal relief, in fact, are available to children, including political asylum, Special Immigrant Juvenile (SIJ) status visas, visas for victims of Trafficking (T visas), family sponsorship, the Violence Against Women Act (VAWA), as well as temporary statuses such as Deferred Action for Childhood Arrivals (DACA) or Temporary Protective Status (TPS). Migrants can move in and out of lawful immigration status over time. At the same time, the state can also repeal one's legality or grant graduated benefits and rights contingent on the type of lawful status. However, for the multiple structural, cultural, linguistic, and developmental reasons I will discuss, there are proportionately few children who benefit from these legal statuses.

Despite the malleability of one's legal status, the practices of law enforcement historically have treated detained migrant children as inherently illegal, blocking children's access to forms of legal relief from which they could otherwise benefit outside of the "care and custody" of the federal government. In immigration law, which lacks a legal recognition of a child's individual relationship to the state, unaccompanied children must rely on an adult or guardian as a proxy to petition state courts for a dependency finding that could lead to legal status. In family reunification petitions, for example, a parent can petition for his or her child as "derivatives" of an asylum application; however, a child as a principal applicant cannot petition for his or her parents until the child becomes a U.S. citizen *and* reaches age twenty-one. Absent a legally recognized parent or guardian, the state serves in loco parentis, and, as such, until recently, ICE served as gatekeeper for those seeking access to the law. Children had been required to seek "special consent" from the Department of Homeland Security in order to enter state court and ultimately to pursue the SIJS visa, a principal for unaccompanied children who have been abandoned, abused, or neglected. ICE's policies and practices have been inconsistent and convoluted in regard to specific consent in which a single individual maintains the authority to grant or to deny children's petitions to enter state court. From January 2001 until August 2006, the national juvenile coordinator at ICE approved only 70 percent of special consent petitions, many of which, advocates contend, came too late to affect a child's legal claim (Marlan 2006). Once they reach eighteen, children typically cannot obtain the needed orders in most state courts (Junck 2012). In practice, ICE's national juvenile coordinator would prejudge cases, often freezing their illegal status by limiting their ability to file a petition in state court. Through outright denials, delaying applications for sometimes up to six months, or by waiting until a child turned eighteen, the coordinator served as lawyer, judge, and jury with no mechanism for appeal. Children were held in a catch-22—unable to access the law because of their minor status and because the state as parent did not grant permission to such access. By restricting children's access to the courts, ICE prevented the opportunity to regularize legal status. The law enforcement approach to unaccompanied children fixed the criminality of unauthorized migrant children, hedging out potential humanitarian forms of legal relief to child migrants in the name of safety and the security of the nation. Law enforcement practices effectively invented permanent illegality and inherent criminality, not unlike the way turn-of-the-century reformers invented delinquency as ascribed to behaviors of lower-class and immigrant children (Platt 1969). In 2008, pressure brought by federal litigation seeking to change practices that made illegality and criminality inherent qualities of unaccompanied migrant children led to shifts in ICE's gatekeeping of state courts. Following federal litigation of *Perez-Olano v. Gonzales et al.*, unaccompanied children must now seek permission from ORR rather than ICE.[2] For the moment, ORR in loco parentis has maintained an open access policy permitting all children the "privilege" (although not a "right") of filing a petition in state court. However, in practice, ORR subcontracted nongovernmental organizations often restrict access, as they will not serve as guardian for the purposes of SIJ while youth are held in their facilities, leaving detained children unable to pursue this principal legal remedy and ensuing benefits.

Critical to the functionality of this sensibility are the ways law enforcement views the relationship between migrant children and their parents.

Those whose parents are identifiable are seen as reproductions of their parents' illegal or criminal behavior, destined to reproduce the same pathological behaviors embodied in their illicit presence in the United States. In this view, deceptive parents pay smugglers to transport their children illegally to the United States, knowingly violating the law. Children unaccompanied by an adult caregiver are seen as lacking the parental relationship necessary for effective socialization and governance. For many unaccompanied children, law enforcement and advocates alike assume that their parents have abandoned them, forcing them to live on the streets and to turn to a life of crime. Migration becomes an indicator of family rupture. Without parents to socialize youth into productive citizens effectively, the unaccompanied child remains pathologically independent and in need of state intervention and discipline. However, there is a critical contradiction in this perspective: ICE considers some children products of their parents' poor decisions, and in this way divorces children from any social agency to make their own decisions or to contribute to familial migration decisions. At the same time, unaccompanied children are held no less responsible for the outcomes of those decisions even if the decisions are viewed as not of their own making.

In a second overlapping sensibility, law enforcement concretizes the linkage between unauthorized migration and the criminalization of youth of color by comparing "illegal" immigration with issues of urban crime and gang violence; in each case, predominantly male youth are framed as exhibiting antisocial behavior and existing outside the law. While different bodies of law guide immigration and state court decisions, both systems draw from the analogous public and institutional narratives that criminalize youths of color. Contemporary American courts contend with multiple layers of norms and values, which inform notions of pathology in relation to multiple and often overlapping terms of race, ethnicity, and poverty (Bortner, Zatz, and Hawkins 2000; Shook 2005: 465). Public perceptions of the criminality and delinquency of youth create tremendous fear, as in cases of highly publicized school shootings or gang violence (Adelman and Yalda 2000: 37; Giroux 2000: 15). High rates of teen pregnancy and school dropouts, particularly in African American and Latino communities, have led some to call for simultaneous policy reform and institutional interventions to "save" troubled youth (Giroux 1998) while the state bolsters enforcement efforts to allay public anxieties.

Some scholars have attempted to contextualize youth delinquency through studies focusing on how youth experience the law through lenses of race, ethnicity, gender, education level, or socioeconomic status. Mike Males (1999), for example, argues that by controlling for race in instances of juvenile crime, income inequality becomes the prominent determinant, not ethnic or racial differences. Given that more people of color in the United States live in poverty, it remains unsurprising that youth of color are more frequently arrested for criminal activity. Pete Edelman (2002) terms these inequalities the "duality of youth," suggesting that there is a division along racial/ethnic and class lines that signals the disparate social and economic support accessible to and ultimately received by youth (Shook 2005: 469). Ann Ferguson's (2001) ethnography traces how race and gender identities shape whether the school system labels African American youth as either "troublemakers" or "school boys." She argues that albeit a fiction, race continues "as a system for organizing social difference and as a device for reproducing inequality in contemporary United States" (2001: 17). This criminalization of youth of color folds comfortably into the national public discourses that associate Latinos and African Americans with social ills such as poor schools, poverty and unemployment, crime, overpopulation, and public health crises (Inda 2011: 77; see also Coutin 2011). The state contributes to and exacerbates the marginality of youth of color through unequal access to employment, education, and health care and disproportionate attention from law enforcement officers, as evidenced by Mario's "Broken Dreams" in this chapter's opening interlude. In U.S. conceptualizations of delinquency, differences in economic status are integrally intertwined with race and ethnicity; variation in skin color becomes a visible means by which to identify delinquent youth, marking those who require punishment and those who warrant leniency.

The juvenile court has shifted from a model based on the tutelary complex as a means of distributing social services to a more punitive mechanism of social control that ignores mediating conditions of structural poverty and racism, yet the conditions under which the court must operate also have changed. Jeffrey Shook (2005) traces how legislative changes in the United States blur the boundaries between juvenile and criminal courts, not only shifting the court's focus to "more punitive and control-oriented goals" but also revealing changes in social attitudes toward delinquency of children and youth (461). The increased ease with which children are transferred from juvenile courts to the adult criminal justice system signals a contestation in the meanings of childhood and adolescence by policymakers and judicial authorities (462; see also Jensen and Howard 1998). Individual U.S. states may ignore the legal provision youth maintain as minors, trying them as adult offenders and incarcerating them in adult state prisons, and, in other words, claiming that a child is no longer a child. "Supported by images of youth as 'superpredators' or otherwise violent and 'dangerous,' transfer [to adult courts] denotes the point where youth have crossed over the line into adulthood" (Shook 2005: 462–63). Acts of violence destabilize the notion of the child's innate innocence because the child has acquired "adult knowl-edge" with which he willingly and with full awareness commits social trans-gressions. Courts may view juveniles as competent and capable actors responsible for their actions, though youth are not granted such an indepen-dent standing in other areas of contemporary social life. In spite of a dra-matic expansion of child protective services, such transfer practices are emblematic of how the state "redraw[s] the boundaries between childhood and adulthood in contradictory ways" (Tilton 2010: 11). Although youth as problematic or as pathological is not a new phenomenon, the treatment of unaccompanied children as if they possess attributes of certain criminal be-haviors associated with adults speaks to the disproportionate consequences for unauthorized children (see, e.g., Finn 2001). Through the lens of race, unaccompanied migrants enter the carceral complex in the United States, which disproportionately detains young men of color with little hope of re-habilitation (e.g., Davis 1999; Schlosser 1998). For unaccompanied migrant youth, the state's presumption is that they are an inherent risk to public safety and, as a result, forfeit any opportunity for rehabilitation. Instead, by governing through crime, the state easily can remove them from the "home-land," while those who are citizens remain incarcerated with little potential for rehabilitation (e.g., Simon 1997).

Under both the presidencies of George W. Bush and Barack Obama, the repertoire of enforcement measures that criminalize migrants has diversi-fied and expanded. Surveillance of the U.S.-Mexico border has become in-creasingly militarized. There has been an expansion of workplace raids, both large and small. ICE campaigns such as 287(g)[3] and Secure Communities[4] have formalized partnerships between state and local law enforcement and federal immigration authorities. Since 2000, criminal prosecutions have in-creased, and misdemeanors that are neither "aggravated" nor "felonies" have transformed into aggravated felonies with mandatory deportation orders.[5] Despite claims to a progressive agenda, the Obama administration has de-ported over 1.06 million migrants in two and one-half years—in comparison to 1.57 million deportations during Bush's two presidential terms—a peculiar and underpublicized milestone for a Democratic president with significant support from Latino constituents (O'Toole 2011). The Department of Homeland Security has exceeded Bush-era rates of deportation with nearly 400,000 individuals deported annually (Spencer and Becker 2010). Mass incarceration of unauthorized migrants has become a multibillion-dollar industry in the United States. At the same time, there is a decreased availability of visas and waivers, and new laws increasingly obstruct the ability of migrants to secure and maintain legal status. Regardless of their legal status, children are impacted disproportionately by the enforcement and deportation regime that may target them individually or divide their families based on differing legal status. As a result, the enforcement regime has produced a class of irregular migrants, many of whom are children.

The "war on terror" has only exaggerated enforcement-only measures. Following the September 11, 2001, terrorist attacks on the World Trade Center in New York, a third sensibility consolidated the conflation of the immigrant with the criminal alien or terrorist. The sentiment has gained significant traction, most notably in the 2001 USA PATRIOT Act and the 2002 Homeland Security Act. Escalating terror-alert warnings—from yellow to orange to red—broadcast at airports, in convention centers, and on the radio and television marked the imminence of attack on native soil. Announcements on highway traffic boards, on public transportation, and in airport terminals encouraged citizens to be aware of suspicious packages, activities, or people. ICE issued a special registration program for male youths over sixteen from predominantly Muslim countries, further institutionalizing the criminalization of young men of color, of foreign origin, and of particular faiths. "Capillary" surveillance à la Foucault was in full force.[6]

The lack of knowledge about terrorists, their motivations, and their potential for violent action has led some behavioral and social scientists to draw insights and model intervention strategies from criminal street gangs, leading to a stronger racialization of criminal behavior associated with youth (see, e.g., Turnley and Smrcka 2002). Racial profiling, particularly of young men, became acceptable in an indefinite war on a still-amorphous enemy. In the ensuing anti-immigrant context, smugglers are agents of terrorism and immigrants are potential terrorists. In 2005 former Speaker of the House Newt Gingrich warned, "fueled by the global nature of the drug trade, gangs are increasingly international operations, with many of the largest and most vicious gangs operating in America hailing from South America. With the infrastructure in place to move and distribute drugs from across the border,

the danger exists that they will use their network to, for the right price, traffic terrorists and weapons into the country" (Gingrich 2005). Central American gangs, in particular, are cast as a growing threat to national security
and as requiring increased levels of surveillance and intervention along the
border and within the interior of the country. A 2007 guilty verdict against
former Chicago Latin Disciples gang member Jose Padilla for his support of
terrorism overseas linked Latino youth, gang activity, and terrorism specifically to the Midwestern landscape during my fieldwork.

In addition to being subjected to the vicissitudes of the war on terror and
the war on immigrants, unaccompanied children also exist as a particular
kind of palpable threat to the body politic. The view that children are somehow in the process of becoming and of being not yet socialized translates
into the contested potentiality of migrant youth. On the one hand, the potential for socialization and rehabilitation offers some assurances to the state,
which seeks their allegiance; on the other, the malleability of impressionable
youth leaves them open to forming suspicious or even dangerous allegiances
with other states, criminals, or terrorists.[7] The diffuseness of terrorism
leaves those allegiances simultaneously undetermined yet, in many respects,
inconsequential. It is the fear of the realization of their potential, influenced
by violent terrorist organizations, that warrants additional attention and
containment. Images of child soldiers from conflicts around the world and
headlines about children as young as fourteen training to be suicide bombers
in Gaza, Pakistan, Iraq, and Afghanistan offer the public further proof of the
capacity of children to commit terrorism. Unaccompanied migrant youths
become yet another group of unencumbered, untrustworthy, brown men requiring law enforcement intervention to control the threat to the nation (e.g.,
Bernstein and Lichtblau 2005). While seemingly irreconcilable with the image of the hardened criminal incapable of rehabilitation, the still-malleable
youth as a potential homegrown terrorist stems from social anxieties of violence and xenophobia. The out-of-place migrant youth transforms from *at*
risk to *the* risk.

These overlapping and emergent sensibilities and sentiments woven
throughout law enforcement practices historically have overridden the best
interests standard, which dictates child welfare practices for children in state
court. The very "shelters" designed as a less restrictive environment than INS
immigration jails that detained children just a decade prior have become
"total institutions" that not only control and document everyday behaviors,
conversations, interactions, and activities but also restrict knowledge from

the very children whose fate hangs in the balance (Goffman 1961). As a Border Patrol officer surveilling the Texas-Mexico border remarked to me, "But these are not *our* children"; in fact, migrant children are not seen as possessing the vulnerability or rights of children at all. The detention, containment, and removal of the Other are palpable. The illegality and perceived innate criminality of migrant youth have become the preeminent factor in the ways they are apprehended, detained, and cared for by both law enforcement and child welfare authorities.

A Humanitarian Response?

In most nations the history of immigration law is at a minimum a catalog of strategic and intricate interventions to shape or to control flows of people and goods across national borders. Yet, we should not assume that these interventions derive from a unified or coherent state strategy or that the law itself is necessarily complete or definitive (De Genova 2002: 424). Instead, as Nicholas De Genova argues in his review of migrant illegality, "the intricate history of law-making is distinguished above all by the constitutive restlessness and relative incoherence of various strategies, tactics, and compromises that nation-states implement at particular historical moments, precisely to mediate the contradictions immanent in social crises and political struggles" (2002: 425). The 1997 Flores Settlement Agreement was such a historical moment in the legal lives of unaccompanied children.

In 1985 the California-based Center for Human Rights and Constitutional Law filed a class action lawsuit against the INS, *Flores et al. v. Janet Reno*, because of the INS policies of detaining, processing, and releasing unaccompanied children.[8] The case challenged a new INS policy that would release youth only to "a parent or legal guardian." The U.S. District Court ruled against the plaintiffs, declaring that the INS detention and release policies were constitutional and that institutional custody, though not the preferred method, was not unconstitutional. In the absence of documented parents, the state as *parens patriae*, or "parent of the nation," was entitled to intervene and institutionalize unaccompanied youth. According to the court, such an intervention was not a limitation on the migrant children's rights as their advocates had maintained. Despite the verdict, the INS was willing to negotiate a settlement decree, known as the 1997 Flores Agreement, which continues to set the minimum standards for the care and release of detained unaccompanied children under the ORR.[9] The decree is based on the premise that the U.S. government must treat children in immigration custody with "dignity, respect and special concern for their vulnerability as minors." In particular, the agreement stipulated that the INS must: (1) ensure the prompt release of children from immigration detention; (2) for those with a pending release from detention, place children in the "least restrictive setting appropriate to the minor's age and special needs"; and (3) implement basic standards of care and treatment of children in immigration detention, including a range of requirements for mental health services, health care, education, recreation, religious services, access to legal representation, telephones, and transportation arrangements.

In the 1997 Flores Agreement, the practices of care and protection are exclusively predicated on the child as victim devoid of social agency and do not apply to those who have been charged or *potentially* face a chargeable offense; have committed or threaten to commit a violent act against themselves or others; have proven disruptive; are escape risks; or must be held for their own safety (VII (21)). In spite of a wide range of interpretations of those exceptions, each restricts a child's social agency exclusively to potential destructiveness, thus necessitating heightened restrictions.

While advocates continue to hail the Flores Agreement as a victory that improved the standards and conditions of housing and release for unaccompanied children, it has not been a panacea for the identification and treatment of unaccompanied migrant children. While binding, the recommendations are still subject to considerable interpretation and elective implementation by both INS/ICE and ORR. In fiscal 2000 alone there were 1,933 children held in juvenile detention facilities, of which 1,569 were nondelinquent (OIG 2001a). In 2001, for example, thirty-four of the fifty-seven detention facilities housing unaccompanied minors could not guarantee that delinquent and nondelinquent minors would not be commingled. In spite of the Flores Agreement and with limited oversight, the INS treated children minimally different from juvenile offenders.

Since the 2003 transition of care and custody of unaccompanied children from INS/ICE to ORR, unaccompanied children have fared better but law enforcement practices pervade in both structural ways and everyday practices. For example, ICE consistently refuses to transfer children who face a chargeable offense to ORR; for many youths, it is sufficient that they are accused of a crime, whether a minor drug possession, curfew violations, or driving without a license, even if the charges are dismissed or never filed.

For ORR, youth exhibiting or even potentially exhibiting "delinquent" behaviors translates into more secure placements reserved for youth with a
"criminal background." In more diffuse ways, nongovernmental subcontractors also absorb the law enforcement mentality. Across multiple sites, facility staff consistently consider any child with an impending deportation order
as a flight risk, often refusing children phone calls to family members, con-
fiscating a child's shoes to deter flight, and subjecting children either individually or collectively to "lockdown" in facilities. In some respects, the staff
considers all unaccompanied children as flight risks and, as a result, regularly restricts knowledge of their family reunification options, withholds
updates on one's "case" or release, and denies access to the Internet or e-mail.
By tightly controlling the dissemination of information, claiming the child's
own best interests and safety, ORR and the facility staff are able to control a
child's delinquent tendencies embodied in the very agency that brought the
child to the United States as an unaccompanied minor. For unauthorized
children, agency becomes quickly diverted from discussions of empower-
ment of individual youth to questions of accountability and the need for
containment (e.g., Bluebond-Langner and Korbin 2007; Hecht 1998; Terrio
2008: 876).

Notably, advocates enlisted the Flores Agreement to untangle the child
from the migrant adult and from illegality. By instantiating the dependency
of children who require care within a language of vulnerability, the agreement forced the image of the vulnerable, migrant child in need of a humanitarian intervention into direct opposition with the criminalized "alien" who
is subject to removal. Vulnerability became an explicitly defined quality of
apprehended migrant children forced to flee war, violence, abuse, depravity,
and the street. Mobility was a symptom of their vulnerability as children
and a condemnation of the conditions spurring their migration. Claims of a
troubling increase in the migration of children were not based on historical
fact but on a constructivist approach to child migration as a social problem.
Drawing from a perception of increased movement of children across international borders, advocates have come to frame this movement as representative of a rupture in the family unit. The discourses of "lost childhoods"
and social anxieties around the "lost generation" gained traction as advocates publicized the victimization of child migrants, abandoned children,
and trafficking victims (Stephens 1995). However, as Joel Best (1990) cautions, we must look at why and how these anxieties emerged in the first place
rather than exclusively the social concern that advocates seek to remedy.

What are the factors that resulted in a surge in interest in child migration as a social phenomenon? How has the image of the child "menaced by deviants" (J. Best 1990: 6) shaped expressions of care? How do American social values shape cultural and economic values of migrant families in their countries of origin? (see, e.g., Boehm 2008, 2012). How has capitalism's impact on the economic functionality of the nuclear family shaped child circulation? In response to the imaginaries depicting youth as threatening and in need of containment, advocates framed migrant children as the "ideal victim"—"a person or a category of individuals who—when hit by crime—most readily are given the complete and legitimate status of being a victim" (Christie 1986: 18). The humanitarian response to child migration continues to be predicated on an understanding of children as dependent on adults and the welfare state and on a culturally situated understanding of childhood as necessarily shielded from adult responsibilities of caregiving and labor (Horton 2008: 929; see also Moreno 2005).

In many ways, the law requires victimhood as constitutive of the migrant child. Particularly in immigration law, the independent migrant child cannot exist and yet, an increasing number of unaccompanied youth enter court dockets each year. As legal scholar Jaqueline Bhabha (2008: 2) argues, a child "can never consent to an exploitative migration facilitated by intermediaries."[10] But at the same time, the unlawful and independent presence of an unaccompanied child forces a production of self that does not reconcile with the ways institutions and the state have produced them. The paradox, though unresolved, then manifests itself in seeking an explanation that builds on the child as victim and the migrant as exploited; only in this way can the nonexistent, nonagentic migrant child occupy a place in the juridical system.

The debate between law enforcement and immigrant advocates escalated in the early years of the twenty-first century over the state's failure to recognize the innate vulnerability of child migrants and to provide safeguards became a judgment on the values of the nation. The state's failure to protect the most vulnerable population of youth because of their legality called into question national values of inclusiveness and multiculturalism as well as the presumed U.S. heritage as a "nation of immigrants."[11] The United States, a nation founded on the premise of protecting of the most vulnerable from harm in the spirit of Emma Lazarus's "New Colossus" brazened on the pedestal of the Statue of Liberty, failed to protect the "littlest of immigrants."[12] In a 2002 report entitled *Prison Guard or Parent?*, the Commission for Refugee Women and Children claimed, "One true measure of a society is its treatment of children. The United States must acknowledge and uphold the rights and needs of newcomer children in order to live up to its reputation as a leader in human rights and a nation that protects children" (3). This accusation has particular resonance in the U.S. context, as the country is one of only two nations not signatory to the UN Convention on the Rights of the Child.[13] Instead of protecting children against the dangers of smugglers and traffickers as well as from abusive parents, the state had developed an extensive apparatus of law enforcement, courts, and legal provisions, and had funded the expansive private prison industry to detain children on the sole basis of their alienage without consideration of their status as legal minors. The accusation unfolded as a condemnation of the state's willful and discriminatory negligence of the child and of the Other.

In this key moment, we see very explicitly the interests of the state and the best interests of the child diverge. Advocates argued that the state had a moral imperative to care for unaccompanied children as victims, whether documented or not, but the state's interests to secure its borders and control migratory flows were and continue to be paramount. The public persona of the unaccompanied child was preeminent in shaping legislation and judicial practice. If delinquent, illegal, and potentially terrorist, unaccompanied children were not deserving of specialized care and limited government resources. The state viewed some unaccompanied children—those who came from countries where the United States maintained critical political interest—as uniquely deserving of special protection. Children from Cuba and the Soviet Union received special treatment and status under the law, while children from Latin America, primarily, Central America and Mexico, were and are treated as criminalized adults who transgressed the laws of the state. Where the political interests of the state in combating communism and the individual child align, the migrant child becomes particularly deserving of specialized accommodations, care, and legal status.

"I Walked Their Geography"

To illustrate the ways these competing regimes trap migrant youth in untenable situations, I turn to the narrative of Mario, a lanky youth of fifteen from El Salvador, whose poem opened the chapter. When I first met Mario, he was dressed in a neon blue sweatshirt with matching pants and black plastic flip-flops provided to him by the facility where he resided. In June's

El Paso heat, Mario incessantly wiped the sweat from his brow onto his right sleeve. The facility's director explained that the fluorescent-colored clothing—red, blue, yellow, and green—allowed staff to easily identify children who attempted to escape the federal facility where they were detained. The sandals were also standard-issue flip-flops to deter fast-footed children from getting very far along the gravel road connecting the facility to the interstate. The facility was at the time one of thirty-six federal shelters in which the ORR subcontracts NGOs to provide housing and social services to unaccompanied or trafficked children apprehended by ICE.[14]

At the time the convoluted network of government departments, federal government agencies, and myriad voluntary agencies involved in the care and custody of apprehended unaccompanied children was indecipherable to Mario. In his mounting frustration with his "captivity" at the facility, Mario remarked, "I am ashamed that I got caught. I made my decision, had everything organized, had my plan, and now what? I am trapped here in this place. My debt is increasing as I sit here wasting my time learning geography. They must think I'm stupid. I walked their geography."

Although Mario's reputation as a talented student and responsible worker had brought him school awards for excellence and stable employment as a dishwasher and an occasional carpenter in his hometown of Santa Ines, it also brought him to the attention of the "Joker," the local Mara Salvatrucha (also known as MS-13) gang leader, whose first contact with Mario was to demand the new tennis shoes Mario had purchased with his earnings. Later, demands came for sex with his girlfriend and participation in gang activities. Each threat was met with Mario's scared though firm and sometimes belligerent refusal. "I am not interested in your *babosadas* [stupidity or rubbish]," he told them. On three occasions, several gang members beat Mario, with the "Joker" directing each blow. They would wait for Mario outside school, his place of work, and even church on Sunday. At times Mario left through an alternate door, climbed a fence behind the school, or ran to escape these confrontations, but often without success. "It was hard to hide from them," Mario remarked on his efforts to avoid gang members in his community. "I'm taller than most people in my town. It's kind of hard for me to blend in."

Mario contributed to his family's food and to schooling expenses for his six younger siblings. His two elder sisters, now married and with children, had limited capacity to contribute to the household's needs. Mario's stepfather had intermittent employment as a truck driver, which varied with the demand for timber from neighboring Honduras, Guatemala, and Nicaragua and with his bouts of heavy drinking; he was verbally and physically abusive. After a particularly brutal beating by the "Joker" and three of his fellow gang members that resulted in Mario's arm being broken, Mario stopped attending school and work, only leaving the house once in six weeks to have his cast removed. "I tried to become invisible," he explained. He slept most of the day or watched Hollywood films on a small television set in the living room, attempting to avoid the gaze of his stepfather who fortunately was working in Honduras for several weeks at a time during that period. Gang members would regularly pass Mario's home and yell threats through the windows. On one occasion Joker knocked on the door. When Mario's mother answered, she said Mario had left for the United States—a decision Mario had been contemplating for several months. Mario recalled this period of hiding: "There was nothing for me there. I couldn't work; I couldn't study; I couldn't protect my mom from my stepfather or even myself [from my stepfather]. I had to hide to survive; that is no way to live."

After six weeks of retreat, Mario and his mother began discussing his journey to the United States. She had located a distant uncle of Mario's who had moved to Maryland eight years earlier and called him on Mario's behalf requesting help. Mario's uncle agreed to secure him employment and provide him a place to live if he could get to Maryland on his own. Mario borrowed $6,000 from a local police officer for whom he had done some carpentry work but who could not provide him protection from the MS-13 recruitment apparatus. The police officer introduced Mario to his brother, a broker for *coyotes* who smuggled migrants through Guatemala and Mexico into the United States. Mario's $3,000 down payment assured him passage to the U.S.-Mexico border, or so he thought.

His departure from Santa Ines marked Mario's entrance into a liminal period of transit, whereby he was simultaneously *outside* of the nation because he is devoid of state protections and *inside* because he is physically present and moving through the nation (Coutin 2005: 196). Susan Coutin adds, "Because their presence is prohibited, unauthorized migrants do not fully arrive even when they reach their destinations," thus they are "present in yet absent from nations" (Coutin 2005: 195). He journeyed for three weeks—by bus through Guatemala, by car and by train through Mexico, and eventually by foot into the United States. The success of Mario's journey was predicated on his hiding in ditches along the road, on the top of trains, and in the back of vans. He rarely spoke for fear of passers-by detecting his Salvadoran accent and vocabulary. "I imagined I was a superhero in a comic book, you know, who had the power to make himself invisible. No one could see me. I never spoke. It is like I wasn't even there. Besides, it all seems like a bad nightmare now. I try not to think about it. It never really happened." Mario entered another dimension in an effort to absent himself while in transit. Susan Coutin (2005) analyzes how "clandestinity" is a public secret, a known social reality in which unauthorized migrants must be "absent from the spaces they occupy" (2005: 195). For unauthorized migrants arriving in the United States, the law becomes a mechanism by which the state may make legally *absent* those who are physically present through prohibition of unauthorized entrance or denial of certain rights and services. The state may also make physically absent, via detention or deportation, those who are unlawfully living within national borders (196).

On crossing the territorial boundary between Mexico and the United States, Mario entered a new juridical space. Mario shifted his principal legal identity from that of a citizen of El Salvador to that of an *illegal alien* with limited access to rights and services in the United States. Within three days of Mario's crossing the border by foot near McAllen, Texas, U.S. Border Patrol agents apprehended him en route to Houston. They interrogated him for two hours and held him for eight days in a small cell with six other migrants. Eventually, because of his age and his presence without a legal guardian, Mario was transferred to an ORR facility for unaccompanied children.

In order to remain in the United States, the most viable legal option for Mario was to petition for a Special Immigrant Juvenile visa, in which he had to detail how his father abandoned him at a young age and the abuse he and his siblings received at the hands of his stepfather from which his mother could not or chose not to protect him. Mario had to publicly claim that he was "abused, neglected, or abandoned" by his family—a claim that, according to Mario, was not only emotionally inaccurate but also undermined his personal and financial commitment to his mother and siblings. "I just can't say those bad things about my family to a room of people, to a judge. You just don't do that. They are my family." According to Mario's former employer in Santa Ines, the physical abuse was public knowledge but something not discussed or addressed. He said, "It [domestic violence] happens. I know it happens but it is a family affair. [Mario] never said anything to me, but I knew what was going on. We all knew."

After two months of meeting with Mario in an ORR facility, I traveled to El Salvador to speak with family and community members of detained youth in the United States and to continue my work with two youths who had since been deported to El Salvador. In my conversation with Mario's mother in their family home, she explained, "It was tough for him here. He is smart and he didn't have options." In addition to the lack of opportunity, she framed his migration north as a rite of passage. "His uncles went to *el Norte* [the North]; many of his cousins did; his father—even if he doesn't remember him." Migration was one alternative within a catalog of choices that Mario's father, extended family members, and now Mario had enlisted.

In my time in Santa Ines, even casual conversations were marked by a migration narrative—either of the individual with whom I spoke or of a close friend or family member. As Douglas Massey and his coauthors (1993) detail, a culture of migration develops over time and becomes a social value. "For young men, and in many settings young women as well, migration becomes a rite of passage, and those who do not attempt to elevate their status through international movements are considered lazy, unenterprising, and undesirable" (Massey et al. 1993: 452–53). What remains striking, though, is that what spurred Mario's migration—his social agency, entrepreneurialism, and fundamental concern for his own physical safety and his family's well-being—is turned on its head on arrival in the United States. Mario is viewed as delinquent and undesirable in the U.S. context, denied the acclaimed American virtues of hard work, innovation, self-reliance, and family values, attributes that describe Mario's character. Savvy to this contradiction, Mario articulated the greatest weakness ascribed to him: "my worst enemy is always by my side. I am Latino and an immigrant."

The quickly growing network of ORR facilities for unaccompanied children might suggest that the law has begun to recognize the social agency of an entrepreneurial youth who orchestrates his own transnational journey, although the bureaucratic processes and institutional practices are predicated exclusively on children as undeveloped and dependent on adults. More frequently the law and lawlike processes frame agency in terms of delinquency, perhaps a contributing factor to why gang-based asylum claims have limited success. Mario's pro bono attorney attempted to convince him that proving abuse, abandonment, or neglect in the form of SIJ status was a more viable option than political asylum, though he could have pursued both simultaneously. She remarked to me, "In court, child abuse is more palatable than gangs."

From the moment Mario became visible to the state, immigration authorities treated him as a criminal without rights and privileges. Shackled at the point of apprehension, he and others like him were detained in prison cells and interrogated by uniformed U.S. Border Patrol officers. "No matter what I say, they [Border Patrol] don't believe me. I am fifteen. I am hungry. I cannot go back [to El Salvador]. I am telling the truth. I cannot go back." Mario's desperation clashed with the institutional perception of Mario that he was somehow dangerous—evidenced by the facility and ORR's repeated reference to alleged drug use and "gang involvement," which he consistently denied. The overlapping categories of race, age, gender, and delinquency create a youth who is not to be trusted and in many instances is a person to fear. On the other hand, legal advocates consistently position migrant youths as victims to seek certain rights on their behalf. In contrast to his state-issued sweatsuits and sandals, which marked Mario as a prisoner, his attorney also sought to physically and symbolically dress him as a sympathetic child victim, worthy of the court's sympathies. His attorney explained, "If you have a client who comes into the courtroom with muscles, visible tattoos, or even just a bad attitude, you will have an extremely difficult time convincing the judge that your client is sufficiently sympathetic and deserving of asylum. However irrelevant to your legal claim, your client must play into a more sympathetic image of the victim—docile, quiet, and sufficiently fearful." By doing so, attorneys deemphasize the sophisticated decision-making processes and social agency Mario required not only to cross vast distances but also to survive with some level of mental and physical integrity. A debilitated victim, particularly a child victim, cannot exercise such significant displays of individual social agency and is cast as isolated from collective dimensions of social agency. In part the singular depiction of the youth as victim undermines the credibility of the unaccompanied child, whose narrative becomes an irreconcilable account of passivity and agency.

Saskia Sassen (1999) argues that migrations are highly selective, structured processes in which migrants travel along specific routes for specific reasons. Mario came to the United States with clearly articulated motivations, not blindly or haphazardly propelled northward. Laura Agustin (2003) highlights the fact that "Individual personalities play their part, differences such as self-confidence, willingness to take risks and adaptability in the face of change. Being in a structurally less powerful position than people in the First World does not mean that one is not making decisions, and that those decisions are influenced by a vast multiplicity of circumstance, including individual desire. Being poor does not make people poor in spirit" (32). Mario does not see himself as a passive victim without options; instead, he considers himself a survivor of persecution, as a provider for his family, as a protector of his mother, and as a future car mechanic. "I am here [in the United States] for me, my future, and my family," he explained later while at his uncle's home in suburban Maryland. He has exercised his social agency in his decision to leave home and journey north. He solicited knowledge from other migrants as to which *coyotes* were reliable, borrowed large sums of money to fund his journey, and clandestinely crossed three national borders. While I do not wish to suggest that agency equates with autonomous decision making amid an abundance of choices or that his situation is necessarily of his own making, Mario understands his reasons for migration in ways consistent with other decision-making processes in his life—to pursue an education, to support his family, and "for a better tomorrow." He is making the most of his limited options.

No Fault of Their Own

To contextualize the denial of agency specific to child and youth migrants, I now turn to another crucial legal ruling, *Plyler v. Doe*, which laid the foundation for the current impasses between enforcement and humanitarianism even beyond the detention context.[15] In 1982, the U.S. Supreme Court struck down a 1975 Texas state statute that denied state K-12 educational funding based on a child's (il)legal status and attempted to charge tuition to unauthorized students. In a 5-4 majority ruling, the U.S. Supreme Court found that the law was in violation of the Fourteenth Amendment because it targeted children and "impose[d] its discriminatory burden on the basis of a legal characteristic over which children can have little control." At the most basic level, the ruling was the first to acknowledge that an unauthorized child is a person—in some ways distinct from his or her parents. However, while granting access to education for all children, regardless of legal status, this ruling did not extend education as a *right* to unauthorized children. Such a ruling would have formalized a relationship based on rights and obligations between an unauthorized child and the state.[16] Instead, the court maintained that parents are mediators between the child and the state, acknowledging a child's presence only as a result of a parent's illegal movements or poor decisions. The court argued that children "can affect neither their parents' conduct nor their own status" and should not be punished for the decisions of their parents. The Court further stated that holding children responsible for the actions of their parents "does not comport with fundamental conceptions of justice." Unauthorized children were seen as "blameless" for actions of migration across national borders, denying children the capacity of exercising any agency.

The Court argued that denying education to unauthorized children would result in "the creation and perpetuation of a subclass of illiterates within our boundaries, surely adding to the problems and costs of unemployment, welfare, and crime." The state has an integral role in protecting children from the tenuous border between becoming an educated member of society and a criminal in a permanent underclass, or "shadow population." In this view, the welfare state must protect children from the consequences of their parents' poor decisions and criminal acts, socializing potential citizens through education while protecting that state's interests in public safety and fiscal responsibility.

This language absenting a child's social agency has continued in over a decade of iterations of the Development, Relief, and Education for Alien Minors Act (DREAM Act), whereby children, "through no fault of their own," are unauthorized in the United States, and thus deserving of in-state tuition for higher education and a pathway to citizenship. Both *Plyler v. Doe* and the DREAM Act cast the child as lacking any agency or decision-making power and as becoming victims of "the sins of their fathers." The responsibility lies in the hands of the parents or the state in lieu of the parent, which frees the state to provide some forms of relief or specialized services to children. DREAMers themselves question the wisdom of agencyless depictions of the deserving victim, whereby youth who do not fulfill the pristine image of the migrant valedictorian are excluded from benefiting from legislation. As Jorge, a youth leader, told me, "I am a normal teen, but getting in trouble is a luxury for me." Being an innocent victim became the legislative gold standard.

The vocal and highly visible activism of DREAMers undermines the image of the docile dependent child as depicted in *Flores v. Reno* and *Plyler v. Doe*. Modeled after the lesbian, gay, bisexual, and transgender communities, unauthorized youth began to "come out" publicly regarding their (un)documented status. In public rallies, congressional sit-ins, teach-ins, and online, youth have emerged from the proverbial shadows of their parents, out of both desperation and hope that they may live lawfully and permanently in the country where they were raised. Educated and socialized in America, DREAMers embrace political participation as the vehicle for social change and publicly demand resolution to their tentative legal status in the United

States. In a rally of DREAMers, another youth, Sofia, declared in defiance, "You gave me this label without asking my permission." Sofia was denouncing not the actions of her parents who brought her to the United States at age ten but the law and its apparatus that sought to strip her of agency and limit her capacity for self-actualization. She went on to describe how her illegality was an emotional paralysis passed from one generation to the next in which she moved through the shadows with her head held down, never making contact with the police despite a pressing need to do so in her gang-affected neighborhood. "In coming out about my status, I stand before you, not powerless but powerful, not vulnerable but fierce, not a criminal but an activist, not afraid but committed to a better tomorrow." Sofia resists the law labeling her simultaneously as a powerless victim of her parents' decisions and as an outlaw hiding from the long arm of the law.

Ascribing agency only in terms of delinquency or moral rectitude not only fails to reflect the realities of youth like Mario, Jorge, and Sofia, but also carries considerable risks. Without an acknowledgment of how knowledge, responsibility, and choice are culturally and collectively informed notions, advocates and law enforcement alike misrepresent a child or youth's agency and ultimately misunderstand the reasons for child migration. The humanitarian regime explicitly summons a restoration of the blameless approach toward delinquency, in which structural inequality and implicitly racist policies create delinquency and in which a child's agency is only marginally relevant, if at all. The child victim in need of saving usurps power from the child and places it in the hands of the advocate "to give voice" to victimized children. As Laura Agustin (2003) argues, victimization as a strategy has become a way of characterizing people with structurally less access to power. In the context of migrating children, this strategy explicitly ignores that children make decisions and that those decisions are influenced by a variety of factors and relationships. On the other hand, the law enforcement regime maintains a child's agency as equivalent to responsibility for one's criminal actions, whether real or potential. The two approaches are at such loggerheads that it emboldens the perception that the legal and child welfare systems must necessarily remain irreconcilable. Out of frustration with ongoing complaints of ICE treatment of unaccompanied children at a national conference, the ICE national juvenile coordinator responded, "I challenge you all, frankly I would welcome it, to come up with a system to deal with UACs [unaccompanied alien children] the way it should. The current system apparently doesn't . . . I invite you."

The ways both advocates for unaccompanied youth and law enforcement enlist agency highlights the complexity and, at times, nontranslatability of the concept of pure agency into law. Legal argumentation makes use of claims to agency or a lack of agency to secure or to deny particular rights for subjects. In the Flores Agreement, advocates emphasized the lack of social agency in order to secure additional legal rights and custody accommodations for unaccompanied children but only for those without a criminal background that would undermine their agencyless framework. There is a moral weight or value assigned to agency by both advocates and law enforcement alike that shifts contingent on the context of the law and the particular legal struggles of youth. As explicitly seen in the Flores Settlement Agreement, *Plyler v. Doe*, Mario's narrative, and the activism of DREAMers, the notion of agency shifts ground and valence as it rubs against different sorts of claims and interests that also run through the law. Without a historically situated and culturally informed discussion of child migration, the highly politicized and moralized debates over social agency and responsibility force children "along a road with no exit."

CHAPTER 3

───

Youth at the Intersection of Family and the State

INTERLUDE

Dear *Mama*,

    I hope you are not mad. I want to help you but it's complicated. I go to school everyday. I am learning English but it is hard. I am not working. I want to but it's prohibited. I promise you that I will do my best in everything I do. I will find a way to help you. I will not forget you.

    I like my mother here but you are my real mother. You will always be my real mom.

    I love you.

—Johanna, sixteen-year-old Mexican girl in foster care

The relationship between the state, the family, and the child is a fundamental unit of analysis in society. The law and social norms that shape this triad inform the ways adults provide for and parent their children and the ways children are socialized into the community, allowing for social continuity over time and space. In the United States, the nature of this relationship has shifted over time as have the roles that children are recognized as playing in this relationship. When there is a perceived rupture in the social norm of the nuclear family, particularly in moments of crisis, such as parental death, abandonment, divorce, abuse, or neglect, the state often enters as mediator of domestic relations (Mason 1994: xiv–xv; see, e.g., Coe et al. 2011). An evolving series of actions and interventions have been designed to evaluate the competence and fitness of parents and make custody determinations. While the courts have waxed and waned from granting maternal and biological deference in custody determinations, they have become increasingly reliant on social and behavioral scientists to determine what is in the best interests of the child (see, e.g., Donzelot 1979).

In this chapter, I detail the historical, political, economic, and social factors that shape the relationship between the child, the family, and the state, and the ways migrant children's lives have come to be defined and contested. The legal identity of migrant children is socially situated within a history that intertwines social movements of helping professionals, legal jurisdictions characterized by increasingly intolerant approaches to juveniles, and shifts in the treatment of unauthorized migrant youth under immigration law over time. In a globalized world, this triangular relationship between children, families, and the state becomes increasingly complex and dynamic. Social policies and legal norms often lag far behind the diverse and fluid domestic arrangements of transnational family ties. I begin by tracing how the creation of the juvenile court and the emergence of the tutelary complex have radically shifted the notion of children as legal subjects in the United States. Through the legal case of *Polovchak v. Meese* and the advent of the Special Immigrant Juvenile (SIJ) status, I argue that the law and institutional practices ensnare youth between competing allegiances to the state and to the family. While the focus of this ethnography remains the narratives and social agency of children, it is critical to understand the gravity of these forces on the ways youth navigate the complex and uneven terrain of everyday life—a commitment I return to in the remaining chapters.

Children as Legal Subjects?

Colonial law in America conceived of the family as a unit of labor led by the male head of household with the wife and children as subordinate members who maintained no independent power. Fathers maintained "an almost limitless right to the custody of their minor legitimate children" (Murray 1996: 54). The state relied on family unity as a mechanism for economic and social governance in which the patriarch wielded uncontested power in the domestic sphere. Nineteenth-century family law followed the tradition of

English law in not recognizing children as individual rights holders independent of their parents; instead, the interests of the family were seen as synonymous with the patriarch's wishes. According to Michael Grossberg's (1985) study of nineteenth-century family law, the law considered children as wage-earning assets of their fathers, in which "their services, earnings and the like became the property of their paternal masters in exchange for life and maintenance" (25). In moments of transgression of the law, children were acknowledged as individuals, but there was minimal distinction between children and adults, subjecting children as young as seven to the harsh gaze of adult criminal courts.

The nineteenth century was marked a critical shift in the ways both women and children were viewed. What Stanley Cohen termed a profound "moral panic" emerged concerning gangs of children overstepping the confines of childhood and threatening "societal values and interests," particularly among new immigrant communities (Cohen 1972: 9; Davin 1990; Pearson 1985: 63). The financial demands on working- and lower-class immigrant households often necessitated that both parents work multiple jobs, leaving children in the care of others or depending on divergent notions of care and child independence, at times unattended with limited supervision. Children's exposure to peers and to the street was perceived as a strong enticement into bad habits. Specialized police organizations emerged to track crime, while philanthropic and religious organizations developed special schools and programs to inoculate against the contagions of youth delinquency. Through monitoring of and controlling the negative habits of youth, a specialized pedagogy emerged to intervene in the lives of children "beyond parental control" (Rose 1989: 156).

From the 1820s to the 1920s, the child-saving movement coalesced into which middle- and upper-class American reformers sought a humanitarian response to youth delinquency. The reformers, who came to be known as the "child savers," sought to protect children from both the vagaries of the street and increased automobile traffic, which claimed the lives of an increasing number of immigrant children accustomed to playing in the streets (Zelizer 1985). Through restricting children's movements to schools, playgrounds, and playrooms in the name of their own safety and well-being, the child savers sought to provide children moral education and to instill social behavioral standards. They labored to ensure the "salvation" of troublesome youth through institutional interventions designed to safeguard children against parental inattention and neglect. By the twentieth century, reformers had established settlement houses—large homes in densely populated urban areas where predominantly immigrant families could engage in education, seek repose from factory life, and receive medical care. In Chicago, Hull House, founded by Jane Addams and Ellen Gates Starr, is the most notable example.

Anthony Platt (1969) has convincingly argued that in their quest to preserve the purity and innocence of childhood, the child savers "invented new categories of youthful misbehavior" that corresponded to the behaviors of youth in predominantly urban, immigrant ghettos (3). Recognizing the family as the primary means of instilling morality and social values, the child savers developed a series of programs for children and families to instill American values in newly arrived immigrant families. For those families requiring more substantial intervention and rehabilitation, the child savers developed reformatory schools to serve as surrogate families for youth, shaping impressionable children to an ethic of obedience, labor, discipline, and morality. By the early twentieth century, Progressive Era reformers had fundamentally altered the relationship between the state, the family, and the child—no longer did a patriarch have absolute possession and control over his child, but the state began to monitor the community's social investment in the child.

Michel Foucault's concept of governmentality is useful in interrogating this shift in the state's configuration toward a pedagogical model, which relied heavily on governance of the self. Foucault enlists the term "governmentality" as a "guideline" in analyzing the period from ancient Greece through modern neoliberalism, arguing that the study of technologies of power requires an analysis of the political rationality that buttresses them (1997: 67). As such, Foucault understands government not as a central or singular state authority, as it is commonly understood in the twenty-first century, but as a historically informed and systematized mode of power (technology) that pursues a particular form of rationality to achieve a specific end. In other words, governmentality, or the "art of government," becomes the ways governments produce citizens tailored to fulfill government interests and the practices, techniques and strategies through which subjects are governed. Foucault expands a singular or hierarchical understanding of state power to the forms of *social* control embedded in social institutions such as schools, hospitals, psychiatric institutions, and jails. Through the production of knowledge and the internalization of social discourses, individuals regulate their own and others' behaviors—a more efficient form of social control and governance. By linking the technologies of the self with technologies of dominance, Foucault argues that the modern sovereign state and the modern autonomous individual are dynamically and mutually constitutive (1982: 220–21).

The transition to the pedagogical state at the turn of the century in the United States exemplifies this dynamic relationship through the institutionalization and dissemination of self-governance, guidance of the family and children, management of the household, and care of the soul at a particular historical moment. The child savers and the courts began to speak a "politics of truth," generating new forms of knowledge and news technologies of regulation and intervention. Perhaps the most lauded innovation of early reformers was the establishment of the first juvenile court in Illinois in 1899 and its transformation into a national system in 1908. The juvenile court was founded on the British legal doctrine of *parens patrie*, "parent of the nation," in which the state serves as the metaphoric head of household. The court's founding act claims that the institution's goal was "to regulate the treatment and control of dependent, neglected, and delinquent children" (Illinois Juvenile Court Act of 1899, 1899 Ill. Laws 131, cited in Schultz 1973: 458). The juvenile courts brought together a spectrum of children viewed as delinquents and as victims of parental neglect. Previously, cases involving children and youth were brought before a local criminal court, which issued rulings based on laws also regulating adult actions. The act not only created a separate court with a single judge to adjudicate claims of children under age sixteen, but also provided for a separate space for proceedings, for prohibitions on children under twelve serving jail time, and for a court-appointed probation officer not paid by the state to represent the interests of the child before the court (Illinois Juvenile Court Act of 1899, 1899 Ill. Laws 131, cited in Schultz 1973: 458). In court a perception of "parental neglect" justified the active involvement of the state as a means of safeguarding the lives of children. Philanthropic organizations not only became instrumental in defining the criteria of neglect and proper expressions of care, but also became folded into the institutional apparatus of the state by serving as probation officers, directly shaping the court's decisions in cases of neglect and delinquency. Philanthropic organizations were a form of government concerned with "the conduct of conduct" governing both themselves and others (Gordon 1991: 48). The categories of care and protection began to move more fluidly across philanthropic and state boundaries, laying the foundation for the emergence of a shadow state of civil society. At the same time, the courts and philanthropic organizations became instrumental in shifting the responsibility for these newly defined behaviors and social risks, be they delinquency, illness, or poverty, from the state to the individual subject (and family) responsible for his or her care.

Since its inception, the juvenile court has expanded its interventionist role within the family in the interest of, as officers of the court see it, the well-being of the child (Lloyd 2006).[1] Child savers argued that juvenile courts were a revolutionary innovation that provided needed diagnosis of and training to delinquent youth. Imbued with progressive ideals, the court was designed to respond to delinquency by viewing the criminality of youth as a consequence of psychological problems spurred by familial neglect and not as a manifestation of a child's depraved nature. Whether youth appeared before the courts at the initial stages of neglect or after years of emotional and physical disturbance now manifested in criminal conduct, the court's goals were primarily conceived of as charitable. Seeking to protect and provide for this inherently vulnerable population, the court began to emphasize children's rights, which "operated both as standards for parental behavior and as limitations on parental power. Parental failure to live up to these standards violated children's rights and justified community intervention" (Woodhouse 1992: 1052; see, e.g., Thronson 2002: 979). Further, by distinguishing between adults and children, juvenile courts sought to shield youth from the harmful gaze of the criminal courts and to offer tailored interventions focused on the needs of the child instead of the offense (Grossberg 2002; Sutton 1988: 108). Child savers argued that by focusing on the underlying problem instead of on the manifested behaviors, the courts sought to act in the "best interests of the child," the legal principle that still prevails in contemporary juvenile courts. Under this rubric the state could interject itself directly into family life to assure appropriate therapeutic interventions for children.

More recently, historians have argued that the invention of the juvenile court system emerged from public doubts concerning the effectiveness of the institutional protection and care of juveniles provided by the child savers and that, in fact, the new court was "an institutional compromise" that relied on legal norms to legitimize the discretionary control of social service agencies over the activities of youth (Fox 1970: 1226–27). Rooted in a medical model of deviance that viewed "abnormal" behavior as a dysfunction of the individual, the juvenile courts provided a technology for charitable organizations not only to control delinquent youth socially through the law but also to shape the normative structure of the court (Sutton 1988: 109).

Platt further argues that the juvenile court movement in the United States extended beyond a purely humanitarian concern for adolescents and became a mechanism for assimilation. He writes, "It was not by accident that the behavior selected for penalization by the child savers—drinking, begging, roaming the streets, frequenting dance halls and movies, fighting, sexuality, staying out late at night, and incorrigibility—was primarily attributable to the children of lower-class migrant and immigrant families" (Platt 1969: 139).

The concluding section of the Illinois Juvenile Court Act of 1899 reads, "This act shall be liberally construed, to the end that its purpose may be carried out, to wit: that the care, custody, and discipline of a child shall approximate as nearly as may be that which should be given by its parents, and in all cases where it can properly be done the child be placed in an improved family home and become a member of the family by legal adoption or otherwise" (cited in Schultz 1973: 458). In effect the state via the courts broke from its paternalistic position to a metaphoric head of household, distributing justice or punishment as "should be given by its parents." When the "care, custody, and discipline" did not approximate that of a parent, the court could intervene as a parent "should" to preserve the mental and physical hygiene of the child. This constellation of spatial, social, and legal reforms marked a critical shift in allegiance in which a child's "highest duty was no longer obedience to parents, but preparation for citizenship" (Woodhouse 1992: 1051). The culturally normative position of the law and the juvenile court framed deviance of youth behavior and of parenting practices as a justification for the state's intervention in family life, disproportionately affecting immigrant families whose domestic arrangements and practices differed. The law becomes a critical site that reflects broader changes in the forms of care, discipline, and governance that emerged from the state and charitable organizations during this time period.

The juvenile court became "a visible form of the state-as-family" through the *tutelary complex*, an apparatus of laws and helping professionals, ranging from psychiatrists to social workers to judges, who determined the spectrum of norms and deviance in children (Donzelot 1979: 104). Public supervision of children and their families through clinical observation, psychiatric evaluation, social work visitation, and court hearings replaced customary means of discipline and punishment of children in reformatory schools, mental institutions, prisons, and work camps. Professionals claiming to know the natural state of childhood and the proper behaviors of youth aided in the rehabilitation of deviant youth, the supposed aim of the juvenile court system. By focusing efforts on the child as a subject instead of on the act, as adult courts did, the tutelary complex institutionalized childhood through the state, family, and education system beyond the normalization tactics it enacted, thus raising panopticism to a new level.

In *The Policing of Families*, Jacques Donzelot argues that the liberal state was caught between two inclinations: on the one hand to preserve social order and on the other to maintain the autonomy found in the private lives of families (1979: 48, 52). With the hope that private consumption of their moral guidance would yield public good, philanthropic organizations understood families as a site of social intervention, distributing advice on financial savings or targeting the housing of the poor with medical and hygienic sanitation interventions (92). Despite strategies of resistance, the family became a mechanism for mediation between individuals and the state (94). Donzelot argues that "government through families" replaced "government of families" (48).

Donzelot's genealogy of the social control of the family remains relevant in the United States today not only for its delineation of the ways charitable organizations serve as an extension of and vital informant to legal judgments but also for its insight into how the family is subject to the state's impersonal regulation of private life. Particularly for unaccompanied children, subcontracted NGOs serve at once as prison guards, rehabilitative experts, and probation officers. In the absence of family, family reunification specialists, social workers, and clinicians become regulators of children's behaviors and of the legitimacy and quality of parenting practices. There is an institutional presumption that parents of unaccompanied migrant children are unfit by virtue of the children's status as "unaccompanied"—at the moment of apprehension, a child was not in the custody of a parent or customary care provider. Constructed as it may be, the juridical category of the "unaccompanied alien child" marks a rupture in the social unit of the nuclear family and calls into question a parent's capacity to attend to the child's "care, custody, and discipline." Only though completing a rigorous series of institutional paperwork and enduring scrutiny by charitable organizations may parents regain custody of their children from the federal government. In the interim, facility staff are charged with the education, socialization, and monitoring of children's behaviors.

In the 1960s, we see another shift in the courts from a pedagogical to an increasingly punitive approach to youth. High levels of incarceration, zero-tolerance policies, and fast-track adjudication point to those courts' contemporary concerns with prosecuting youth instead of providing excessive counseling. Juvenile courts in the United States continue to request the supervision and rehabilitative services of social service agencies, but organizations remain overwhelmed by the demand and are underfunded and understaffed. Distinct from earlier claims of saving youth or of preserving childhood, the current U.S. court system reveals repressive and controlling tactics. The increasing notoriety of both the police and the prosecutors who investigate and arrest youth positions juvenile justice in a new light in contrast to the early twentieth-century emphasis of the courts as in loco parentis.

Contrary to the turn-of-the-century child savers who sought to moderate children's and families' behaviors through pedagogical interventions, civil libertarians of the 1960s and 1970s advocated for a rights-based approach (H. Cohen 1980; Farson 1974; Holt 1974). Liberationists claimed that children should have all of the rights of adults and decried the imposition of child labor laws, compulsory schooling, and juvenile courts. Liberationists framed earlier reformist efforts as disrespectful of children's rights as citizens and as unduly constraining of their liberty. In their view, the juvenile court was not rehabilitative as reformers had claimed; in fact, the courts were punitive and provided no due process rights to children, instead relying on the judge as a paternal authority that failed to identify and respond to the complex needs of the individual child. "Drawing on works by Jean-Jacques Rousseau and John Dewey, liberationists argued that children desire to participate fully in society—to speak, to vote, to choose, and to work. Perceptions of children as dependent reflected histories of subjugation" (Minow 1995: 1575). Some liberationists argued that children would be the basis of the next civil rights movement following African Americans and women (Holt 1974). However, finding it difficult to convince the public that the law should treat infants and adults equally, early liberationists instead concentrated their efforts on adolescents, advocating for more personal and individual participation for these youths in decisions affecting their everyday lives. Youth, then, moved center stage, becoming a particularly contested group in which advocates, legislature, courts, and families all staked particular and at times conflicting claims to their best interests, a contestation that continues to pervade contemporary discussions of the rights and responsibilities of youth.

During the same time period, the U.S. Supreme Court teetered between granting some essential rights to children as liberationists had advocated and repealing other provisions affecting children's equal standing in the courts. The landmark 1967 decision in the case of *In re Gault*[2] was handed down by the Supreme Court (reversing the earlier decision by the Arizona Supreme Court that affirmed the dismissal of the habeas petition by the parents of the boy, Gerald Gault), ruling that a child has a constitutional guarantee to protection and to due process when he or she is committed to a state institution such as a juvenile detention facility. The juvenile court must afford children a notice of charges, a right to counsel, the right to confront and cross-examine witnesses, and the right against self-incrimination. Yet, in 1971, the Supreme Court denied a child's right to a trial by jury. As legal scholar Martha Minow argues, the court made a fundamental distinction: "As persons, children should benefit from the basic legal protections against abusive governmental power. Yet, as young persons, children should benefit from the guiding authority of juvenile courts, schools, and parents. In this view, children need rights when they are constrained in the ways adults could be constrained, but they do not need rights when they are constrained the way children *need* constraint" (1995: 1577, emphasis added). In other words, children possess rights only inasmuch as they do not conflict with the priorities and social expectations of the state's behavioral norms and expectations of children located in the family and society. When children appear to exist outside these structures, the law and the courts must bring them back into the fold or remove them from society.[3]

The Supreme Court has observed that children possess a special status under the law: "Our history is replete with laws and judicial recognition that minors, especially in their earlier years, generally are less mature and responsible than adults. Particularly during the formative years of childhood and adolescence, minors often lack the experience, perspective and judgment expected of adults" (Bien 2004: 831).[4] In many ways these early rulings not only further institutionalized a cultural construction of childhood that was put forward by the early reformers but also relegated children to second-class citizenship within the state. Contemporary state and federal courts consistently view children as individuals who do not possess rights and agency equivalent to those of adults. Furthermore, while such rulings do make special accommodations and distinctions in the treatment of children as distinct from adults, it is critical to note that these provisions are not binding in federal immigration courts in their treatment of unauthorized children. The few rights granted to youth in state and federal courts do not extend to unauthorized youth in immigration court.

Historically, youth has been a contentious category in which the members benefit from some specialized provisions due to their perceived dependence and vulnerability, while they are simultaneously excluded from the rights afforded adults. The courts have increasingly assumed an interventionist role in the domestic sphere, attempting to protect children from abusive parents. The 1980s and early 1990s brought a renewed emphasis on and sensitivity toward child abuse.[5] While laudable, it bolstered the state's ability to intervene in a parent-child relationship particularly in cases of abuse and of dangerous or inadequate parenting.[6] Congress "created incentives for states to provide permanency for children on whose behalf the state had intervened to sever the family relationship" (Lloyd 2006: 237–38). Unauthorized children who are abused, abandoned, or neglected are in theory subject to state intervention similar to that accorded to documented youth.

While the expansion of state intervention in the domestic sphere of the family explicitly and profoundly shapes the lives of all youth, in many ways unauthorized migrant youth are excluded from any of the positive measures such strategies may have. We see how the conditions of intervention are predicated on middle-class norms of childhood and parenting practices that place immigrant youth in a marginalized and often tenuous position in relationship to their families and to the state. This is particularly acute for unauthorized children who do not benefit from unconditional protection from the state due to their unauthorized presence in the United States. The state child welfare system can remove a child, documented or undocumented, from an abusive parent and provide care through state foster care programs, but on their eighteenth birthday, unauthorized children return to their status as "illegal aliens," unable to live or work lawfully in the United States. In spite of the legal justification for state intervention and its intense and sustained involvement, which includes removing children from their parents, the state effectively abandons such children on their eighteenth birthday. The protection of children from abusive families and from the state that seeks to deport them is predicated on children's ability to navigate the law amid restricted rights, limited accommodations, and marginal standing in the courts. This fluctuating relationship between the child and the state becomes particularly problematic for the ways in which youth conceive of their future selves amid significant uncertainty.

Contemporary federal immigration law still frames immigrant children as objects, analogous to now-discarded notions of children as property, recognizing the identity of a child only inasmuch as that child is a derivative of the actions, legal status, and presence of his or her parent(s).[7] U.S. immigration law is predominantly family-based, presuming that adults are the decision makers and providers for children. Children exist as derivatives of adult petitions or as dependents who are petitioned for by their parent or legal guardian in family reunification applications. Given this, children must rely on their parents to access the law, and forfeit any individual relationship to the state in immigration law. In the context of immigration law, children are not acknowledged as individuals, nor do they possess specific rights or social agency autonomously. Immigration law is an anomaly—the exclusive form of law that does not consider or even acknowledge the status or needs of children outside their relationship to their parents. To be clear, other areas of law have not necessarily gotten it right or are unworthy of critique.[8]

Immigration law remains the only area of law that has made no legally binding distinction between adults and children in the adjudication of legal petitions. Immigration law does not provide any compulsory child-specific accommodations customary in family and juvenile courts. Under these laws children do not have a right to state-funded attorneys but must secure and pay for their own representation during immigration proceedings; there is no best-interest legal standard that takes into account the safety and well-being of the child; the rules of evidence remain the same for children and adults, forcing children to meet the same credibility and evidentiary requirements as adults; and child applicants cannot petition for their siblings or parents as derivatives in their applications for political asylum (see, e.g., Nessell 2005). As one attorney remarked, "You can put a baby in a basinet before an immigration judge and she would have to make her claim just like a forty-five-year-old man would." However, court records are abundant with examples of youth challenging this static framework. The sheer presence of a growing number of unaccompanied children speaks to the legal challenges that result from ignoring youth as rights holders capable of social and political agency. The case of Walter Polovchak is one such example.

The Littlest Defector

In January 1980, two citizens of the Soviet Union, Michael and Anna Polovchak, came to the United States with their three children, residing temporarily in Chicago. After a few months, they decided to return to the USSR, but their two eldest children, Nataly (seventeen) and Walter (twelve), refused to return with them. Nataly and Walter left the family home in Chicago to live with a cousin. Disagreeing with their decision, Michael and Anna Polovchak asked the police to force Walter to return to their home in Chicago. The police took Walter from his cousin's home, but instead of returning him to his parents, they held him because he feared his parents would force him to return to the Soviet Union. After consulting with the State Department and the INS, the police initiated custody proceedings in Cook County Circuit Court. The trial judge temporarily placed Walter in the state's custody, "as a minor in need of supervision." "Later that same day Walter, with his attorney but without his parents, filed an application for asylum with the regional INS office" (*Polovchak v. Meese*, 774 F. 2d 731 (7th Cir. 1985), §§2–3). Walter's application for asylum was granted and in October 1981 his status was changed to that of "permanent resident alien." The state trial court held a hearing on Walter's wardship and eventually adjudicated both Walter and Nataly as wards of the court, removing them from their parents' custody. The Illinois Appellate Court reversed that decision in December 1981, "determining that the Polovchaks should not have been deprived of parental custody" (*Polovchak v. Meese*, §5), but the parents had returned to the Soviet Union by that time. The Illinois Supreme Court affirmed the appellate court's decision in May 1983.

The district court initially determined that "the private interest of . . . Walter . . . is by its very nature considerably less than that of his parents" (*Polovchak v. Meese*, §16). In the absence of his parents, who, as the adult family members, maintained Walter's legal status and to whom his lawful presence was contingent, Walter was unauthorized to remain in the United States. A fierce and very public debate ensued. In the context of Cold War politics, protecting a child who chose "freedom" over "communism" raised the stakes.

In the Illinois Appellate Court's view, Walter's parents had a fundamental right to make decisions about their child's care and custody and, given his young age of twelve, those rights superseded Walter's desire to remain in the United States. Walter's age became the centerpiece of a debate on parental rights. Just five years older, Nataly maintained a visa independent of her parents, and, as a result, her parents did not legally contest her decision to remain in the United States. However, the appellate court ruling was later complicated by Walter's petition for political asylum in federal immigration court based on his fear of persecution as a practicing Baptist in the Soviet Union. Walter was quickly granted political asylum and, in the Cold War context, heralded as "the littlest defector." Discontented with the ruling, Walter's parents petitioned the federal court, stating that "the grant of asylum violated substantive constitutional rights protecting their privacy and the integrity of their family, as well as their right to raise and control their son and to participate in his major life decisions" (*Polovchak v. Meese*, §6).

The tensions that emerge in this case reverberate through the lives of unaccompanied children more than twenty-five years later. The *Polovchak v. Meese* case illustrates the still conflicting and disparate conceptualizations of a child's legal identity between family and immigration courts and the legislators that guide their rulings. State family courts traditionally adjudicate family disputes, given their recognized expertise in child welfare and the organizational apparatus in which to provide services and monitor compliance. By granting Walter political asylum, the federal government in effect made a custody determination, not only denying the parents legal standing but also ultimately conflicting with their wishes. Under the Refugee Act of 1980, the federal government is obliged to provide protection to those who are persecuted in their country of origin. While parental rights ultimately were not terminated in this case, Walter was temporarily deemed a ward of the state prior to receiving political asylum. Without receiving notice from the court, his parents, who had returned to the Soviet Union, had been excluded from the political asylum process affecting their son. When the parent is absent, the state serves as the legal guardian with the autonomy to decide what is in the best interest of the child, which necessarily coincides with the best interests of the state. The federal government uncomfortably became the mediator of domestic relationships in an explicit and highly political way. In Walter's case, a child's decision to petition for asylum for political reasons placed his wishes in direct confrontation with a parent's right to determine the proper living environment for the child.

Polovchak v. Meese is also a critical precursor to contemporary context affecting unaccompanied children because of the politicization of the migrant child and how these conditions shape the choices available to youth. The notoriety of Walter's asylum petition reached the floor of the U.S. Senate and the news media. Particularly during the Cold War era, the political implications of revoking Walter's grant of asylum and returning him to his parents would have adversely affected the United States as a nation of refuge and reliability. However, in the circuit court's view, recognizing parents' unchecked right to remove their children from the United States forcibly would unnecessarily commodify children as property of their parents, subjecting children exclusively to the decisions of their parents, instead of recognizing them as individual rights holders. It is important to recall that there were no special provisions or procedures in the immigration court enlisted to treat Walter any differently from an adult asylum seeker, yet the court's rulings had real implications on the feasibility of the Polovchak family's future visitations and communication. The Asylum Office and Executive Office of Immigration Review (EOIR), which adjudicate asylum petitions, do not have authority to make custody determinations. However, by granting Walter political asylum in the absence of his parents' consent, the court's ruling had significant implications for parental custody and family unity.

Because of Walter's status as a minor, the case raises concerns about the child's independent relationship to the state (Schneider 1968). As Evelyn Glenn (2002) convincingly argues, independence is a "key ideological concept anchoring citizenship," manifested in rights such as property ownership, voting, and recognition as decision makers (27). At the same time the family becomes the mediator of the state's investment in the child as a future citizen. Because of this presumed dependence, children must rely on their parents as proxies before the law, restricting their independent access to the state (Jans 2004; Leiter, McDonald, and Jacobson 2006; O'Neil 1997; Thronson 2002). In *Polovchek v. Meese*, Walter's wishes directly contradicted his parents' decisions about their minor child, which unsettles the state's perception that children are necessarily and exclusively dependent and cannot forge an independent relationship with the state. In this view, to claim political agency (in the form of a political asylum petition), Walter must be shorn of his kinship ties and become a dependent of the state.

Walter's independent desire to remain in the United States in spite of his parents' desire for his return to the USSR marks a deviation in the social norms of a dependent child. The site of the family as mediator of the law for the child was called into question. Walter's illegality and physical presence in the absence of his family complicated the state's response—which was to bounce Walter between legal systems that struggled to respond to the state's diverging obligations to provide sanctuary (via immigration law), to not intervene in family matters, and to ensure the safety and well-being of children (via family law). Because of his status as a child and as an unauthorized migrant, Walter's case crossed over multiple domains of the law that conflict in the treatment of and obligation to a child. In a liberationist approach, the child's rights would be preeminent, but are further complicated by culturally situated views of child agency and the legal restrictions of the child's rights.

For unaccompanied children the inability to access the state and the law directly becomes highly problematic. Immigration law consistently frames children as variables or liminal figures and not as actors in or involved contributors to migration decisions. The law does not view children as autonomous individuals from birth, but sees them as beings that families must socialize into mature adults. The law views unaccompanied children without a legally recognized caregiver as existing alone though paradoxically still dependent. Without a recognizable parent, the child cannot access the state to petition for legal relief. At the same time, the legal identity of unaccompanied children is contingent because of their illegal presence in the United States. Unaccompanied children are "impossible subjects," to enlist Mae Ngai's (2004) term. Their presence is "simultaneously a social reality and a legal impossibility—a subject barred from citizenship and without rights" (4).

Were the child in question an adult with recognizable rights, agency, and a defined relationship to the state, the circumstances would be quite different. Take Walter's sister Nataly, who maintained her own legal status and was already positioned in the upper end of "an age range in which a minor may be mature enough to assert certain individual rights that equal or override those of his parents," in contrast to Walter who, at twelve, was identified by the court as at "the lower end of an age range" (*Polovchak v. Meese*, §17). Walter Polovchak's case bounced between state and federal courts involving seven different lawsuits until the asylum adjudication process was complete on the eve of his eighteenth birthday in 1985. His right to protection in the form of political asylum was augmented with his age. It was reasoned that, as an adult, Walter was legally allowed to make his own decisions. In the U.S. Senate chamber, legislators celebrated Walter's eighteenth birthday with a "birthday party of freedom" in his honor.

Special Immigrant Juvenile Status

Cases such as those of Walter Polovchak and Elian Gonzalez have given rise to new legal avenues that seek to remedy the legal and institutional tensions that emerge in a child's independent and unlawful presence in the United States. Historically, the state has defined and positioned unaccompanied youth largely through the law, or by legislating citizenship, labor, or eligibility for government programs (Garcia 2006; Hagan 1994; Orellana et al. 2001). Shifts in immigration law for unaccompanied children have begun to guarantee some measure of legal relief for minors through the introduction of Special Immigrant Juvenile status. While SIJ has existed since the early 1990s, advocates have increasingly used this tool since 2000.

The SIJ legislation initially emerged when child welfare advocates in Santa Clara County, California, began applying for amnesty under the 1986 Immigration Reform and Control Act (IRCA) for unauthorized children who were dependents of the county's Department of Children and Family Services (DCFS). In an interview with one of the drafters, he explained, "When the [immigration] amnesty came, I was working with twenty children dependent on DCFS who qualified for amnesty. I, as the prudent parent and as the guardian ad litem, thought I had the right to apply for them, and so I applied for all of the children in the Santa Clara child welfare system. I got most of them through, but one immigration officer refused the last two children. The legislation emerged as a clean-up measure. The initial impact was not that much. It was relatively obscure at the time."

Even amid a growing anti-immigrant climate in the late 1980s, the SIJ legislation was remarkably inclusive of unauthorized children and might have served as a legal remedy for cases like that of Walter Polovchak in the 1980s. Early provisions of the law stipulated that unauthorized youth must be (1) a dependent of the juvenile court, (2) deemed eligible for long-term foster care due to abuse, neglect, or abandonment, and (3) a youth for whom return to his or her home country is not in the best interests of the child.[9] The legislation did not require the abuse or neglect to occur in U.S. territory or that the offending parent have legal status. Furthermore, SIJ initially included children who had never been involved with the immigration system, though this was amended in the 1997 revision amid concerns about potential abuse of SIJ.

While in many ways SIJ is consistent with immigration law's view that children are necessarily dependent, it did open a critical window through which advocates began to push for expanded rights of children and initially a more nuanced perspective on migrant children. SIJ is the only provision in immigration law that considers the best interests of the child, creating a unique hybrid of state courts and federal immigration law, which provides certain unauthorized children with an avenue to citizenship. The mechanism of the best interests standard with the SIJ petition is one of the few ways by which the voice of the child might figure into immigration proceedings. While SIJ might suggest recognition of children as independent social actors or agents at least of their own migration, initial discussions of SIJ applicants operated on the assumption that children could not be responsible for migration decisions, whether lawful or unlawful. In the SIJ regulations the INS insisted, "A child in need of the care and protection of the juvenile court should be precluded from obtaining Special Immigrant Status because of the actions of an irresponsible parent or other adult" (Lloyd 2006: 243). In the INS view, not only could the migrant child not make autonomous migratory decisions but also the child's unlawful presence was evidence of the condemnable behavior of the child's parents.

However, SIJ is an insufficient remedy for unauthorized children in the United States. As Ani Ajemian (2007) reminds us, "While this opportunity for legal status [via SIJ] appears an appropriate solution to the unaccompanied child problem, it is still fairly narrow in its application and fails to take into account a number of child-specific harms no less deserving of protection" (25). Unaccompanied migrant children may also seek political asylum, but the obstacles are significant. As mentioned previously, the rules of evidence and testimony do not distinguish a child from an adult, forcing children to meet the levels of detail and credibility standards of adults. Furthermore, immigration law does not easily recognize child-specific persecution, including social phenomena such as child soldiers, street children, youth resisting gang membership, or even youth as political activists. Advocates have experienced some success in petitioning for children by rooting their legal claims in discourses of human rights instead of framing their claims as child-specific persecution.[10]

While Congress's original intent in SIJ was to defer to the expertise of the juvenile court in determining the best interests of the child, conflicts have ensued over jurisdiction (see, e.g., Hamm 2004).[11] The state court may make recommendations on the proper care and best interests of the child, at times finding the child a dependent of the court. However, when the federal government takes a child into custody, the state court no longer maintains jurisdiction over the child regardless of his or her needs, because federal immigration proceedings preempt state court proceedings. As a result, many state court judges are unwilling to make the necessary findings indicating a child is dependent on the court while not providing any services or oversight of the child's permanency planning.

In addition, while the legislative history gives no indication of a distinction between detained and nondetained youth, the INS explicitly distinguished between the two populations, stating, "The INS will seek revocation of any juvenile court dependency order issued for a detained alien juvenile [as such] juveniles are not eligible for long-term foster care because of their federal detention" (INS general counsel, cited in Lloyd 2006: 244). The INS argued that state courts could not find a child dependent if that child was under the care and custody of the federal government, in practice, preventing detained children from seeking SIJ. Although the 1997 amendments clarified that no distinction should be made between detained and nondetained youth, the vestiges of this distinction persist in practice in the contemporary relationship between ICE, ORR, and state courts whereby detained youth who have been abused, abandoned, or neglected do not necessarily have open access to family courts to protect them.[12] They face significant political and economic resistance from state welfare authorities, judges, and state's attorneys involved in state court proceedings.

Following numerous complaints and lawsuits, Congress revisited SIJ in subsequent efforts to clarify its intent in 1997, 2003, and 2009. These court cases and legislative modifications clarified some of the jurisdictional issues, accelerated or resolved delays in processing applications, attended to age-out provisions, which deemed youth with a pending application who reached eighteen as ineligible, and addressed the issue of "specific consent" procedures.

Despite various revisions, the fundamental principle underlying SIJ has only become concretized: children claiming SIJ must be shorn of kinship ties and become dependents of the state (via its proxy as the ORR or the juvenile court).[13] Under SIJ a child forfeits any right to petition for his or her parents or siblings to immigrate. Furthermore, since a special immigrant juvenile status recipient is "no longer the 'child' of an abusive parent, the CIS [U.S. Citizenship and Immigration Services] may assert that he or she no longer has any sibling relationship with brothers and sisters" (Kinoshita and Brady 2005: 9). As such, SIJ suffers from a "legal aconsanguinity" in which "immigration policies nullify legal legitimacy of some kinship ties" (Coutin 2000: 32–33; De Genova 2002: 427).[14]

Not only does SIJ prohibit simultaneity of allegiance to kinship networks and to the state, it also requires children seeking SIJ to, in effect, sustain legal charges against their parent or parents. Children who are abused, abandoned, or neglected by one parent become a public charge of the state, a relevant factor in the parent's petition for legal relief. If a child receives SIJ status, the immigration court may deem the parent as exhibiting moral turpitude, an irreconcilable value with granting legal status and citizenship to the parent.

Lucia, a thirty-four-year-old Mexican woman, was convicted of a series of shoplifting offenses and sent to jail, leaving her daughter Leticia a dependent of the court. On Lucia's release, she later told me, "I thought Leticia would be better without me. I had no money, nowhere to live and no papers." A child protective services (CPS) agency petitioned for SIJ for Leticia based on abandonment by her mother. Lucia eventually secured employment and had two more children with her U.S.-citizen husband. In evaluating her petition to adjust her status, ICE discovered that Leticia received SIJ and claimed that on the grounds of moral turpitude of abandoning her child, Lucia's application for lawful permanent residency was denied. The legal issues facing unaccompanied children, whether detained or not, have grave implications for the entire family system. "Who are the perpetrators? Who are the victims? It is hardly ever clear . . . and these families don't have the money to clean this up," lamented a social worker.

Johanna's letter to her mother that opened this chapter explaining her inability to remit money speaks to how youth are caught between familial obligations, legal permanency via the state, and the subsequent institutional practices shaping their everyday lives. In initial meetings with her attorneys, Johanna did not believe her mother had abused, abandoned, or neglected her. "I did what I wanted to do. My mom did not control me. She worked hard to provide for us. My problems are my responsibilities. It has nothing to do with her." Unbeknown to her mother, Johanna had been sexually abused by a neighbor, and on the basis of her mother's failure to protect Johanna from the repeated abuse, attorneys identified Johanna as eligible for SIJ. Initially resistant, Johanna asked, "She is not a bad person. She didn't know. How could she do anything to stop it?" Gradually understanding that her release from detention and placement in foster care was contingent on her claim of SIJ, Johanna astutely explained to me, "My mom has to be the bad one. She wants the best for me. She will understand." Since her placement in federal foster care, Johanna has been reluctant to explain that she cannot extend her legal status to her mother or siblings, instead continuing to promise to bring them to the United States. Her inability to remit money to support her family, a restriction of the federal foster care program, has only frustrated Johanna's relationship with her mother. "She wonders if I love her anymore. She thinks I have a new family." Her mother's request for financial support resulted in the state's monitoring of their phone calls for six weeks rather than Johanna's assistance in meeting her social and financial obligations to her family. Struggling with her inability to assist her mother and three siblings, Johanna drafted a letter in her journal to convey her ongoing commitment to her "real mother" in spite of her inability to fulfill her responsibilities to them.

In this chapter, I have argued that recent changes in immigration law for unaccompanied children, including provisions for SIJ status, have shifted the relationship between the state, the family, and the child, positioning the state at odds with lived kinship structures. Without an individual relationship to the state or recognition of their legal rights, unauthorized youth are forced to choose between the state (and partial citizenship) and existing kinship ties. The following chapter examines in detail the narrative of Deruba, a Guatemalan youth, as he confronts this stark choice.

CHAPTER 4

Forced to Choose

INTERLUDE

Participant Personal Property Form

From the "Participant Personal Property Form" listing the belongings at intake of Deruba, a Guatemalan youth. Deruba traveled from Guatemala through Mexico and was apprehended by Border Patrol shortly after crossing into the United States. He was transferred to the custody of the Office of Refugee Resettlement and initially placed in a facility in south Texas.

Participant Name: _____

A# _____

Participant Clothing:
- · 1 blue windbreaker
- · 1 light blue jeans
- · 2 t-shirts (both gray with logos)
- · 2 pairs of white socks with black stripe
- · 1 compass
- · 1 small green backpack
- · 1 rosary (cloth)

Participant Money: $1 \times 4 = \$4$ (USD)

                     30 *quetzales*

Comments: Quiet, observant, calm. Child reported hunger and a series of cuts on his feet.

Arrival Date and Time: _____

Participant Signature: _____

Staff Signature: _____

The study of migration invariably involves discussions of law—immigration processes, agreements between nations, human rights, and interventions of civil society—all related to the flow of people across national boundaries. In the exploration of child migration, the law provides an essential site for probing the tension between the unauthorized presence of migrant children and the social norms of children and the family embedded in legal discourses. The law is a potent force shaping the everyday lives of child migrants—where they circulate, how they engage with or evade the state, how and where they access resources and opportunities, with whom they construct social networks, and how they envision their futures. However, much of the current scholarship views the law and youth as separate lines of inquiry that converge only when youth come into conflict with the law. Few practitioners or scholars have reflected on how youth engage with the law outside common tropes of the juvenile delinquent and the child victim, failing to ask essential questions. How do youth make sense of the law? How do they mediate conflict and interact with the policies and practices of legal institutions? How do they shape the legal codes and practices that affect their daily lives? Are there multiple, contested interpretations of a youth's legal identity? As social actors, migrant children and youth push back, resist, and challenge the law explicitly in their unauthorized and independent presence and implicitly in the ways they move through multiple geographic and institutional sites in search of care, education, or employment.

Informed by this deficiency, this chapter traces the journey of a Guatemalan youth named Deruba from his hometown in Guatemala to a county courtroom in Illinois. I detail how Deruba navigates the complex network of actors and institutions in pursuit of safety and employment and the ways the law affords him some rights by virtue of his being a child while restricting other rights due to his independent presence in the United States. Deruba's circulation between the street, institutions, and other caregiving arrangements becomes pathologized as an inability to develop appropriate attachment relationships—a simultaneous justification for rehabilitative efforts and for containment. Deruba's narrative reveals how he negotiates the imposition of the law on his everyday life. Perceived as unruly, delinquent, and somehow dangerous to society and the nation-state, he embodies the intersection of the law's attempts to contain and to reintegrate those existing outside the law. Embedded in his marginalization are the ways institutional actors conceptualize risk and rehabilitation, which intersect with discourses on gender, race, poverty, and (il)legality. At the same time Deruba is not merely a passive recipient of the law but actively shapes legal discourses on migration in his everyday negotiations of institutional and community networks.

On the Move

In his first two months at the immigration detention facility, Deruba consumed his daily lessons of vocabulary and math. "Good morning. My name is Deruba. What is your name?" he would chant. "I am from Guatemala. Where are you from?" "Good afternoon. How are you? I am fine." He had only attended school for four years in Guatemala before his parents died in a bus accident, forcing him to support his younger sister, Isura. "It was not a good time. We did not have anybody. No aunts, no uncles to help us. My grandparents died long ago. I don't even remember them. It was just me and my little sister." Deruba, a thirteen-year-old Garifuna[1] youth at the time, and Isura, then eleven, lived on the streets of Livingston, Guatemala, for over two years. Amid a population of 14,500 residents, Deruba worked as a boat hand on *lanchas* (boats) transporting tourists to Livingston; he also painted cars at a small auto body shop and sold marijuana to young German and American tourists coming to soak up Livingston's bohemian environs.

On a map of Livingston that I had from my previous work in the region, Deruba showed me where he and Isura had lived on the outskirts of town in an abandoned house, seeking protection with a small group of youths who circulated on the streets. "I did not worry too much about trouble. As long as we stuck with the group, we were okay, but it was not good for my sister. It was fine for me. I could survive. She was so young. I had to protect her." Earning money became increasingly difficult, leaving Deruba and Isura without food for several days. "We chewed [cactus leaves] to help our stomachs." Feeling fatigued, they moved to Guatemala City with two other youths, where, with a population of 3.3 million in the Guatemala City metropolitan area, they hoped for greater opportunities. "We had nothing [in Livingston]. No house. No food. No parents. No family. Just bad memories. Why not?" he explained to me while detained in an ORR facility. With increasing violent crime, unemployment, and pervasive poverty exacerbated by heightened migration to the capital city, Guatemala City would prove much tougher terrain for hustling tourists.[2]

By 2005, when Deruba and Isura arrived in Guatemala City, political
violence targeting activists and human rights organizations as well as gener-
alized violent crime were escalating. Matched with sensationalist media accounts of gang violence, several high profile cases of gang shootouts, and
general marginalization of youth, this reality had resulted in the government's renewed *mano dura* (strong hand or iron fist) policies, pervasive during Guatemala's thirty-six-year civil war. A rash of killings in Guatemala
City by unknown men in white paneled vehicles incited fears that death
squads had returned to Guatemala's political landscape. This reminiscent
pattern of mysterious deaths spurred rumors that social cleansing campaigns
had returned, yet there was a noticeable shift from the state-sponsored campaigns of the civil war era to one with more private-sector features. Security
guards, many of them former members of the armed forces, became assassins
for hire, adding to an emerging conglomeration of political killings, gang violence, and organized crime (see, e.g., Godoy 2006). Street children became
the targets of the private sector seeking to "clean up" the business sector, while
police forces also sponsored intermittent raids in high-crime areas, rounding
up children, making allegations of gang involvement, and removing them from
the city center. Death squads targeted and "disappeared" street children in
many of the same ways government death squads operated against the rebel
forces of the Guatemalan National Revolutionary Unity (Unidad Revolucio-
naria Nacional Guatemalteca, URNG) during the civil war. Youth—whether
on the street or as members of gangs—became a new social problem, necessitating, as many hard-line politicians argued, a swift, iron-fist response from
the state.

Amid the environment of escalating violence and with limited social and
financial resources, Deruba and Isura hesitantly decided to enter a private
shelter for street children in Guatemala City.[3] Deruba explained his motivation for entering the shelter: "I had to look for a place for [Isura] because I had
lived *bastante* [enough]. I couldn't do it anymore, but [at the shelter], I didn't
sleep much either. I had to protect her." Despite the staff's efforts to curb violence and drugs in the shelter, "when you bring street children together under
one roof, you aren't going to rehabilitate them overnight," explained a former
shelter social worker, when I visited the now-defunct shelter in Guatemala
City. "We have gang members, drug traffickers, and innocent children in one
place. No matter what measures we take, there will be problems." Despite a
generally talkative and gregarious personality, Deruba was uncharacteristi-
cally silent about his time at the shelter. "It was a bad time," he often told me.

"Malísimo." He eventually disclosed that he was sexually abused by a staff member at the Guatemalan shelter, and when he disclosed the abuse to a supervisor, he was forced to eat his own feces as a form of punishment.

Only a few months after entering the shelter, Deruba was caught in the government's anti-gang campaign, which indiscriminately apprehended street youths and accused them of gang involvement. Deruba recounted how soldiers apprehended him along with eight other youths in a raid on gangs while he and Isura scavenged for food at the Mercado Central. Under the state's justification that the police are ill equipped to confront such well-armed insurgents as the gangs, the armed forces have increasingly participated in anti-gang raids.[4] Accused of belonging to Mara Salvatrucha (MS-18), Deruba was held for six weeks in an adult prison in Guatemala City. Deruba recalled to me, "I didn't know what happened to Isura. She was only thirteen. She didn't know how to get back from the market to the [shelter]. That was the last time I saw her."

Just as he was indiscriminately detained, Deruba was unceremoniously released. "It was dark already and they just told me to leave. I didn't know why they let me leave. I didn't ask," he explained to his incredulous American attorneys, as they assembled his narrative piecemeal from his responses to their questions. During his detention, Deruba said he realized that he could neither continue to provide for Isura nor protect himself. "[At the shelter], she had food, a bed, and she went to school for the first time. I could not give that to her. She was better off there for now." Despite his own abuse, Deruba convinced himself that his sister was safer in the short term than if she risked the treacherous journey to *el Norte*. Following his release from jail, Deruba did not return to the shelter to find his sister, telling himself he would return for her eventually. Instead, he traveled to nearby Antigua, an affluent tourist locale forty-five minutes outside Guatemala City, where he once again would work odd jobs and run errands.

Deruba spent several months in Antigua, where he was befriended by a restaurant owner from Cuba who allowed him to live in a back room of his compound in exchange for janitorial services. "Uncle Luis, he was good to me. He is black like me," reasoned Deruba for Luis's generosity. From detention, Deruba would use his weekly call to contact Luis but had not reached him in months. I, too, was unable to reach him over a six-month period. "It is the only number I have. Everyone else is calling his mom or grandma. I have Luis," he explained as to why he continued to call despite the automated message indicating the phone was no longer in service.

After several months Deruba found this work arrangement limiting. "A copper will not make sound by itself" he explained using a Garifuna proverb. "Uncle Luis was kind but it was not a place [to bring] Isura." After seeing the wealthy American tourists in Antigua, Deruba decided he would travel to the United States to earn a living, eventually returning for Isura when he had enough money to build a house. From his conversations with Luis, Deruba calculated that he would need 45,000 *quetzales* (approximately U.S.$6,000), about two years of work in the United States. "Once Isura has a *cédula* [Guatemalan state identity document] that says she is eighteen, I can get her out of [the shelter], and we can live in our new house." Deruba was unambiguous in his plan to return for his sister. "She is all I have left. I am here for her. I wonder if she thinks about me. I wonder if she knows I am alive. Maybe she thinks I was killed; she hasn't seen me in so long." When I met Deruba on the first day of his detention in Illinois, he asked the staff to help him locate his sister. "All I want is to tell her I'm alive. I'm here. I haven't forgotten her." After Deruba had spent several weeks in both the Texas and Illinois facilities, no one had yet attempted to locate Isura. Facility staff and the pro bono legal service provider claimed it was outside the confines of their roles. At Deruba's request I inquired with former colleagues of mine in Guatemala City and in Panajachel, who were able to find out that after a month of Deruba's absence Isura was transferred to a program for girls in the Departamento de Sololá, where she lived for a year before moving to a third shelter in the Guatemala highlands, where she resided as of late 2012. After over a year without contact, Deruba spoke with Isura in Guatemala. "I couldn't stop crying. She could not stop crying. She is alive and safe and she knows now that I will come back for her." In a phone conversation with Isura months later, she told me, "I didn't believe [the social worker] that Deruba was on the phone. No one has ever called me and now it was [my brother] who I think is dead. . . . I thank the Lord Jesus Christ for that phone call. I may not see him this year or even next year, but now I have a reason to continue."

"I Didn't Come Here to Eat a Bag of Chips"

Deruba told me that he borrowed 2,000 *quetzales* (about $250) from Luis and set out for the United States. His journey took eight months. Of the youths participating in my larger, multisited ethnography, those without a strong social network that could support their journeys north either financially or

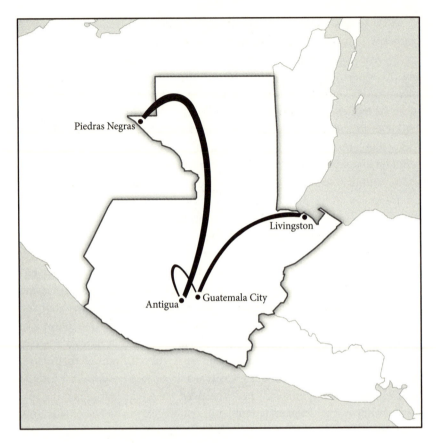

Figure 2. Deruba's circulation through Guatemala.

logistically took from two months to two years. Several were apprehended by Mexican authorities and deported to Guatemala; others lived in Mexico for a time, working to earn enough to continue their journeys or initially choosing to live in Mexico. In 2006 Deruba traveled by bus to Piedras Negras in the Departamento de Péten, Guatemala's northernmost point bordering Mexico. Perhaps simple good fortune allowed him to evade apprehension while crossing the Mexican border. With increased funding and political pressure on Mexico from the United States to curb Central American migration in combination with the 2006 election of enforcement-minded Mexican president Felipe Calderón, surveillance and containment efforts had substantially increased. There were additional soldiers and federal police patrolling the border and more frequent immigration checkpoints in the south of Mexico. Deruba stopped intermittently to earn money and to beg for or steal food, hopping trains northward. "I didn't know what it would be like. I just knew I had to get north and that my fortune would change."

Over the course of several conversations, Deruba spoke about the reasons why he had institutionalized his sister and migrated alone northward. Isura's age and small stature were a practical concern in Deruba's decisions. He said, "I found a place for Isura, I took advantage of the opportunity. Because I am bigger, I can get on the trains. If you are too little, something bad could happen. If you are too young or too little, you can fall underneath the train. The train goes fast and you have to time it right. I wanted to bring her but I couldn't because I couldn't live if she got hurt. She is too young. I couldn't take her out of the home for girls until she has a *cédula* that says she is eighteen. She had to stay there. I had to leave her." His decision to leave his sister was a constant source of anxiety for him. At some moments, he confidently declared that leaving Isura temporarily was the best option and, in fact, an opportunity for her to attend school. Other times, he worried how she might survive alone. "She is my only family. I must take care of her and I failed. But, I will make it right. I will," he promised aloud.

"I spent a lot of time on "El Diablo" [The Devil, the cargo trains running through Mexico]. It was dangerous, but there were a thousand other people riding the trains so there are a lot of people around. I didn't have any problems with the gangs or the police." Also known as El Expreso de la Muerte (Death's Express) or La Bestia (The Beast) among other names, the trains are notoriously perilous for northbound migrants. Migrants board passing trains, waiting at locations where the rails curve and trains slow to fifty kilometers per hour allowing them to grab hold of ladders and pull themselves on top of the trains or stow away in open cars. Migrants risk losing a limb under the moving trains. As one youth told me, "Your feet are just a snack. Your legs are dinner." Once on board, migrants must guard against police raids and the *maras* (gangs) that patrol the tops of trains, robbing migrants and at times throwing them off of the trains. Several young people told me that they had been robbed by gang members, bandits, or police officers who searched their shoes and the lining of their clothes for their small reserves of cash. "I had some clothes but no *cédula*. No money. Even if they tried to rob me, I had nothing," Deruba told the facility caseworker as she cataloged his belongings on the "Participant Personal Property Form" at his initial intake.

Deruba said he was not too concerned about fatigue, which threatens migrants gripping the railings on top of trains. "I am used to sleeping little," he told me, recalling his time living on the streets in Livingston and in the shelter in Guatemala City. "It prepared me for the trains." Low-hanging branches, daily rains, and aging train tracks in disrepair also threaten the bodily integrity of migrants. Many youths, particularly those traveling with the assistance of a *coyote*, or smuggler, view the dangers the trains pose as outweighing the risks of being caught at one of the many immigration checkpoints along bus routes through Mexico.[5]

On his train travels Deruba befriended Ernesto, another youth migrating from Guatemala to Ohio whom I would later meet in an Illinois facility. Ernesto, sixteen, had attempted this journey north on two previous occasions but was deported each time to Guatemala City. With his Maya features and accented Spanish, Ernesto had difficulty persuading immigration authorities he was Mexican. In the absence of documentation, the police and consular officials test an individual's knowledge of language, politics and cultural practices to determine citizenship. When stopped just south of the U.S.-Mexico border, Ernesto said he was unable to sing the Mexican national anthem or recall that the eagle on the Mexican flag rested on a cactus. He was deported to Guatemala. On his second attempt north, Ernesto crossed the Rio Bravo/Rio Grande only to be quickly apprehended by the U.S. Border Patrol. Once again, he was unable to "'speak Mexican correctly,'" an officer had told him. "I was embarrassed to be sent home again. I didn't even go to see my family. I just stayed in Guatemala City for a week and then headed north again." Ernesto said his family had borrowed money from family and neighbors to fund his journey. His family was awaiting a phone call from the United States marking his safe arrival, but it had now been eight months with no communication. When I asked what prevented him from calling his mother, Ernesto insisted he would not call until he could remit money to his parents—an impossibility while he was still in detention.

Ernesto and Deruba rode the trains north to the U.S.-Mexico border, detraining only to avoid immigration checkpoints. They recalled scurrying around the checkpoint and attempting to catch the train on the other side. Ernesto guided Deruba through these movements, avoiding bandits or gang members flanking formal immigration checkpoints. Ernesto told me "I knew how to cross and what to look for." He had missed the train twice previously, deterred by bandits who beat him and robbed him of his tennis shoes in which he hid his last few pesos. Deruba and Ernesto had to penetrate the

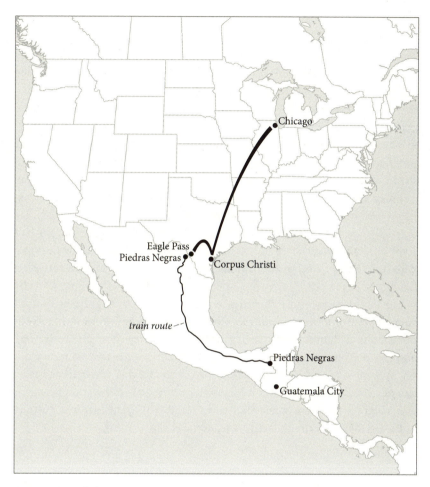

Figure 3. Deruba's circulation through Guatemala, Mexico, and the United States.

border created by the state and shadow-state authorities thwarting north-ward movement and threatening the physical integrity of migrants. "I don't know who wanted us more—the gangs or the immigration police or Los Zetas [a Mexican drug cartel]," Ernesto told me. "We may get robbed or beaten by either. The gangs and *narcos* [narcotraffickers] may have killed me, but at least they wouldn't send me back to Guatemala." Ernesto and Deruba would travel north together for two more months, and, although they were sepa-rated en route, they met again months later in a facility for unaccompanied children in Illinois.

On reaching Piedras Negras in the northernmost state of Coahuila, Mexico, Deruba rested for three days in a migrant shelter run by Catholic missionaries. "Everyone there tried to convince me to stay. Not to go north. They said that I was too young, too little, that it was too dangerous to pass. They told me every bad story to try to stop me, but when I told them about my life, they knew." Information circulates quite fluidly among migrants about the perils of migration, and, while the information deters many, it aided Deruba to make preparations for his solo crossing by knowing how to ration his water, to remain clothed despite the desire to disrobe in such heat, and to shadow the main roads so as not to get lost. Because he had no money to pay a smuggler, Deruba crossed alone from the town of Piedras Negras along Eagle Pass into Texas. "No one was with me but I had one of those things that tells you the direction. I just kept walking north for two days. I had some food and water with me, though." The compass, provided by Luis as a departing gift, proved to be invaluable to Deruba's survival while crossing the desert in the 110°F July heat. After a day and a half of walking, Deruba found the highway and followed it northbound. A passing driver noticed him, stopped to give him food and water, and called the Border Patrol to apprehend him. "I didn't know what happened until they [Border Patrol] came and got me. I was eating some chips and drinking water and then they put me in handcuffs and pushed me into the car. . . . I didn't come here to eat a bag of chips." Two officers took Deruba to a Border Patrol station where he was jailed for two days before they transferred him to the care and custody of the ORR at a children's facility in south Texas.

Navigating Rights and Race

In the Texas facility, Deruba was one of thirty-five boys and seven girls. "It was a fine place. There was food, clean clothes, and I had my own bed. I was there for one month and seven days before they kicked me out." Deruba had a confrontation with a facility caseworker, which was recorded in a significant incident report (SIR) in his institutional file as "inappropriate and threatening behavior." Deruba explained, "[The caseworker] was giving everyone else dessert, a piece of chocolate cake, but wouldn't give me any. I don't know why she wouldn't. I got mad. She hadn't let me play basketball either. Everyone was eating dessert, but she wouldn't give it to me. I had a right to dessert just like everyone else. The lawyers told me I did, so I told her. She didn't like that, so she sent me [to the staff-secure facility]." Deruba believed from what he had learned in the Know Your Rights presentation from the local legal assistance provider that he had both fundamental human rights as well as certain legal rights at the facility and that these rights extended to equal treatment in access to activities and food. This incident came on the heels of Deruba's touching of the caseworker's blond hair. "I just wanted to see how it felt, but she didn't like that, either." The caseworker reported that Deruba had assaulted her, requesting that ORR transfer him, or "step him up," to a staff-secure facility where there were greater restrictions and monitoring of movement, a lower staff-to-child ratio, and alarmed or locked windows and doors.

Many of the youths who were detained at the staff-secure facility and with whom I worked had accusations but no criminal charges pressed against them. The criminal charges had either never been filed or been dropped, or the children had served their sentences, and then ICE placed a retainer on them because of their unauthorized presence, sending them to facilities for unaccompanied minors, despite parents known to live locally. Others had pending criminal charges but were unable to attend court proceedings because they remained in federal immigration detention with no information provided by the federal government to state courts. In the child's absence, state courts would issue a warrant for the child's arrest, which awaited him or her on release. Children would be rearrested by state authorities, continuing the revolving door of arrests and institutionalizations between the state and federal systems. Still others did not know why they were placed in a staff-secure shelter rather than a "regular shelter." The variation in the reasons children who are classified into staff-secure facilities is substantial; there is a tremendous amount of personal and organizational discretion for requesting staff-secure placement for a child. According to ORR, staff-secure facilities are for children who are identified (by ICE, ORR, or facility staff) as having behavioral issues or criminal concerns or who are considered a flight risk.

After Deruba had spent a week at the staff-secure shelter in Illinois, one of his teachers commented to me, "Deruba doesn't belong here. He may be mischievous but he isn't a criminal. But here, the accusation is enough." While the policy remains that transfer decisions are made in collaboration with facility staff, voluntary agencies, and ORR federal field specialists, the final decision lies with ORR, which can recommend transfers or prevent a child from "stepping down" to a less restrictive shelter facility. As ORR is the legal guardian for all unaccompanied children in their care, it makes all final determinations, at times with unchecked authority and at times discordant with child welfare law and best practices.

When I spoke with the Texas supervisor who had requested the step up, she remarked offhandedly, "Deruba is the only black kid in the program. He just doesn't belong here." There is tremendous variation between facilities in ORR's network, spanning from some agencies with a long history of providing culturally sensitive services to a diverse population of immigrant youths to others that follow a law enforcement model in an effort to detain and control this population of "illegal" youth, who are often framed as inherently delinquent or criminal due to their unauthorized presence. Factors such as access to interpreters, education level and training of staff, state child welfare laws that license facilities, organizational leadership and philosophies, and local politics all shape the models of care that affect children's experiences of detention.

While remarks such as the Texas facility's caseworker regarding Deruba's dark skin color as a racist justification for his transfer are not always so explicit, bias and inequity are woven into the institutional practices and procedures of ORR, ICE, immigration judges, and immigration law based on a child's illegality and country of origin. There was an institutional presumption that all Chinese and Indian children are trafficked and thus require a "suitability assessment" of potential sponsors or family members, a ninety-day assessment. Such rigorous screening processes have not historically nor with such uniformity applied to Mexican and Central American youth, who are presumed to migrate for economic reasons or to reunify with family members already in the United States. Since the time of my research, the policy requiring suitability assessments for all Chinese and Indian children has changed only in institutional language to "countries known to traffic children." In practice, the presumptions remain embedded in everyday institutional practices under which virtually all children form India and China receive forty-five-day suitability assessments on nonparent sponsors. Karen Bastia (2005) questions the usefulness of the term "child trafficking" in the context of teenage Bolivian migrants in Argentina, where the distinctions between smuggling and trafficking are unstable and often shift on a continuum of exploitive labor arrangements. In many ways the consolidation of difference in the juridical category of unaccompanied children shapes institutional practices that mask the diverse realities of these children, regardless of their country of origin.

There are layers of scrutiny of parents to determine their suitability as care providers, particularly for children with any special needs, mental health issues, delinquency background, or prolonged separation from a parent who may have preceded them in migration. While the institutional claim is to safeguard against placing children with abusive or neglectful parents, suitability assessments necessitate that a child remains detained for the duration of the investigation. In contrast, the domestic child welfare system presumes a parent is suitable unless there is an accusation of abuse, abandonment, or neglect; and investigations take several days rather than several months to minimize the traumatic separation of a child from his or her parents.

After the mandatory three months at the staff-secure shelter, Deruba "stepped down" to a second facility in Illinois, where he joined fifty-three other children, principally from Mexico, Central America, and China.[6] It provided a less restrictive environment, allowing for more outings to a local YMCA for swimming, basketball, and soccer or for fieldtrips to area museums. After several months at the third facility, Deruba still felt thwarted. "You can tell his waning motivation by the way he wears his pants," explained a supervisor. "They are too low when he has a bad attitude and doesn't want to be here and at a normal level when he is more optimistic about his options." In the year and a half since, Deruba had met with his two attorneys on five occasions to develop his legal case; however, he was uncertain whether to stay in the United States. His desire to stay ebbed the longer he remained detained.

The Law and Its Possibilities

In Deruba's initial meetings with his pro bono attorneys, he struggled to understand the implications of the legal alternatives that his lawyers presented to him. "When can I leave this place [the detention facility]? When can I start working? When can I go back to Guatemala? When can I see my sister?" Deruba grappled with the inconsistencies in their responses to his questions. "It depends" seemed to be the mantra he heard from his attorneys. "You need to ask your lawyers. Every case is different," explained the facility caseworker. "Guatemalans are treated differently than Mexicans," remarked a Honduran youth detained at the facility. Despite the consolidation of difference within a single juridical category of the "unaccompanied alien child" and within detention facilities, the range of legal remedies available to each youth is quite vast. For example, a child's experience of persecution by the armed forces in Uganda may allow him to secure political asylum, while persecution by a gang in El Salvador or even the local police may be insufficient for making a viable claim for asylum. In other cases a child who is trafficked may be granted a nonimmigrant status visa for victims of trafficking (T visa), while another child, despite her the exploitative labor arrangement, may be classified as smuggled and have no legal remedies available to her.

Deruba struggled alongside his attorneys as to what forms of legal relief to pursue. Political asylum was perhaps the most difficult to secure, despite his persecution by death squads while he was living on the street and his detention in a Guatemala City jail. Deruba had no evidence, no documents, and no witnesses to his detention, just secondhand accounts from his sister, whom he had not seen in a year, and from Luis, who did not answer his phone. Limited evidence is not uncommon in asylum cases due to the nature of violence and persecution that spur flight from one's home country. Deruba's case was compounded by his inconsistent and at-times nonchronological narrative. Few rights and protections are afforded to adults in immigration proceedings, and children fare no better than adults. As I have argued, the absence of specialized provisions for children derives from the belief that a child cannot exist without a parent. In the absence of his parents, Deruba had to meet the same standards of evidence and the same levels of credibility as an adult would.

A second option was SIJ status. Deruba would have to petition the Illinois state court to find him dependent on the court. Such a finding would require that he prove that his parents "abandoned" him in their death; that returning home—regardless whether that home was in Guatemala, or the United States, or his "last habitual residence," Mexico—was no longer a viable option; and that he qualified for long-term foster care.[7] SIJ does not alter immigration law but defers dependency decisions to state courts, which maintain an expertise in child welfare, while federal immigration courts maintain control over determining immigration benefits. With this finding, Deruba had to file an application for the SIJ visa with the U.S. Citizenship and Immigration Services (USCIS). Only then and with this visa, could he later adjust his status to legal permanent resident and apply for citizenship in five years.

It is important to recall that a finding of dependency must not alter custody. According to ORR, for a child to petition for SIJ, a state court's finding of dependency must not alter ORR's legal custody of children; this directly contests the ways many state courts conceive of dependency. Deruba was caught in a catch 22. A dependency finding would signify that he had been abused, abandoned, or neglected and had no one to provide for him other than the state of Illinois. But, since Deruba was under federal custody and ORR was providing shelter and care, the agents of the court reasoned that the court need not intervene regardless of the untenability of permanent care in immigration detention. This has led to significant variation in the ways individual jurisdictions respond to petitions for SIJ. For example, the Indiana legislature, arguing that the federal not the state government should be responsible for unauthorized children, has determined that it will not grant any SIJ petitions statewide. Until recently, Texas had never granted a single SIJ petition despite the significant number of unaccompanied children residing both in and outside ORR facilities. Now, some jurisdictions in Texas are known for their successful SIJ findings amid the state's generally conservative political landscape. On the other hand, while there were only 900 SIJ visas issued nationally in 2008, Los Angeles alone granted over 500 petitions, establishing a specific office in the Los Angeles Department of Children and Family Services (DCFS) to facilitate applications for dependent unauthorized children in state care. Illinois, once admired for its relatively fluid working relationship between state courts and immigration advocates, currently has far fewer possibilities for SIJ despite an increased population of children such as Deruba who would otherwise qualify. Much of the variation seems contingent on state and local attitudes toward unauthorized migration as well as state budget restrictions, which seek to distribute or entirely negate responsibility for noncitizens.

Despite his attorneys' efforts to convince him otherwise, Deruba initially and vehemently refused to consider SIJ as an option, just as Mario had done (see Chapter 2). If Deruba secured SIJ status, a process that can take six months to two years in many county jurisdictions, Deruba could leave the facility and could legally work; however, he would not be able to reunite with his sister in the United States or to safely return to Guatemala for at least a year until he had secured legal residency in the United States. If granted SIJ, Deruba could not extend his new legal benefit to Isura despite their shared life experiences of losing their parents and living on the street. Since the SIJ recipient is no longer the child of an abusive or neglectful parent, the USCIS may assert that he or she no longer has a sibling relationship with brothers or sisters (Center for Human Rights and Constitutional Law 2004). In effect, SIJ voids Deruba's relationship to his parents and any other family members. In the eyes of the state, he no longer has biological siblings or relatives who might otherwise benefit from his legal status, even though his sister remains in the same quandary, without an extensive social network or resources in Guatemala. Deruba, tormented by the prospect of never seeing his sister again, asked his attorney, "How do you expect me to leave her with no one? She has already lost my parents. She already thinks she lost me. Now, she really will."

SIJ is consistent with the ways immigration law conceives of migrant children as exclusively dependent and incomplete, not afforded the same access and rights as adults. Yet unaccompanied children challenge this legal framework—with their unlawful, physical, and independent presence—by occupying spaces the law reserves exclusively for adults. Even SIJ, hailed by many legal advocates and legislators as a step to incorporating into immigration law the best-interest standards prevalent in state courts, suffers from restricted conceptualizations of children as without social agency and devoid of kinship ties.

One of the youths at the facility, Sergio, also known as *el notario* among the children for the legal savvy and advice he offered them, explained that Deruba could pay a *coyote* to transport Isura to the United States. "The most important thing is that you are together, no? That you see her and she knows you are alive. It doesn't matter how it happens, just that it happens." He explained that with legal status Deruba could work and Isura could go to school. "She doesn't need papers," he explained. "I don't have them, and I went to school until I came [to the detention facility]. I was in tenth grade already. . . . Besides, the lawyers could get her status once she is here," he added. Deruba worried about his sister migrating alone even with the assistance of a smuggler. Stories of the ways smugglers mistreated and violated girls in particular circulated throughout the facility daily. A number of children had been held captive by smugglers who extorted additional funds from family members in the United States and in the child's home country.

Deruba's third legal option was voluntary departure or deportation, which his attorneys rarely discussed as an option. Deruba did not want to return to Guatemala, repeating that he had nowhere to live, but as months passed at the facility and other children circulated through, he began considering it more earnestly. "I don't want to go back, but how can I stay here one more day?" Foster care is designed to remedy prolonged stays. For both articulated and unarticulated reasons federal foster care is not deemed appropriate for all unaccompanied children. In Deruba's case, ORR referred to his institutional file, where Deruba had spoken with the facility's therapist about sniffing inhalants and negotiating with gangs while living in Guatemala City. Deruba's history of "drug abuse" and his interactions with gangs in Guatemala were sufficiently alarming to the ORR federal field specialist that foster care initially was not considered a viable alternative for Deruba. With no family reunification options, Deruba remained at the facility awaiting his legal case. The short-term institutional model of care and custody for unaccompanied children does not graph onto the lengthy timelines of hearings in state and federal court, which can span several months to several years, excluding appeals. A facility supervisor speculated that ORR was unwilling to risk its "limited number of foster families with a child like Deruba who has a history of drug abuse and gang activity." An ORR supervisor remarked that "recruiting foster families to care for teenage males coming from countries where gangs are everywhere is a real challenge, not to mention children with special mental health needs or physical disabilities. We have only one foster family for every forty-five children in our care. We try, but it just isn't as much as we need." More recently, ORR has developed group homes primarily for male teenagers who, as another ORR supervisor proclaimed, "just don't want another mother"—as if an unaccompanied male youth cannot be encumbered by a nurturing family environment. Furthermore, per ORR policy, only youths under seventeen and one-half qualify for foster care or group homes, which eventually excluded Deruba from renewed attempts for foster care, extended care, or group homes despite a record with only SIR from his first placement, leaving Deruba to languish in a detention facility for the duration of his legal case or until he "aged out" on his eighteenth birthday. Various stakeholders involved in decisions regarding Deruba's care arrangements had transformed notes from his presumed-confidential therapy session into indisputable facts that impeded his release. What was in Deruba's best interests came into conflict with the state's need to ration limited resources.

A final unspoken option was that Deruba could abscond from the detention facility. In the third facility, where he ultimately resided for much of a year, two of the doors remained unlocked, though tightly monitored, and he knew the direction of the busiest street—the best route to escape—from occasional outings. While gardening in the front courtyard of the facility, when the teacher's back was turned, Deruba touched the handle to the gate, saying under his breath, "It would be so easy. I would be gone." Looking at me standing next to him, he assured himself, "I know you won't stop me." Two other youths had recently escaped from a nearby staff-secure facility. They managed to return to their families in San Francisco, avoiding deportation to Honduras scheduled for the following month. If Deruba had fled, as ten other youths had while I conducted my research, and been reapprehended, he would have been placed in a secure facility, akin to a juvenile jail. But after nearly a year and a half, Deruba still had not run. Instead, he found himself back in state court.

Today Is *the* Day . . .

"Today is the day," his attorney said to him, patting him on the back as he entered the courtroom. Deruba shrugged. This was the fourth time he had been in the juvenile court. Each court date was "*the* day," he later remarked with sarcasm, but never *the* day when he would receive a legal decision on his case. "It's all a game for them: beating the clock, beating the other lawyers, beating the system," Deruba remarked about his team of young attorneys. The two attorneys from a prestigious private law firm had experience in tax law and contract law, but Deruba's case was their first time representing a child and practicing in juvenile court.

Standing to the left of the judge was the assistant state's attorney, a junior attorney from her office, two attorneys from the Illinois Department of Children and Family Services, and two attorneys from the Cook County Office of the Public Guardian. To the right of the judge were Deruba's two attorneys and their supervisor. The nine attorneys stood before the judge, each with a vested interest in Deruba's case, there to advocate for their interpretation of his best interests. The four court clerks scurried back and forth assembling paperwork for the afternoon cases and responding to requests from the judge and various attorneys.

Deruba sat on a bench alone in the back of the courtroom picking invisible lint off his light blue polo shirt and borrowed jeans; his hair greased back with copious amounts of hair gel—a highly coveted award for maintaining a clean room at the facility. Deruba was awarded 32 ounces of neon-colored hair gel only intermittently with his waning motivation to adhere to the facility's requirements for good behavior. It was often more effective with recent arrivals. After months at the facility, these prizes lost their allure. He had borrowed the gel from his roommate that day. Deruba's English language skills were rudimentary and his Spanish basic, though improving. Despite increased emigration of the Garinagu in the past five decades to urban locales, namely, New York, Los Angeles, and Chicago, the court's efforts to secure a Garifuna interpreter were unfruitful. In his first court hearing over a year earlier, Deruba strained to understand English, occasionally asking his attorney to explain who the people were and what they said. Now, in his fourth hearing, Deruba watched, disinterested and uninquisitive. He sat linguistically isolated in a room full of English-speakers with no official interpretation of the proceedings determining his fate.

But, today had to be *the* day. Deruba was turning eighteen next week. After five years of moving between households, the street, and five shelters in four cities and three countries, Deruba would find his legal fate decided. If he was not granted a dependency finding from the juvenile court judge, his birthday would bring a chocolate cake for lunch, and in the afternoon ICE officers would accompany him to the county jail where ICE detained unauthorized adult migrants. As he sat in the courtroom with his shoulders slumped forward, his small frame and young age belied his life experiences in Guatemala, Mexico, and now the United States.

The assistant state's attorney, who very rarely attended such seemingly insignificant hearings, "was ready for a showdown," she remarked to no one in particular. Her office had declined to endorse Deruba's petition for dependency, leaving his attorneys to bring the case on his behalf. While any individual can petition the court, proceeding without the support of the state's attorney's office makes the process significantly more difficult. The state's attorney typically screens cases following an investigation by DCFS into allegations of abuse, neglect, or abandonment. In Illinois, DCFS often declines to send an investigator to the facilities, reasoning that unless the accusations are about abuse at the facility, the child is in a safe environment, secure from the abusers. A DCFS supervisor in California explained that much of the resistance nationwide stems from "using local resources for what is seen as a federal problem" of unauthorized children. The federal government "has custody of these children. They should be responsible for them, not us. Why should we be compelled to provide services if the child is safe just because ORR doesn't want to follow through with the responsibilities of being a legal guardian?"

If DCFS does not receive notification of abuse through "regular abuse channels"—a telephone hotline—bringing in a case such as Deruba's through an alternate route communicates to the judge a need for additional scrutiny. One state's attorney explained, "We don't bring in a child [to DCFS custody] just because a child is dependent on someone other than their parents—a grandmother or aunt and uncle—we don't bring them in when family is a safe and viable alternative. This is a disservice to the child and to the family. We only bring in very few cases where their living situation is not viable. On some occasions we will have situations where abuse is alleged years and years ago or in a different country but we have no way to investigate or to determine because all witnesses are gone, and there is no evidence and no police investigation." Another assistant state's attorney elaborated, "At [the ORR facility], they are safe, fed, housed. Why would we go knocking on the door asking if they want to come into court when there is no danger to their personhood just so that they can get an immigration visa?" For both attorneys from the state's attorney's office, the concern is for the imminent danger and the proper expressions of care represented by the provision of shelter and food, but they willfully choose to ignore the fact that federal immigration detention is a restrictive living environment in which the state has affixed itself as parent to migrant children; instead they assume that the federal government is the utmost trustworthy guardian.[8] According to the regulations framing SIJ, children may not petition the court for dependency with the intent of seeking immigration relief. That attorneys representing Deruba were without the backing of the state's attorney's office did not bode well for his chances of securing a dependency finding.

As a guardian ad litem remarked, if a child comes through "the regular channels, then no problem, but it is when you have a kid who says 'I left Guatemala four years ago because my father was beating me. I have been living alone. I have been hustling. I took the train here.' It is unbelievable that a fifteen- or sixteen-year-old could do this alone." Just as Deruba's experience was out of the ordinary for the nine attorneys in the courtroom, his physical presence was indisputable—standing before the law, independent, abandoned, and meeting the legal criteria for SIJ. Yet the agents of the law, informed by their own cultural conceptions of childhood and social agency, stood in disbelief that this young, wiry youth could make a rational decision to institutionalize his sister, be released from a Guatemalan jail without a court hearing, travel on top of trains while evading state and extra-state authorities in Mexico, and eventually arrive in an Illinois courtroom. The impossibility and subsequent invisibility of the child as a legal subject does not reconcile with the material presence of the child.

Violent Collisions: State/Federal and National/Transnational

Poignantly, Deruba's person became the site of a violent collision between legal systems of state family law and federal immigration law and between their willingness and capacities to respond to the transnationalization of kinship ties. The transnational nature of the lives of migrant youths is a complicating factor that contributes to the situation in which they are considered to be a social and potentially irresolvable problematic. To some extent immigration law acknowledges both the logistical challenges of securing evidence from one's home country—particularly when state authorities are the perpetrators of torture and persecution—and the lack of witnesses due to the transnational nature of the persecution. However, juvenile and family courts are ill equipped to manage the transnational lives of immigrant youths in a number of ways. First, documents may be scarce and witnesses unlikely. Child Protective Services agencies are often unable to investigate the abuse, to ascertain its truth, since the abuse may have happened in another country or even several years ago. While the federal statute does not require that abuse must occur in the United States, state court judges have difficulty making a finding of abuse or neglect with minimal corroborating evidence. The assistant state's attorney involved in Deruba's case said: "We rely on the eyes and the ears of the community. But here, there is no community. There is no evidence. There are no witnesses. So, what can I tell the judge? Who do I call as a witness? How do I corroborate the abuse? . . . Besides, sworn affidavits from outside the country, countries that won't extradite their nationals for prosecution, don't stand up under the penalty of perjury."

Deruba's guardian ad litem explained: "Many times, I only have the child's word saying he was beaten with a stick every night for ten years. I may get an affidavit from the parent saying 'Yes, I was an alcoholic, and, yes, I did this,' but for the judge and the state's attorney, these affidavits are self-serving. We are trying to get the kid a visa. Now if you have three neighbors who saw dad beating his kids and the neighbors are willing to stand up here and testify, you have a better case. But because [Deruba's] abuse happened over the hills, through the woods, during the rainy season seven hours from a phone in Guatemala, he has no chance."

International home studies by local social service providers are insufficient. As a voluntary agency representative commented, "If either ICE or state's attorneys ask for a home study, they aren't going to like what they find. And whose standards are the local social workers using? Suitability assessments here among my own staff are value judgments on what makes a good home. It functions in this country because we have standards, but how could it possibly work outside the American system?" While the law does not make a spatial distinction on the location of abuse (instead foregrounding the act of abuse or the absence of parental care), spatiality takes center stage in the institutional practices of truth seeking.

In addition, the courts have culturally informed biases of the spatial distribution of kinship, conceiving of family as living in a singular national territory. The transnational character of kinship ties of unaccompanied youth problematizes the ways state courts respond to migrant children—regardless of immigration status or (un)accompanied status. With increased immigration raids and escalating rates of deportation, what continue to rise to the surface are the complex arrangements of mixed-status families. The variation in legal statuses in families forces state and immigration courts into an uneasy relationship where immigration rulings have profound implications on family integrity and where state court jurisdiction may impede federal enforcement of immigration law.

For Deruba the process of seeking legal relief was marred by the politics of immigration reform and a conflict between the multiheaded apparatus of the state. Under the rubric of the best interests of the child, state court judges have tremendous latitude to assess the stability of a household in which immigration status may play an important role, yet U.S. family law does not permit judges to adjudicate claims based on immigration status. David Thronson (2005) has meticulously documented how state courts often make rulings informed by a child or parent's immigration status. He argues that state courts may make custody determinations through discriminating based on immigration status, manipulating family court findings to assist in obtaining legal status, concealing the influence of immigration status factors in legal decisions, or in some instances modifying requirements based on immigration status and employment authorization (Thronson 2005: 54–75). In practice, family law is predicated on a principle that the best interests of the child should override even the best interests of the state, but, as we have seen in Deruba's case, the practice is quite different.[9]

Postscript

Despite considerable investment of time and resources by Deruba's legal counsel, the state court denied a finding of dependency required to petition the federal government for an SIJ visa. Although his long-term care in federal immigration detention was untenable, the judge found that while Deruba

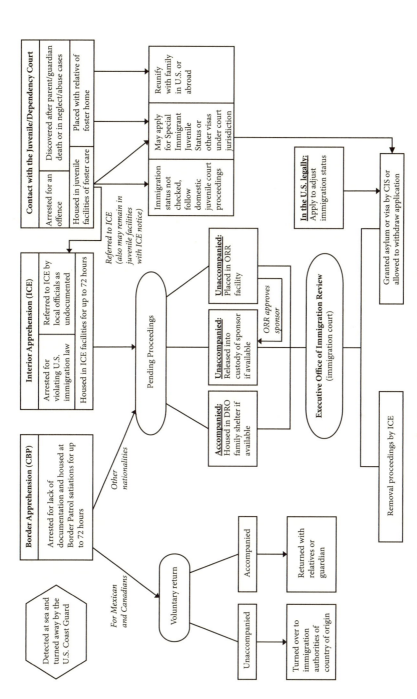

Figure 4. Immigrant children and youth in immigration and juvenile justice systems.

was under federal custody the state court lacked jurisdiction to intervene. Furthermore, it is important to recall that in the SIJ legislation, a child cannot petition for SIJ with the intent of seeking immigration relief. Arguably, as an orphan, Deruba would benefit from state services, but the judge viewed his petition as seeking immigration status. Because Deruba was quickly approaching his eighteenth birthday, the state's attorney argued and the judge agreed that services were not the centerpiece of the petition. The judge's ruling highlights one of the glaring deficiencies in the legislation that create often insurmountable obstacles for a marginalized and vulnerable population of youth who are bereft of most legal protections and rights while in immigration detention.

Deruba remained in federal immigration detention for children until his eighteenth birthday, when ICE agreed to release him on his own recognizance rather than transfer him to adult immigration detention. The county jail was already beyond capacity with adult migrants. Deruba initially entered a transitional housing program but quickly left, finding the restrictions on working without legal authorization stifling. He drifted from job to job, slowly saving to build the house in Guatemala he had dreamed of—all with the singular determination to care for his sister, Isura. Deruba resumed his plan that the federal government and well-intentioned advocates had interrupted in the name of his best interests. He filed for political asylum, and still awaits the results, living in a prolonged, liminal legal space. "Isura is my life now. Everything I do—every job I take—is to build us a family home."

CHAPTER 5

―――――――

The Shadow State

INTERLUDE

There is the righteous one.
Here is a ruined me.
See how far one is from the other.

What links to piety and righteousness have guided my
    way?
There is the sound of the sermon,
I hear the melody of its instrument.

But, my heart grows weary of this cloister,
The hypocrites cloak.
Where is the monastery of the Magi?
Where is the pure wine?

The days of my vision are gone.
Let them be my joyful memories.
Where once was an affectionate glance
Instead, I find reproach.

What can the enemy's heart find in my tired face?
Here in my eyes is the extinguished candle of hope.

                        —Pascal, sixteen-year-old Guinean youth

In this chapter, we enter the labyrinth of federal immigration detention for migrant children called "shelters," in which the federal government subcontracts with NGOs to provide for the everyday needs of children. At the point of apprehension, ICE makes a series of assessments. Is the child accompanied by a family member to whom they can be released? Is the child a Mexican national with no credible fear of return and thus imminently deportable? Does the child pose a threat to the community and warrant ongoing detention? Or, is the child unaccompanied by a parent or guardian necessitating transfer to the ORR Division of Children's Services? As I explained previously, the "unaccompanied alien child" is simultaneously a constructed legal and administrative category and subject to significant discretion by ICE and U.S. Customs and Border Protection. In 2012, ORR maintained custody of over 2,000 children daily in a series of seventy facilities. This has only increased since that time, with an anticipated 26,000 unaccompanied migrant children entering into ORR custody in fiscal year 2013. New facilities open almost monthly. The statistical majority of children entering ORR custody are from Central America and are apprehended crossing the U.S.-Mexico border. However, an increasing number of children are apprehended internally in the United States as a result of increased workplace raids, partnerships between local law enforcement and federal immigration authorities, and collaboration between the juvenile justice system and immigration enforcement. As a result, recently arrived migrant children are commingled with youth who have grown up in the United States from a very young age. The result is a complex and dynamic population of children and youth (ranging up to eighteen years old) from around the globe placed in programs that struggle to provide for the diverse social, cultural, therapeutic, developmental, and legal needs of children and youth. In some instances, U.S. citizen infants are held in immigration detention facilities to preserve the parent-child unity while detaining the parenting teenager.

Facility sizes range from ten beds in programs working with homeless and "troubled" youth to three hundred beds in facilities exclusively for unauthorized children. Despite its being perpetually in "draft" form, ORR has developed a set of national protocols and procedures that guide subcontracted NGOs to provide daily care, including education, recreation, medical care, and mental health services. Charged with implementing the conditions of the Flores Settlement Agreement, facility staff takes seriously their commitment to provide for the physical needs of children and attempt to provide a safe place where children can heal from their journeys and pursue renunciation with family members or a sponsor. In addition to obligations of care, facility staff are also responsible for detaining children, restricting their movements, regulating behavior, closely monitoring their communication with others, and evaluating a child's suitability for sponsorship or limited placements in foster care or group homes. While this decentralized network of facilities functions with limited supervision from ORR or from states licensers, my research has identified patterns of care and strategies of control across multiple sites over time.

Through four ethnographic vignettes that exemplify these trends, I demonstrate the tensions between how the state structures interventions, how organizations imagine a child's well-being, and how children exercise their social agency. I detail how ORR policies and the everyday practices of their subcontractors pathologize children's mobility and negate their social agency in order to curb perceived "problematic" and "unattached" behaviors; at the same time, these policies and practices structurally reinforce these behaviors. In many ways, youth agency is highly constructed and scripted by the rules and regulations of facility life, yet youth creatively adapt given their variable resources. Within the shelter milieu, children develop sophisticated mechanisms to manage and to resist a context of limited information and structural powerlessness. I trace how these strategies circulate between children across age, gender, and nationality in ways that undermine the "rehabilitative" efforts and disciplinary practices of the state and civil society. As the narratives below demonstrate, some children navigate these spaces more adeptly than others, sensing the fluctuating dynamics and institutional complexity and making critical adjustments to ensure access to information and desired outcomes.

In spite of a mission to provide a humanitarian response to the unlawful presence of children as migrants, ORR policies and procedures and their implementation by nongovernmental organizations establish what Erving Goffman (1961) has termed a "total institution." Across facilities, children find themselves "cleanly stripped of any of [their] accustomed affirmations, satisfactions, and defenses, and is subject to a rather full set of mortifying experiences: restriction of free movement, communal living, diffuse authority of a whole echelon of people, and so on. Here one begins to learn about the limited extent to which a conception of oneself can be sustained when the usual setting of supports for it are suddenly removed" (1961: 148). While migration is often framed as a disturbance, trauma, or rupture in the lives of children, detention becomes a traumatic experience marked by anxiety, uncertainty, and powerlessness in ways migration may not be for many youths. Juridically and spatially removed from communities and families, children must navigate these "mortifying experiences" by relying on their individual strengths and capacities and their ability to quickly develop social networks among their peers. Through the everyday experiences of Raul, Manuel, Sergio, and Pascal, I argue that rather than reinforcing the distinctions between the moral, ethical, and legal obligations to children, ORR policies and organizational practices blur the bright line between the humanitarian and law enforcement regimes in their treatment of migrant children and youth.

Raul: "Hardly Home"

The immigration officer opened the van door and removed Raul's handcuffs. "*Aquí estás* [here you are]," said a second officer, who remained in the driver's seat. The officer accompanied Raul to a wrought-iron gate on a tree-lined residential street in Chicago. A red mailbox hung next to a well-worn intercom, which regulated entry. This former nursing home spanning three city lots would be Raul's home for the next four months. His feet ached from his recent journey from Honduras through Mexico and across the Sonoran Desert into Arizona; small lacerations riddled his feet from the stones and plants he stepped on as the soles of his tennis shoes deteriorated with each step. "They were new, too. My brother sent them from Ohio, but they didn't last. Next time I will get boots," Raul later recalled.

The buzzer sounded. The officer pushed open the gate, motioning for Raul to enter the small courtyard. He rang the doorbell next to the oversized wooden door and waited patiently. No answer. By the third insistent ring, a supervisor, Alicia, opened the door and welcomed Raul by name. The officer followed Raul, entering a bright hallway—white floor tiles, white ceramic wall tiles, white paint—all cast yellow from the flickering fluorescent lights overhead. The officer told Raul to sit on the array of couches, as he and Alicia exchanged signatures on a series of forms. The smell of burnt coffee wafted from the nearby conference room. Raul stared blankly at the framed posters— "Human Rights is in our DNA" above a multicolored helix and "The United Nations Declaration of Human Rights" surrounded by multicolored hands. Bright colors were strewn on posters and bulletin boards throughout the three-story building.

After escorting the officer to the front door, Alicia returned, asking Raul, "When was the last time you ate?" Taking hold of Raul's black trash bag of belongings, she led him downstairs to the dining hall. It had been three days since ICE apprehended Raul—he spent the first two days in a small jail cell in Arizona and the third on his first airline flight. "I knew I was in Chicago because I saw a sign at the airport, but I didn't know anything else—where I was, how long I would be here, or even when I could finally take a shower. Nobody would tell me anything," he recounted to Alicia as I observed. Raul's stomach growled as if on cue. "I had some crackers on the plane. And a couple of burritos when I was in jail."

In the large basement room, lined with small windows along the top of the brick walls, Alicia prepared a plate of pancakes and eggs still warm from breakfast and a tall glass of milk. Raul hated milk but would learn to force himself to drink the required glass at each meal. "I would love a cup of hot coffee," he remarked as he stared at the poster of a cup of coffee hanging on the cafeteria wall. He would come to find out that "the only coffee in this place is on the wall," as other youths had joked. As Raul took a heaping bite of eggs, Alicia explained that, although he was no longer in the custody of ICE, he could not leave. "We will provide you with a place to sleep, clean clothes, plenty of food, English classes, and help you to get in touch with your family. This is your new home while we help to sort out your case. We will be your family while you are here." Raul seemed skeptical that this woman, who had just signed his transfer papers with the ICE officer, was telling the truth. There were sixteen cameras strategically located throughout the facility, monitoring his every movement. "Hardly home," he murmured under his breath. Raul had learned to question everyone and everything. "The *coyotes* taught me to never believe what you see." The scars on his feet would remind him lest he forget.

After wincingly drinking the last drops of his milk, Raul was accompanied upstairs by Alicia, who introduced him to a caseworker who began the program's extensive intake process. The process involved dozens of questions regarding the child's history, migration, and family composition; bathing, disinfecting, and distribution of institution-issued clothing with identifying numbers; confiscation of personal property, cataloged and held in inaccessible storage; orientation to the program rules and regulations; and a series of education, mental health, and medical assessments. As Goffman (1961: 16) observes, "Admission procedures might better be called 'trimming' or 'programming' because in thus being squared away the new arrival allows himself to be shared and coded into an object that can be fed into the administrative machinery of the establishment, to be worked on smoothly by routine operations." Raul later reflected that the most frustrating aspect of his lengthy intake process was that the facility staff refused to use his correct name. The transfer documents Alicia signed used an alias Raul had provided when apprehended. Until the Mexican consulate could confirm the authenticity of his last name, the caseworker said she was obliged to use the name on his ICE transfer forms. Goffman (1961: 18) reflects, "Perhaps the most significant of these possessions is not physical at all, one's full name; whatever one is thereafter called, loss of one's name can be a great curtailment of the self." Raul would come to find out that the intake procedures were just one of many behavioral management techniques enlisted to foster pliancy among "program participants."

The Continuum of Detention

Since 2003, the ORR Division of Children's Services[1] has developed a national network of facilities and programs that include large residential centers, staff-secure shelters, therapeutic shelters, residential treatment centers, group homes, juvenile jails, and community-based group foster care and family foster care programs. Although facility and program staff are employed by the individual nongovernmental organizations, funding, policy setting, and decision making descend exclusively from ORR headquarters in Washington, D.C. And, while NGOs that run the facilities provide for the children's everyday needs, the experience of "shelter life" is not benign. Children constantly are monitored by security cameras, watched and counted continuously by staff, permitted to leave the facility only when supervised at particular staff-to-child ratios, restricted to communication with one or two preapproved family members by phone for twenty minutes a week. Most facilities have locked, alarmed doors and windows. Staff members document medical and mental health sessions, behaviors, personal communication, phone calls, and visits with advocates in the child's institutional file, which is freely shared with law enforcement on request. As a *total institution*, every action and reaction is subject to surveillance and documentation in the child's ORR file. Staff members remind children that misbehavior will affect their "case," widely understood by children as their release and long-term permanency in the United States.

The "shelter" as a site of inquiry is of particular importance because, analogous to airports, ORR facilities are simultaneously located within and outside national territories. Unaccompanied children are held betwixt and between in federal facilities that are geographically in United States territory but without access to the rights and services afforded to citizens (Turner 1967). They are not able to leave the facility without certain documentation the state has deemed essential (e.g., a legal passport, an original birth certificate, a permanent residency card, etc.), yet they are not entitled and have very limited access to such documentation due to their unlawful presence in the United States and their inability to secure the documents while in detention. As a result, unaccompanied children are confined to federal "shelters" for much longer than their counterparts in the domestic child welfare system, because, among other reasons, they lack the proper documentation to enter national spaces. In effect, children are fixed in spaces of nonexistence. While Guantanamo Bay has become synonymous with the spectacle of state abuse, torture, and indefinite detention of enemy combatants, the existing immigration detention apparatus for children shares in the complex web of legal contingencies that creates a situation of indefinite detention with limited external oversight.[2]

The ORR detention facilities are an explicit example of the state in loco parentis. The director of the Division of Children's Services is the legal guardian of all children in ORR care; the federal government pays nonprofit caregivers to provide for the everyday needs of children; ORR makes determinations on children's futures based on claims to their best interests as a parent would. The state establishes the parameters and expectations of everyday life, enforces compliance to nutritional regimens and to participation in education and recreation, and evaluates which social and kinship relationships children may maintain or must temporarily sever. ORR funds all facilities, legal assistance programs that provide "Know Your Rights" presentations and legal screenings to unaccompanied children detained in ORR facilities, a pilot project appointing guardians ad litem, and voluntary agencies involved in the placement of children with sponsors, family members, foster care, or group homes. In the envisioned model, the partnership between the state and civil society allows the state to oversee the care of unauthorized migrant children, while local organizations provide the child welfare expertise to nurture children in need. Seen as a less restrictive environment than juvenile jails as called for by the Flores Settlement Agreement, facilities provide a "homelike" setting. Albeit unintended, this funding and operational

model has resulted in a patronage relationship between the state and civil
society in which advocates do not challenge ORR's unilateral decisions on
specific children's cases without jeopardizing their organization's fiscal survival. As ORR has contracted its funding priorities to legal providers to
screen detained children, even legal advocates are resistant to challenge or
to sue ORR over discriminatory practices or abuse of power, violations of
child welfare best practices, prolonged detention, denial of parental rights,
or violations of due process and state and federal confidentiality laws for
fear of losing limited funding. In 2013, the Senate is considering legislation
that would relocate legal and child advocate services to the Department of
Justice in order to remedy this monopoly of power and resources. Until legislation is passed, there remains no independent actor or agency involved in
the daily lives of detained children to contest ORR's unilateral decisions and
organizations are left jockeying for limited resources. Further, parents are
systematically excluded from decisions regarding their children's education,
legal rights and options, and medical and mental health care, with only very
limited control over custodial decisions if parents provide the requisite documents to ORR. A local DCFS social worker explained, "ORR has become a
shadow welfare system that makes its own rules as it goes along with no regard
to existing child welfare practices and expertise. No one is willing to shine
the light on what ORR really is—a glorified warden." With limited oversight
and with a financial stronghold over legal and social service providers, ORR
has established a federal welfare system for unauthorized youth who, because
of their detention in federal facilities instead of state-run programs, do not
meaningfully intersect with the knowledge and expertise of the domestic
child welfare system.

With increased immigration raids, higher apprehension rates since 2007,
direr poverty levels in Central America, and increased cartel violence in
Mexico, the population of detained migrant children has grown, as have the
demands on ORR to expand its capacity. What was initially imagined as
small programs in residential settings has transformed into the institutionalization of unauthorized children. Funding for ORR's programs has only
marginally increased to match the growing demand for facilities, resulting
in rising demands on nonprofit personnel to provide for a larger number of
children from a greater diversity of countries and complex mental health and
legal needs with even fewer resources at their disposal. As a result, facilities
have grown in size but diminished in capacity to provide individualized
care for migrant children. For example, in Texas and Arizona, the largest

facilities maintain 160 beds, with "emergency facilities" in Texas housing upward of 300 children temporarily in multibuilding complexes; in Illinois, the largest of the seven facilities is licensed for 250 beds in a single building. "Shelters," the lowest level of security, average 50 beds, while secure facilities are typically rented bed space in domestic juvenile jails. "Shelters" have become holding facilities in which a small number of staff monitor and control an increasing population of youth. The surveillance responsibilities once held by ICE in detention facilities have transferred to nonprofit staff who must serve as prison officers, restrict movement, monitor behavior, control circulation of information, and recapture children who attempt to abscond from facilities. A supervisor at a California facility lamented, "It is all a ruse. We may call ourselves a shelter, but we are a detention facility. I am not supposed to admit it, but we don't have time or resources to rehabilitate these kids. We just keep them in a holding pattern until they get deported or go back to living with their families [as] before they were apprehended." In a Texas facility, the executive director of the shelter was married to the ICE regional supervisor; particularly along the U.S.-Mexico border, the personal and professional lines between civil society and law enforcement blur frequently. Facilities regularly hire off-duty police officers, former Border Patrol agents, and former members of the armed services to staff new facilities. As Raul noted, Alicia's signature on institutional paperwork was a signal to him that nothing was as it seemed—that ICE, ORR, and civil society were part of a continuum of detention and surveillance that, as he would come to discover, would shape his life in meaningful ways even beyond his physical confinement at the facility.

Manuel: "No Sé. No Sé Nada"

Exasperated, Manuel told me, "I can't sleep because I think I may leave tomorrow. I get so excited to see my brothers and my sister. But then I am disappointed because I don't leave. I don't know what is going on." Manuel had come to the United States from a village in the state of Guanajuato in Mexico to work at an apple orchard where four elder siblings had worked since the late 1990s. At fourteen, Manuel had a slight build but was accustomed to the physical demands of migrant labor from his work on a local plantation in Mexico. With his mother's emotional support and his sister's financial assistance, Manuel journeyed north and reunited with his siblings in Michigan. After eight months, "a policeman pulled me and my brother-in-law over because we are Mexican. He called *la migra* [immigration enforcement] who came to get us on the side of the road." The police officer did not explain the reasons for pulling them over nor did he issue a citation to Manuel's brother-in-law. That "we are Mexican," as Manuel observed, was sufficient for local police to assume the role of immigration enforcement, an increasingly common practice under the ICE Agreements of Cooperation in Communities to Enhance Safety and Security (ICE ACCESS)[3] program, which trains state, local, and tribal officers to enforce immigration law. Within a week, Manuel's brother-in-law was deported to Mexico; because of his minor status, Manuel was sent to an ORR facility in Illinois.

Manuel is one of a minority of Mexican youths who enter ORR custody. For most, their removal from the United States typically occurs within seventy-two hours. The Contiguous Territory Agreement between the United States, Canada, and Mexico allows for the administrative removal of children, in practice limiting children's access to family, legal counsel, and social services and bypassing a hearing before a judge. A popular rumor circulated among Mexican youth in Midwestern facilities where I conducted research: "If you get north of the Mason-Dixon, you come here [to the detention facility]. If not, you get deported," as Manuel explained. The analogy to the U.S. Civil War era border delineating the free North and the slave South speaks to a perceived racialization of some groups and the privileging of others within the networks of institutional and state actors engaged in the apprehension and placement of migrant children.

Manuel remained in the facility while his family reunification application was assembled so that he might be released to his sister-in-law, who is a lawful permanent resident. Ironically, Manuel had lived with his brother and sister-in-law in Michigan, but the administrative procedures to authenticate their relationship and to assess their willingness and ability to care for Manuel meant that he remained in the facility for four months while a series of individuals and organizations assembled and evaluated his application to ORR. Manuel's apprehension and detention became an interruption in the stability of family life he had enjoyed in Michigan.

Before each meeting with a new supervisor, whether from the facility, voluntary agencies, or ORR, Manuel had become hopeful that he would return to his family, yet each interview brought additional questioning and layers of evaluation. Following his meeting with ORR's federal field specialist, Manuel told me, "She says she doesn't know anything about my case even though she has my file right in front of her. She asked me all the same questions that everyone else has asked me. Who is making the decision anyway? If it isn't here [at the shelter], if it isn't anyone I have met, if it isn't her, if it isn't immigration, if isn't my brother, and it sure isn't me, then who? Just tell me, who?" Manuel experienced the flexible detention of ORR facilities in which the length of his presence was not based on a fixed sentence common in criminal proceedings, but continually shifted contingent on the length of time it took for a number of actors and agencies to collect and evaluate his paperwork. For Manuel, the continued circulation of his institutional file was both the obstacle to the decision-making process and evidence of collusion among institutional actors preventing his release.

Sitting in the back row of the classroom with Manuel during a break from his English class, I asked him what the family reunification specialist had told him. Manuel responded, "Nothing. He says any day now, but that he doesn't have any information . . . that they are waiting for one more person to approve the papers. Why is it taking so long? Why do so many people need to approve that I live with my brother who I lived with before for months. He is family. I don't understand it. *No sé. No sé nada* [I don't know. I don't know anything]." Manuel's language acquisition was once lauded as a sign of his adaptability and potential, while his lack of participation was now a problem according to his teacher. When called on in class, Manuel repeated, "*No sé. No sé nada.*" Manuel rested his head on the table in the back of the classroom.

Everyday practices of facility's staff are motivated by a desire for children to acquire new skills and knowledge that may improve their future "quality of life"—a culturally situated and class-based assessment. Manuel's presence at the facility is framed as an opportunity for him to learn proper social behavior, personal hygiene, and consumption practices—all essential components for his success. Staff instructed him on the proper way to make his bed each morning "to impress your mother at how responsible you are. It is a sign of respect to your mother who has more important things to do than to clean up after you," explained a caseworker. Manuel was taught proper hygiene. "Only drug users have a long [pinky] nail like that," remarked a night supervisor when Manuel protested cutting his nails. In their daily lessons, teachers emphasized that learning English grammar would facilitate future success for youth either in the United States or in their home countries. When students grumbled as the teacher asked them to take out their notebooks, the teacher lectured, "When you are trying to find a job, you are just like all of the other kids in your neighborhood who want to work. But, if you speak English, you stand out. You show them that you are smart, that you can learn, and that you will be a good employee." On several occasions, staff would remind youth that they were lucky to be at the detention facility, with food, shelter, and education. At a "house meeting," a supervisor scolded children for not taking a full plate of food at mealtimes. "There are children starving all over the world and you don't take food. You need to fill your plate with one of everything and drink your milk at each meal." As I sat down to eat the next day, Manuel picked at his food and remarked, "Instead of telling us that children are starving, we know that already. Why don't we take what we can eat and they just cook less? They can save the money they spend on groceries and send it to the starving kids. Eating my plate will not solve hunger in Mexico."

In spite of the rhetoric on the power of knowledge and the opportunity for self-making, children are left with little information, access to decision-makers, and input on their futures. The obfuscation and restriction of certain types of information is a daily practice at the facilities in which staff withhold information about activities of daily living. "I know we are going out. Why don't you just tell me," asked Manuel of a teacher. "I don't know yet," the teacher lied. To no one in particular, Manuel asked, "Why don't they just tell us? It isn't that big of a deal." The teacher later explained, "Once they know what we are doing, you have to watch them even closer in case they are planning to escape or cause trouble." Keeping activities of daily living unpredictable is justified by the desire to protect children from an amorphous and undisclosed threat but also serves as a valuable tool of controlling a growing population of children in the facility. The control of youth in shelter facilities is predicated on the staff's ability to shape information and veil it from youth. With the justification of minimizing a child's opportunity to abscond, shelter staff do not inform children that they will be returned to their countries of origin until moments before leaving for the airport, creating a constant climate of uncertainty and anxiety. Particularly for children who have suffered traumatic losses, the inability to psychologically plan for change—even if desired—maintains significant potential for retraumatization.

A teacher at the facility explained to me the challenges of the multiplicity of roles:

> Kids don't understand that I am a teacher but I am also security. I have to see the big picture. I can't tell them certain things. I can't let

them do certain things. There are so many things not even under my control. Kids get frustrated with being here, but there is nothing I can do about it. Some kids explode and get angry at me. I try not to take it personally. I have to be professional, but I am waking the kids up, feeding them, teaching them, joking with them, disciplining them. . . . I am a teacher. I am a parent. I am a mentor. I am a security guard.

There are some forms of restricted information, such as a sponsor's personal finances or criminal history, that staff frame as an ethical response to the privacy rights of adult sponsors to the inquiries of individual children. However, children from whom the information is solicited or about whom it affects have very limited access to any information. The staff limit children's access to the telephone and closely monitor their communication. They listen to personal conversations of individual youth and record it in their institutional file. Because children are not seen as individual right holders and, as a federal agency, ORR does not see itself as bound by state confidentiality laws, confidentiality between NGOs, ORR, and ICE is porous, which, in some instances, has proven detrimental to a child's legal claim. For example, Raul's weekly phone calls to his abusive mother while in immigration detention became ICE evidence of his falsified claims of domestic violence. "How is it that you call this woman who has beaten you for years every single week without fail? Isn't it true that you are making all of this [physical and sexual abuse] up?" pressed the ICE attorney during her cross-examination in court nearly two years later. In contrast to the rhetoric of fostering a "home" and "nurturing" environment for children, children's movements within the facility and their access to communication with the outside world become highly scripted and monitored. What information enters the child's institutional files becomes the state's evidence against individual youth, and yet children cannot access their files while detained.

For detained children, in the absence of the power to influence their legal or family reunification petitions, information is a critical asset. Tight control of the circulation of information becomes an added layer of frustration to their detention. In part, the restriction of information is a symptom of ORR's lack of transparency in the decision-making process regarding family reunification and foster care placements. ORR has come under criticism by the Office of the Inspector General for its often-unwritten rules, arbitrary decisions, and lack of oversight of such processes (OIG 2008). At times, family reunification specialists do not have the information themselves to share with youth, but they also choose not to explain the process adequately to inquiring children. The process is indeed complicated, involving an intricate web of institutions and actors, many of whom the children never meet but who maintain significant decision-making power over their futures. The logistical demands on specialists who are responsible for an increasing number of children limit opportunities to explain the process; nevertheless, as Manuel observed, children are systematically excluded from the decision-making process. Predicated on the notion that children are not informed social actors who contribute to migration and caregiving decisions, children are excluded from accessing information regarding their own future care arrangements and meaningfully contributing to these decisions. The facility staff possess and restrict knowledge that, in many ways, is not theirs to conceal or withhold, information from and about the very children they bypass in the process. In spite of the self-making rhetoric, the little agency afforded to youth is restricted exclusively to a child's potential for disrupting other youth in the facility or escaping from detention.

Pascal: "Here in My Eyes Is the Extinguished Candle of Hope"

Since his arrival at the facility nearly two months earlier, Pascal, a sixteen-year-old Guinean, intermittently has been given "boot camp"—a punishment in which he must awaken early to clean all the bathrooms, assist in the kitchen, and is unable to participate in recreational activities throughout the week. Pascal lost the privilege of outside activity that he had taken for granted before entering immigration detention. After weeks in English and math classes that were far beneath his intellectual and educational experiences, he welcomed the opportunity. "They think it is a punishment, but I would rather be here [in the kitchen] learning Spanish than forced to do long division I learned in fifth grade," he explained. Pascal had come to the United States to pursue his soccer career. He had undergone months of testing, interviews, and screening in Guinea to secure a student visa to study for a year in the United States. With only a few months remaining on his visa, Pascal received a call from his mother saying his father, a community leader, had been assassinated and the family was no longer safe in Guinea. Amid the family's flight, his mother told him not to return to Guinea. Pascal was apprehended by local law enforcement in New Jersey at a routine traffic stop, and when local police realized he was in the United States on an expired student visa, he was transferred to an ORR facility.

Pascal longed for regular phone communication with his family; however, his mother and two younger siblings had gone into hiding, moving from house to house, not able to consistently receive Pascal's weekly phone call at a prearranged time. Children are restricted from making phone calls to individuals who have not met ORR criteria for a verifiable relationship to the child. Such guidelines emerged from a concern for the safety of children from traffickers and smugglers who might seek repayment or retribution for their debts. Pascal asked if he could make a phone call to his aunt who might have contact with his family in Guinea, but without documentation verifying the authenticity of their relationship, he was refused. Exasperated at what he perceived as a double standard, Pascal informed me, "It is clear they don't want to let me leave here. And it is clear they are lying to me. I can't trust anything they say because they have lied to me so many times." When I asked him to clarify which lies, he explained that in over two months at the facility, he was denied access to the telephone, with staff later citing an inability to secure a Kissi interpreter to screen his communication with his aunt to ensure their biological relationship. "What they say and what they do just don't make sense. They say that they can't find a Kissi interpreter but there is one who comes every week as a [child] advocate for [another detained child]. They can use him to communicate with my aunt. If he is approved to work with children at the center, then they must trust him. Why could he not help to make the phone call? If they don't trust him, why is he here? Don't I have a right just like all of the other kids to make a phone call?"

Acutely aware of the disparate treatment he received, Pascal pointed out this inconsistency in the organizational practice of prescreening phone calls to the facility's director, who found his insistence justification for further boot camp. Recognizing his powerlessness at the facility, Pascal opted to employ logic and debate, skills he had learned from his father at a young age in Guinea, to highlight the disparities and inconsistencies in treatment between children and to exercise his rights as he understood them. Unable to respond in a transparent or logical way, staff found themselves frustrated by Pascal's insistence, or in their perspective, his "combative behavior." In many ways, Pascal was correct in his analysis of this situation. Despite the poster on the wall above her head lauding human rights, a caseworker remarked to me, "The reality is he has no rights. He hasn't yet figured out that he is in detention and that in detention, he doesn't get to do what he wants." The value placed on rights, equality, and opportunity espoused by the NGO contradicted Pascal's experiences of everyday life. Pascal was not a passive receptacle of the state or facility rules, but creatively adapted. That he both identified and articulated this contradiction was a form of resistance to the discretionary decision of facility staff to locate a Kissi interpreter and the fallacies in ORR's institutional logic. Attempting to counter his positional powerlessness as a detained minor, Pascal's use of logic and argumentation to lay bare what he viewed as the truth was effective, leaving the director to acknowledge the contradiction or attempt to silence him with additional punitive measures.

Despite an updated computer lab at one of the facilities, Pascal's access to the Internet was also tightly regulated. Website blockers prevent children from accessing personal e-mail accounts or sites such as MapQuest or Google maps for fear of children deciphering the facility's location and orchestrating an escape. Analogous to domestic violence shelters, ORR facilities are confidential sites. When Pascal circumvented the parental controls and printed a picture of his younger brother from his e-mail account, the facility director informed him, "You may be smart, but I am smarter than you." She confiscated his photograph. Staff control is predicated on their ability to restrict both information and access to the outside world—restricting the children's telephone calls and Internet access, denying visitation with family members, and obscuring information about the activities of daily living and about their individual cases. Yet, Pascal's knowledge and ability to outwit even technological restrictions and to access an increasingly interconnected world were a threat to the staff's ability to exercise absolute control over their subjects. Printing a photograph was Pascal's way to undermine staff authority and to demonstrate how he, in many ways, was cleverer than the facility staff. Furthermore, printing a picture of his family member linked Pascal to an extended kinship network whose existence was institutionally discounted. In the staff's view, Pascal's independent presence was evidence of his pathological behavior and justified the facility's rehabilitative efforts to mold him into a pliable subject. Compelling the recognition of his family and its importance to him challenged the facility's claim to serve as "his family for now," as Alicia had told Raul.

The director later told me that Pascal's "problem is that he is just too smart for his own good. He needs to learn to do what he is told and not to question everything. If he keeps it up, he will jeopardize our recommendation for foster care. It is in his best interest to just follow the rules." Pascal's refusal to conform became justification for punishment that would threaten his release. Instead of recognizing that there was a fundamental disconnect between the humanitarian rhetoric espoused by ORR and the NGOs detaining children and the law enforcement approach shaping everyday practices, the facility leadership sought to punish Pascal in the name of his own best interests.

Interestingly, such practices of restricting and obscuring information extend to interactions with other actors and agencies involved in the care of unaccompanied children. Across sites, attorneys and voluntary agencies voice great frustration at the facilities' institutional culture of obfuscation, in which silence and inflexibility are understood as a perversion of their mission to care for and to protect migrant children. Concealing information regarding institutional expansions, restricting visitation policies for attorneys and guardians ad litem, disparate treatment among the children based on nationality, and behavioral modification strategies lead advocates to question the facilities' humanitarian claims. Advocates have accused facility leadership of collusion with ICE, citing what appears to be open communication. In several instances during my research, including for Pascal, the administration initiated and paid a forensic odontologist to conduct a dental examination to verify the age of individuals suspected of lying about their minor status. In five of the six cases, staff considered these children "problem children" or incapable of rehabilitation. For Pascal, the authenticity of his student visa had come under scrutiny, leading facility staff to question his credibility.

The reliance of age determination policies using wrist bone forensics and dental records is highly controversial due to a substantial margin of error of two to three years, particularly in cases of malnutrition and stunted growth—a polemic in regard to many children from Central America, particularly Honduras. Normed on a sample of Caucasian youth in the 1930s, the G&P standard (named after the study's authors Greulich and Pyle), the practice does not account for ethnic, geographic, or socioeconomic variation in pediatric populations. W. R. Maples (1978) claims that age determination is an art in which science, cultural context, and interpretation are equal factors. The reliance on scientific knowledge remains a contested domain between ICE and ORR, in which ICE considers the lower threshold in the range as the child's age, while ORR assumes the higher threshold. For example, if dental exams indicate that a child is between 17 and 18.6 years old, ORR will presume the child is 17, and ICE will contend the child is 18.6. ICE maintains the right to request bone or dental scans but only occasionally requests them for children in ORR custody. "They either don't want the bad press, so err on the side of caution or can't bother putting down their Starbucks to care," speculated a seasoned legal advocate. In the absence of evidence to the contrary, ORR guidelines stipulate that children's age claims should be trusted; however, this rarely applies to youth perceived as untrustworthy or behaviorally delinquent. By initiating such scans, particularly in situations where ICE does not order testing, NGOs solicit the creation of evidence that would otherwise not exist and call for a heightened level of scrutiny under a faulty metric.

The staff gave Pascal, who claimed to be sixteen, two weeks to secure corroborating documentation to demonstrate that he was indeed a legal minor, but without access to e-mail or speech with unscreened family members (namely, his aunt), he was unable to do so. Furthermore, because he feared the Guinean government that his family believed was responsible for the murder of his father, he would not request an interview with the Guinean consulate. The exclusive reliance on scientific knowledge produced by the dental and bone scans to disprove Pascal's age feeds suspicions that ORR possesses a misguided interpretation of the best interests standard. Advocates view the facility staff as leveraging its position as care provider to influence the state's discipline of individual bodies, transforming social service providers into agents of state surveillance in explicit ways. Shortly after his dental examination, two ICE officers escorted Pascal from the shelter to a local adult immigration detention facility, where he remains while he petitions for political asylum.[4]

Sergio: *"El Notario"*

Sergio sat at the lunch table, shifting his food from one side of the plate to the other. "There is too much rice here," he remarked to no one specifically, yet the other four youths at the table and I all nodded in agreement. After six months in the facility, Sergio's frustrations mounted each day: "Why am I here? I am American," he had asked his attorney in the screening interview several months earlier. "My mother immigrated from Mexico before my years of recollection. I think I was seven but I don't know for sure." Sergio explained to me that coming to the United States "seems a world away," as did his suburban life in Cincinnati, his weekend work as an inventory clerk at the local Sportmart, and his friends with whom he regularly skipped school.

Rather than a consequence of his unauthorized status in the United States, Sergio understood his presence at the facility as one of "falling into the wrong crowd." His truancy from school and recreational drug use incited panic in his mother. His mother explained to me, "He wouldn't go to school. I didn't know where he was. He would stay out all night and wouldn't come home. He just wouldn't talk to me about anything. Not even hello. I thought the worst . . . that he was in a gang and selling drugs. My brother died from an overdose in Los Angeles. I needed to do something to save my son." When she found marijuana in his jacket, she said, "It confirmed for me that he was selling. I had no other option. I had to call the police. I knew he might get deported to Mexico, but that was the risk I had to take to save my son. Now, I don't know if it was the right thing."

Isabela and Martín, recent arrivals to the facility from Brazil and Honduras respectively, interrupted Sergio's mealtime routine of organizing and reorganizing the items on his plate, as they talked about their immigration hearing the following day. Sergio perked up. "So are you going to court for the first time?" he inquired.

"Yes," responded Isabela, struggling to understand in her broken Spanish as she tucked her institution-issued green T-shirt into her gray sweatpants. Despite the staff's repeated reissuance of increasingly large shirts and sweatpants, Isabela had managed to fasten her clothes tightly around her body, revealing a figure many of the youth might find provocative, staff feared. One of the supervisors passed the lunch table, removing Isabela's arm from Martín's shoulder. "Behave properly," he remarked and walked away.

Sensing Martín's nervousness at his upcoming court date, Sergio said, "Don't worry. You just go in and the judge asks you your name, your age, and where you are from. Just answer her. That's it."

Martín asked, "And if you want those women to be your lawyers?" referencing the team of attorneys and paralegals from the local legal service provider screening children in ORR facilities. Funded through an ORR subcontractor, the Vera Institute of Justice, the legal program holds the exclusive contract with the facilities to screen and represent detained children. In Illinois, the detention facilities and the legal service provider are programs of the same umbrella NGO, a conflict of interest that harks back to INS conflict of interest. Should an individual child and his family hire an outside attorney, the attorney occasionally may meet with his or her client at an off-site location, but the family must initiate this request amid myriad institutional and logistical obstacles. As a result, nearly all children accept pro bono counsel.

Sergio: "Yeah. That too. I forgot. I have a different lawyer though."
Isabela: "A different lawyer? How did you manage that?"
Sergio: "My mom hired him because I didn't trust the ones here."
Isabela: "Your mom is here? That's great."
Sergio: "Yeah in Cincinnati, but not much good it has done me. Are
    you going to ask for more time? I mean, do you want to try to
    stay here or do you want to go back to Brazil?"
Isabela: "I want to stay, don't you?"
Sergio: "Yeah, I'm from here. I don't know anybody in Mexico, but
    I want to get out of this place. I'm going nuts" (returning to
    his mound of rice now located on the left side of his plate).
Isabela: "But why? What's the rush? Here you have three meals a
    day. A warm place to live. You can learn."
Sergio: "This isn't life here. I am just waiting on my cousin to get his
    papers in order. I'll go to Texas to be with him."

Sergio had chosen to reunify with his cousin instead of his mother in Cincinnati. He explained that he could not trust his mother anymore. He told me, "I know what I was doing was no good, but she is my mother. I still can't believe she would do that [call the police] to me." At fifteen, Sergio struggled with conflicted emotions of love and resentment toward his mother.

Sergio had missed over half of the school year, deciding to spend time with friends, some of whom were members of a *pandilla*.[5]

Martín: "I don't know what I want to do. My family is in Honduras
    but the lawyers tell me I might be able to stay. They say it won't
    be a long time until I get to go home."
Sergio: "Well, you can ask for more time. You can do that three
    times before the judge gets annoyed. The lawyers can do it for
    you. I've asked for more time. But, yeah, they are right, if you
    stay here, you can't go back home. And, sometimes, even if you
    win your case, you can't bring your family here. So, you have to
    think hard. It's a lot of pressure."
Martín: "Maybe I'll ask for more time . . . I don't know."

Sergio: "Well, that's good. The lawyers just do it for you. You barely
    have to talk. She [the immigration judge] will give you another
    three to four weeks and then you have to go back to court
    again."
Isabela: "How long can you do that for?"
Sergio: "Just a few months and then you have to decide if you take
    voluntary [departure] or if they deport you. Of course, you can
    try to stay if your lawyers let you."
Martín: "But Yesinia has been here [in the facility] for 15 months."
Sergio: "Yeah, but her case is different."
Isabela: "But Elena never saw a judge and she got out. And, Julia just
    got sent to [an adult] jail. She woke up and the next thing, they
    are putting her in handcuffs. I saw it from my bedroom
    window."
Sergio: "Every case is different. There are different rules for different
    types of people. If you ask for voluntary [departure], you can
    come back at some point. Or even if you ask for deportation,
    you can switch [to voluntary departure] if you come up with
    the cash [to fly home]."
Isabela: "How much is it?"
Sergio: "Right now it is about $500 to fly back to Mexico. I bet at
    least twice that for Brazil."

Amid the limited access to information and input into his own legal cases,
Sergio became a repository of information and legal knowledge for recently
arrived children. His English language skills and cultural familiarity assisted
him in adeptly navigating facility life and immigration proceedings, resulting in his reputation as *el notario*.[6] While some of his legal advice was not
factually accurate, Sergio had a sophisticated understanding of immigration law, legal proceedings, and his rights, which he freely shared based on
the specific fact patterns of a child's familial context, migration histories,
and past abuses.

With increased immigration raids and enforcement within the interior
of the country, rising numbers of unaccompanied children who have spent
the majority of their lives in the United States are entering into the ORR
shelter network. Principally designed for non-English speakers with limited
educational attainment, the facilities are increasingly challenged to accom-
modate youths such as Sergio, who are culturally American and who have

exposure to the American school system. Sergio developed his skills and knowledge amid an adverse environment with great uncertainties, and he helped Isabela and Martín to compensate for the lack of transparency about their legal and family reunification cases. Attorneys conduct "Know Your Rights" presentations for all youths within two weeks of their arriving at the facility; due to the number of children (at times, upward of 120) they screen, and given that there is only one organization granted routine access to the facilities, the availability of an attorney to respond to individual questions and inquiries does not keep pace with the demand. Furthermore, even if eligible for legal relief, pro bono legal organizations represent only a fraction of children in ORR custody; however, if a child seeks voluntary departure, organizations are obliged by their funders to provide representation. The irony remains that immigration attorneys serving detained children can more readily assist the child in departing the United States than in pursuing legal remedies to remain.

Sergio gained a reputation for his legal savvy, and new arrivals solicited his advice. Sergio instructed Goz to withhold all information such as his parents' identity, country of origin, and current address in New York to minimize the risk of deportation of his parents and younger siblings. Goz was an eleven-year-old child who was detained when his uncle was pulled over by police for expired license plates on his car and could not produce a valid state driver's license. While there are only a few instances in which ICE has used children as bait for unauthorized parents, Sergio knew that Goz's father's criminal history would put him at heightened risk of deportation to Nigeria. Goz's parents later advised him to conceal his family's history and contact information from the facility caseworkers as well. In another instance, Sergio advised sixteen-year-old José to accept voluntary departure to Chiapas, encouraging him to only immigrate once he turned eighteen to avoid another lengthy detention in ORR facilities due to his minor status. "If you are caught when you are eighteen years old," Sergio reasoned, "you will be quickly dumped over the border [to Mexico] and could just come back." In only a short period of time after arrival and with the guidance of other youths, children were able to discern vital information regarding their legal cases and the trustworthiness of actors working in the facilities or with ORR, voluntary agencies, or local legal organizations.

Even from immigration detention, Sergio expressed his cultural belonging to the United States and held out an invitation to others who wished to pursue a life in the United States. He assisted others in navigating the legal and institutional structures that marginalized, pathologized, criminalized, and excluded them from the nation-state.

Pathologization of Mobility

Social and legal policies are indebted, either explicitly or implicitly, to discourses that imagine the child as psychologically vulnerable, pathologizing the child who migrates "alone." Interventions frequently consider child migration in the context of natural or manmade disasters such as famine or war, or as a result of family breakdown; these circumstances are in turn interpreted as leading to the increased vulnerability of children exposed to harsh labor or living conditions (Coe et al. 2011; Hashim 2006: 4; Ressler, Boothby, and Steinbock 1988).

A collection of literature on independent child migration attempts to counter this pathologization by detailing the autonomy of child migrants in their decision-making processes, migration journeys, and settlement practices. Viewed as neither passive nor powerless social actors, children become central to discussions of global inequity, transnationalism, and local culture, whereas their life experiences were previously considered marginal. Unfortunately, this scholarship divorces the child from the family, attributing the child's "premature" independence as either signifying family conflict and dissolution or resulting from parental compulsion or coercion of children to migrate. In addition, the research on independent child migration has become skewed toward those children in the most vulnerable and harshest living and working conditions and those who achieve a certain level of visibility. While it is essential to acknowledge the realities of abuse and victimization of children as they choose or are coerced to move between households, the street, and across national boundaries, often ignored is that neither childhood nor migration is an undifferentiated experience. Ethnicity, gender, socioeconomic status, age, as well as country of origin, destination, and motivation to migrate are some of the myriad factors that texture the day-to-day experiences of migrant children and youth. Focusing on autonomous or independent migration of children who become visible and the types of interventions necessary to reconnect them to the family and to society reinforces the dichotomy of the child as capable of rehabilitation and as a delinquent in need of containment. Some children become defined in pathological terms (such as child soldiers, street children, or trafficking victims), by their engagement in a particular type of labor (e.g., sex workers, agrarian laborers, or factory workers) or by their perceived absence of kinship ties (e.g., orphans and vulnerable children, unaccompanied and separated children). However, the vast majority of migrating children remain invisible or marginal to scholars, institutions, and organizations alike, with minimal analysis of the context of children's movements, why they move, how they move, or how many times they move.

Although there is certainly a growing recognition of child migration as a social phenomenon, there is an institutional consolidation of difference with the juridical category of the "unaccompanied alien minor." For detained migrant children, the facility becomes not only a site of containment and surveillance but also the site in which the state attempts to socialize migrant youth to certain behavioral norms. The migrant child's deviance is predicated on the assumption that the normal environment of the child is to be stable (Fass 2005: 938). High mobility, then, somehow disrupts the health of children and inhibits their ability to form essential social ties. Developmental models of childhood bolster the fear that a displaced child with fractured social ties and a lack of attachment to community results in solitary, detrimental behavior carried into adulthood (Eckenrode et al. 1995). Children who remain highly mobile are seen as missing the opportunity to learn the skills necessary to live a productive life (Sampson 1988). The category of street children demonstrates how institutions attempt to control those "out of place"—those who do not reside in a home with family members, attend regular schooling, participate in proper social activities with peers, and occupy spaces designed for children (Panter-Brick 2002; Zelizer 1985).

ORR policies reflect this problematic presumption shaping the rehabilitative, educational, and socialization efforts. Behavioral management programs reward docility and compliance and punish critical thinking and questioning of authority. Numbing or silencing individual expression becomes a justification to control a growing population of children in large institutional settings and to ensure safety in the name of children's best interests. A daily routine of language and hygiene instruction and skill building are framed as rehabilitative services intended to "develop responsible young people," as a facility therapist explained. Children are presumed to be irresponsible or deviant because of their physical and unlawful presence in the United States; the complex behavioral management programs in which they "participate" and lengthy house rules to which they must obey establish normative behavioral markers that track compliance, deviance, and "improvement" and on which a child's release may be contingent. Yet, these depictions of stability stand in contrast to the historical record, which reveals children circulating throughout time and space. While the norm of stability may be an ideal for childhood, a satisfactory or fulfilling childhood is not necessarily forfeited by a child's mobility. In fact, migration may be a resource to children within a context of global inequities. As with Manuel and Pascal, migration may allow greater access to educational or employment opportunities and facilitate consumption practices otherwise restricted to those more "privileged" (Hannerz 1996).

The diverse reasons for movement may not signify family rupture exclusively but may indicate variations in the ways children navigate limited resources, challenging the notion that dissolution and "failure" are experienced as the sole cause for migratory practices. For example, fostering is a widely recognized tradition in parts of sub-Saharan Africa to "redistribute the costs and benefits of childbearing" (Isiugo-Abanihe 1994: 171; see also Goody 1982; Notermans 2004; Verhoef 2005). Acknowledging the varied reasons for fosterage, such as death, illness, education, divorce, or the reinforcement of family ties, allows us to consider the fluidity of households, which, at times may span great distances, and the social and economic conditions that spur child migration (Young 2004: 472; see, e.g., Eloundou-Enyegue and Stokes 2002). While scholars historically have not considered fostering in terms of migration, contemporary fostering practices have in some ways become more akin to it. Although extended kinship networks often absorb children who find themselves orphaned by illness, in countries such as Uganda, Tanzania, and Zambia, HIV/AIDS has made this practice more difficult, due to fewer resources and more children in need, resulting in new sets of tactics that include migration (Foster and Williamson 2000). In other words, mobility may be sought for strategic purposes to improve quality of life or opportunities. Similarly, unaccompanied migrant children may circulate between households or geographical territories in an effort to satisfy basic needs, assure physical and psychic integrity, or expand educational, professional, or marriage opportunities—often with the explicit or tacit support of their extended kinship networks. Furthermore, anthropologists have begun to trace how the physical and technological mobility of youth shape cultural practices in local settings and transnational contexts (Boehm 2008; Henderson, Taylor, and Thomason 2002; Tully 2002).

The unaccompanied migrant child disrupts cultural constructions of the child as necessarily fixed (stable) and located within a family. Advocates contend that desperation and depravity drive children to take such extraordinary measures, such as migration, not typical of their American counterparts. While there is certainly significant evidence of this, the exclusive emphasis on vulnerability as a cause for migration denies a child's ability to make decisions and to implement a well thought out plan. In the absence of socialization by the nuclear family or in a constant place, a youth who negotiates his own transnational journey becomes untrustworthy, bearing unknown allegiances and requiring particular institutional prescriptions of care and protection. In part, the perception of childhood as protean holds both promise of rehabilitation and threat of the unknown. Institutional prescriptions, often veiled as being in the "best interest of the child," hinge on both the mourning and the pathologization of child agency, not a celebration or even recognition of a child's potential strengths exhibited by his resourcefulness. However, it is critical to recognize that youth are not passive recipients of these discourses. Youth evade, circumvent, resist, and confront such positioning, whether it be through Isabela's tightened clothing, Sergio's preservation and circulation of essential legal knowledge, or Pascal's explicit challenges to illogical institutional policies. Even in an age of deterritorialization, with increased flows of people, goods, labor, and information across borders, facilities continue to pathologize mobility and laud fixity rather than recognizing youth flexibility and fluidity as assets in an increasingly contingent world.

CHAPTER 6

═══════

Reformulating Kinship Ties

INTERLUDE

Parents' Day

When I was young, I lived with my mother and father and I was happy. I had everything spiritually that a child could have—the love of my parents and my grandmother. But, like you know, Central America entered into a difficult stage—the gangs and the drugs contaminated each step. When I was six years old, I received the sad news that my mother and father were going to *el Norte*. They promised me that they would return, but they never came back.

I stayed by my grandmother's side. She taught me about what is right and good in the world, but without the love and understanding of my parents, I rebelled. But who cared? I had no mother or father to worry or to punish me.

In school each year, we had parents' day, but each year my desk stood empty. My grandmother tried to occupy a space for three, but she could not.

One day, my father decided to bring me to the U.S. but he did not realize that I was no longer the boy he had left that day long ago. And, here in this country, I found a mother and father unknown to me and a brother and sister I had never met. Where had they gone? I was confused and did things my grandmother had told me never to do.

And, now that I am returning to my country, my
question is what will happen when I return? I only have
my faith and hope that my grandmother will continue to
fill one of those seats at school. But who will fill the
others?

—Edwin, sixteen-year-old from Guatemala

Unconventional Spokesperson

"Born in the USA. Don't take our moms and dads away," the crowd chanted
during a 2007 immigration rally in Chicago. With much anticipation, Saul
Arellano took the stage. His mother, Elvira Arellano, had rallied a national
call for immigration reform in the United States. Despite Chicago being a
sanctuary city in which municipal funds are not used to enforce federal immigration law, in 2002 Elvira Arellano was arrested along with five hundred
other unauthorized laborers in a raid of Chicago O'Hare International Airport, where she cleaned airplanes. Pleading guilty to document fraud, Arellano was ordered deported to her native Mexico.[1] Instead of returning to
Mexico, she defied the order and sought refuge, first in a Southside Methodist church and later in the Adalberto United Methodist Church in Chicago's
historically Puerto Rican neighborhood of Humboldt Park, in hopes of remaining with her seven-year-old son Saul, a U.S. citizen.

Like Elian Gonzalez nearly a decade prior, Saul came to embody the heated
national debate on immigration reform. Anti-immigrant coalitions claimed
that enlisting a child as a spokesperson not only was abusive and exploitative
but also signaled the movement's desperation. Critics questioned Elvira Arellano's character and parenting practices, indicting her for refusing to leave her
son in the custody of family in the United States or to return with Saul to
Mexico to begin life anew. Unlike Elian, who as a child never spoke to the
public and rarely appeared publicly, Saul was shy but vocal when speaking
about the everyday impact of his mother's illegality. Following the rally, Saul
told a local reporter, "[My mother] can't take me to the store and can't take me
to school. It makes me feel a little bad. My other friends, they have their moms
and their dads. It's different for them" (Cepeda 2007). Standing before thousands, Saul became the unconventional spokesperson for the impact of height-

ened immigration enforcement on immigrant families. Saul spoke to reporters at rallies, to politicians in the nation's capital, and to the Mexican Congress, denouncing workplace raids, collaboration between local law enforcement and federal immigration authorities, surveillance in school districts, the application of federal identity theft laws against workers like his mother, and the ways immigration enforcement divides families.[2]

Through family-based petitions for legal status, U.S. immigration law claims to privilege the nuclear family, yet many families are restricted in the avenues for legal migration necessary to preserve family integrity—waiting in the proverbial (though arguably nonexistent) line to enter the United States lawfully. With limited opportunities to secure legal status, families engage in autonomous family reunification through clandestine migration. As a result, the number of migrant families with complex configurations has increased.

In 2009, the Pew Hispanic Center estimated that nearly 8.8 million people live in mixed-status families, of which 3.8 million are unauthorized adult migrants and half a million are unauthorized children (Passel and Cohn 2009: 18). A mixed-status family consists of members with differing legal statuses, ranging from U.S. or naturalized citizenship, Temporary Protected Status (TPS), lawful permanent residency, student or work visa to undocumented. Increasingly though not exclusively, mixed-status families consist of a child who is a U.S. citizen through jus soli ("right of the soil," or birthright citizenship), while the child's parents and possibly elder siblings may not share in the same legal status. Although living in a single household with identical biological parents and attending the same school, one sibling may have certain legal rights as a citizen, while the child's older unauthorized sibling does not have access to analogous rights and opportunities, including health care, higher education, and authorization to work. Jeffrey Passel and D'Vera Cohn (2009: 18) found that the number of children—both unauthorized and U.S. citizens—in mixed-status families had increased from 3.3 million in 2003 to 4.5 million in 2009, a trend likely to continue absent comprehensive immigration reform. Furthermore, legal status may shift and slide over time: when family members are able to regularize their immigration status; or when a visa expires or federal legislature fails to renew TPS, leading some family members to fall out of status.

Despite the rhetoric that unaccompanied children are untethered to family and act individually, unaccompanied children and youth are intensely embedded in kinship and social networks, which facilitate migration and shape their everyday actions. While there are certainly migrant children who are alone, fleeing abuse, violence, or poverty and seeking employment, education, and opportunity, more commonly children and their families leverage social and financial capital to facilitate their transitional migration and settlement (even if temporarily) in the United States. Scholars have demonstrated how transnational migration itself strengthens, shifts, and at times disintegrates kinship ties (see, e.g., Boehm 2008: 781). Children "left behind" in the country of origin learn to assign meaning to family life in a global context of connectivity, relatedness, and mobility (Olwig 1999; Orellana et al. 2001). Rhacel Parreñas (2001) has traced the ways mothers entrust their children to family members to engage in the work of mothering and caretaking in the global economy. With the feminization of migration over the past several decades, kinship networks fill the caregiving gap during parental absence (Battistella and Conaco 1998; Donato et al. 2006). The contexts encouraging and relationships facilitating child migration are consistent with other patterns of migration, in which kinship networks and social capital are essential assets to transnational migration.

As Deborah Boehm (2008) argues, in an analysis of the changing character of kinship ties amid transnational migration, it is critical to consider change against a backdrop of state power (778). Children, whether unaccompanied or in mixed-status families, feel the profound impact of the law and state policies in their private and public lives. The heavy hand of the state enters everyday life, shaping family integrity, custody arrangements, educational opportunities, occupational choices, access to public benefits for qualified family members, and involvement in the child welfare system (see, e.g., Fix, Zimmerman, and Passel 2001). The contradictory values and practices enshrined in state structures that aim to unify families, whether immigration law, family courts, or ORR sponsorship practices, demonstrate how the state can construct, (re)produce, and divide families.

Rather than preserving family integrity, the law has become a mechanism for dividing migrant families, as with Saul and Elvira Arellano. David Thronson (2006) attributes the rise in mixed-status families to the ways immigration law fails to recognize children as primary applicants in family-based petitions. A U.S. citizen child such as Saul cannot petition for his parent and as such becomes vulnerable to abrupt and often prolonged separation if ICE apprehends his parent. Children whose parents are detained or deported face heightened risks of involvement in the child welfare system, at times calling into question a parent's custodial rights over the children when the parent no longer resides in the United States (Liebmann 2006; Nessell 2008; Thronson 2005). Unauthorized migrant parents and deported parents face significant obstacles to meaningfully accessing court custodial proceedings, participating in the judicial process determining their family's fate, and regaining custody of their children.[3] Both family law and immigration law fail to keep pace with the fluid and complex configurations of migrant families within the United States and across international borders—often with severe consequences for children.

In previous chapters, I have argued that immigration law and institutional practices both fail to recognize children as social agents and as rights holders, and as a result, isolate children from their social and kinship networks in which they are contributing members. In this chapter, I build on that argument by examining how the state (re)constitutes kinship ties for migrant children both within and beyond the confines of immigration detention. I analyze how ORR's sponsorship process, known as "family reunification," structures migrant families, strengthening some relationships while negating others. Through the lenses of race, income, biology, and culture, institutional policies and practices assess who is a "suitable" guardian and what are the conditions for a "proper" childhood. The complex and dynamic lives of children—unaccompanied, unauthorized, or as members in mixed-status families—call into question the legal and institutional imaginaries of children and their families. In light of these state policies and interventions, youth are forced to navigate the shifting terrain of state power by reformulating their families both in the United States and transnationally.

Lourdes and Jesus

One of the few benevolent features of immigration detention is that children may be released to a family member or sponsor while their deportation proceedings continue. In contrast to their adult counterparts, children do not have to pay a bond and are not necessarily detained until their legal cases are adjudicated (though some may be). Instead, their release is contingent on a screening process that assesses and evaluates not only the relationship between the child and the sponsor but also the capacity and competency of the potential sponsor to care for the child. There is a compelling argument for a rigorous screening process to ensure the safety and well-being of the child and to guard against criminal networks that may have a financial investment in children smuggled or trafficked into the United States. However, for detained migrant children and their families, sponsorship can be a long and fraught process. Once a child is apprehended and transferred from ICE to an ORR facility, the child meets with one of the facility's family reunification specialists (herein, "specialist") who evaluates the viability of sponsorship according to ORR guidelines. The specialist attempts to contact individuals that the child identifies as possible sponsors in order to explain the bureaucratic process.

The identification of sponsors in and of itself can be challenging, as many children report losing contact information due to theft or loss along their journeys, inclement weather blurring ink on scraps of paper tucked in their backpacks, or, less frequently, not knowing their final destination. Sponsors may be parents, relatives, or family friends identified by the child or the child's biological parents as someone willing and able to care for the child, though the criteria for each category of relation differs. Making contact with some sponsors is particularly difficult, as they may be apprehensive to answer telephone calls from an unknown source. In the interests of confidentiality, caller identification is blocked on all outgoing calls from the facility. The child must secure the parent's written consent to pursue family reunification with a relative or family friend—a highly problematic prerequisite for children fleeing an abusive parent yet one of the few ways parents are included in a custodial system that largely disregards their rights as parents. After agreeing to sponsor a child, potential sponsors must undergo a lengthy application and review process in which they must provide an original birth certificate (or signed social security card) for themselves, the child, and any family member that can link the child to the sponsor; proof of immigration status; proof of citizenship; bank statements; a rental or mortgage agreement; utility bills; federal income tax returns; pay stubs; and a letter from the sponsor's employer. Sponsors also undergo a fingerprint background check against the database of the FBI National Crime Information Center, the Central Index System and the Deportable Alien Control System. If the sponsor is not a biological parent, everyone residing in the household must also submit to a background check. In addition to the child and the sponsor's anecdotal evidence substantiating the veracity of their relationship typically in the form of parallel factual patterns, specialists must also attempt to verify the relationship between the child and the potential sponsor through corroborating documentation, such as institutional paperwork from the child's country of origin or photographic evidence. For those families able to secure the requisite documents and forms necessary to substantiate a sponsor's relationship to the child, ORR evaluates the suitability of the care provider and the caregiving environment. A sponsor's fitness is determined by a series of factors including the sponsor's deportability or criminal history and the sponsor's ability to meet standards for housing, employment status, financial support, child-care arrangements, and household composition.

At once frightening and onerous to potential guardians and children, the sponsorship process is predicated on biological understandings of relationality. The Convention on the Rights of the Child recognizes a child's right to a family, yet how these families are defined in the U.S. context becomes problematic for migrant children. ORR policies are based on a legal construction of family rooted in the nuclear family as the unit of socialization of children. Family reunification policies fail to recognize other functional kinship arrangements such as same-sex couples, grandparent- or child-headed households, single parent or polygamous households, godparents, or even extended kinship networks when members of that network are undocumented (e.g., Demleitner 2003; King 2010). ORR does maintain the policy that a biological parent's illegality may not be a barrier to sponsorship, in contrast to INS policy prior to 2003; however, in practice, illegality may negate parental claims to custody. Due to their unauthorized status in the United States, some parents are apprehensive about coming forward to claim their child. Disclosing their legal status, place of employment, and home address to the very authorities they fear is counterintuitive. Unlike a child's ORR file that masquerades as confidential, the sponsorship application involves explicit involvement from both ICE and FBI. There is no presumption or claim of confidentiality despite specialists' attempts to allay the fears ICE will use this information to apprehend unauthorized parents. In 2012, advocates reported that ICE has begun using information disclosed by sponsors in raids on workplaces and households, a fact ORR seeks to conceal from potential sponsors, the attorneys contend.

Lourdes, a Nicaraguan woman, explained her hesitation to sponsor her son, Jesus, who was apprehended while crossing the U.S.-Mexico border and placed in an ORR facility in Texas: "I am putting myself at risk and my whole family—my kids and my family in Nicaragua who I support and my children and [my partner] here—to get my son back. If he gets deported, at least he will still have my mother to care for him. If I get deported, who is going to support them? And what happens to [my children and my partner] who live here?" Working in a local Chinese restaurant in a suburb of Chicago, Lourdes and her partner remit over a third of their meager monthly income to Lourdes's parents and her three children in Nicaragua. Following his grandmother's diagnosis of cancer, Jesus migrated to the United States to reunite with his mother who was concerned for her mother's ability to care for a teenage boy. Although Lourdes's partner of three years is a legal permanent resident, Lourdes cannot benefit from her partner's legal status because immigration law historically has not recognized civil unions between homosexuals.[4] Conflicted by her choice between her financial and familial obligations in Nicaragua and the United States and her responsibility and desire to care for her son, Lourdes told me, "Jesus hates me for leaving him five years ago, and I can't bear to leave him again. I will lose him. I know it."

Indeed, Jesus felt betrayed by his mother's unannounced departure from Nicaragua. In the initial screening interview by the local legal service provider, Jesus said, "My mother abandoned me when I was young. I got back from school and my mother had gone. She did not leave a letter. She did not tell me where she went or when she would be back. My [grand]mother told me she left for the United States and was not coming back for me." At the paralegal's probing, Jesus revealed that he was not abandoned in the legal sense of the term because he maintained regular contact with his mother. Nevertheless, he felt emotionally abandoned. He said, "She calls twice a year and she sends me birthday and Christmas gifts, but I do not want them. I want her to act like a mother not to send me things. My grandmother is my mother now." In his biological mother's absence, Jesus was raised by his maternal grandmother with whom he maintained a profound emotional bond, as he envisioned his relationship with Lourdes might have been under different circumstances.

According to Lourdes, she departed Nicaragua out of fear. "Leaving my children that way was so painful, but I had few options. The harassment was getting worse. I didn't know what would happen next." The police and several residents of her small town had accosted Lourdes on several occasions, accusing her of being a lesbian and threatening to kill her if she did not leave the town immediately. Lourdes recalled that her name appeared on a list posted on the bulletin board in the town square—a list of alleged homosexuals wanted for questioning at the police station. Instead of reporting for interrogation for what she believed would translate into imminent incarceration and prolonged brutality, Lourdes fled her hometown that same afternoon.

ORR releases children to a biological parent if given assurances of a child's safety; nonetheless, ORR regularly denies a child's release to a biological parent if the parent has an order of removal or deportation order. In practice, a parent's deportability, which is in the interests of the state, trumps a child's right to family. Furthermore, unauthorized parents must claim their child at ORR subcontracted facilities. Even if sponsors overcome the fear of disclosing their identity and contact information to the federal government, given that 82 percent of beds are located along the southern U.S. border, parents must pass through numerous immigration checkpoints to arrive at detention facilities. They face palpable risks of detention and deportation in order to regain custody of their children. On several occasions, U.S. Customs and Border Protection officers detained unauthorized children in the custody of Texas state child welfare workers. Because ORR cannot ensure that children will not once again become unaccompanied if their parents are detained en route to or departing from the facilities, during the period of this research, in practice ORR did not approve family reunification with unauthorized parents for children detained in Texas and Arizona.[5] Such was the case for Jesus. After Lourdes submitted all identifying documents, according to the federal field specialist, ORR still denied her custody of her son based on the risks of Jesus becoming unaccompanied on leaving the facility. Caught in the crosshairs of the enforcement regime and an institutionally constructed risk, Lourdes's immigration status became a preeminent factor in the state's assessment of her fitness as a parent.[6]

Jesus's mother's failure to gain custody further destabilized Jesus's understanding of social obligation and relatedness. Jesus told me, "Mothers are supposed to care for their children, feed them, support them, hug them when they cry. She says she is my mother but she is not acting like one." While Jesus never openly acknowledged his mother's sexual orientation, his repeated insistence on how his mother's behavior did not coincide with his specific imaginary of motherhood and mothering alluded to his belief that his mother was somehow different from other mothers. Lourdes's repeated failure to comply with such an imaginary, which in many ways she shared with Jesus, was significantly troubling to her and explicitly motivated her sponsorship petition amid the risks to her presence in the United States and the well-being of her family. Lourdes explained, "I want to be the mother I have not been . . . that I could not be." ORR's reunification policies and practices prevented her from having this opportunity; instead, Jesus returned to the care of his ailing (grand)mother in Nicaragua.

Edwin

For Edwin, a sixteen-year-old K'anjobal youth from Guatemala, the sponsorship process led him to question the enduring quality of his kinship ties. Despite having three older siblings in the United States, Edwin found that none of them appeared willing to sponsor him from immigration detention. He said, "For months, I have been sitting here [at the facility] waiting for them to help me. They say 'Yes, yes, we will help you.' But then nothing. [The specialist] says he calls my sister and she says she is almost done with the papers, but I am still here. What am I supposed to believe? That she cares for me? No, I don't think so. That is not how real family acts."

In conversation with Edwin, it became clear that he was only minimally privy to the risks posed to his sister in pursuing sponsorship. He said, "Juan left here to be with his mother. Jesus left with an aunt. Sofia left with a cousin that wasn't even her cousin. Why not me? She is my sister, my family. I thought that has value here." Edwin knew that other detained youth had been released to family members, though neither facility staff nor the ORR federal field specialist explained the risks of sponsorship to him. Beyond the sponsorship requirements that may deter unauthorized family members from completing the process, having information withheld from them on their sponsorship progress leaves children to draw conclusions based on the experiences of their peers. In the absence of an explanation, Edwin's anger and resentment toward his family festered.

Across facilities, the historical illegality of Guatemalans in particular has profound implications on the sponsorship process. In the facilities where I conducted research, specialists were overwhelmed with the volume of "cases"—inundated with phone calls from family members both domestic and abroad, stakeholders, consular officials, ICE, and ORR, as well as with the task of completing and submitting sponsorship packets to ORR. Amid pressure to maintain a low average length-of-stay factor, specialists strategically channeled their energy to "the more promising cases," which translated into those youth with documented sponsors. Edwin's family reunification specialist explained to me, "We are faced with convincing [unauthorized] parents to claim their children when it means risking their livelihood. Nine out of ten cases, they won't do it. And nine out of ten cases where the undocumented sponsor does come forward, ORR won't allow it." Another specialist in an Arizona facility confided to me, "The Guatemalans aren't worth the energy because their cases never work out. If I have eight hours in my day, I am going to spend it on the Mexican and Salvadoran kids who at least have a chance of leaving here." Often unwilling to challenge ORR administrative decisions, specialists tailored petitions to fit ORR's historical patterns of approvals on reunification cases and dissuaded children whose cases did not conform to this history.

Across multiple facilities, I observed specialists consciously and unconsciously weigh which sponsorship petitions were most likely to succeed and thus warranting their limited time and attention. These calculations were rooted in the assumption that Guatemalan sponsors were more likely to be undocumented than other nationalities, and thus children they sponsored were less likely to be released from ORR custody. In contrast, potential Salvadoran and Honduran sponsors were seen as more likely to have legal status, such as Temporary Protective Status or lawful permanent residency, and the Mexican community was almost always presumed to have sponsors available to petition for a child. There is certainly demographic and historical evidence to suggest some veracity to these assumptions. Mexican migrants in the United States far outnumber Central Americans and maintain higher rates of legalization. Guatemalans and Salvadorans systematically were denied asylum until the 1991 *American Baptist Churches v. Thornburgh* settlement agreement recognized the discriminatory practices of the USCIS, the Executive Office of Immigration Review, and the Department of State.[7] The 1997 Nicaraguan Adjustment and Central American Relief Act also recognized some unauthorized migrants from Nicaragua, El Salvador, Guatemala, Cuba, and some former Soviet bloc countries as de facto refugees who had been categorically denied legal status in the 1980s and 1990s. For some families the legalization process has gone on for decades, resulting in a differing prevalence of legality among some Central Americans and among their child beneficiaries who may age out of their parents' petitions for legal status. In this way, the state's historical discrimination against Guatemalans continues to shape contemporary institutional practices toward Guatemalan youth.

There are also structural impediments to the indigenous Guatemalan community that can impede sponsorship. The language barriers between Spanish-speaking staff and some indigenous youth who speak Maya languages pose an additional challenge. Although language hotlines are available to facility staff, they are severely underutilized as they add expense to the facility. For some languages it can be difficult to locate a trained interpreter. Such is the case for children from francophone countries who may not be fluent in French or other indigenous groups such as the Quechua in Ecuador or the Mixtec in Mexico. While detained for six months, Edwin did not have access to a K'anjobal-speaking interpreter, nor did his sister; instead they relied on their limited Spanish to navigate the complex bureaucratic process to reunify. Furthermore, children and family members with limited literacy often find the cumbersome bureaucratic process of sponsorship unmanageable. Several specialists and facility supervisors attributed indigenous children's limited understanding of the sponsorship process to their "unsophisticated cognitive abilities due to a pervasive lack of education," as one supervisor explained, rather than a halting fluency in the Spanish language. These racial, class, and linguistic biases overflow into the courtroom as well. For example, during immigration proceedings for Edwin, the immigration judge remarked, "Guatemalans are so cute. Their feet don't even touch the ground. It is amazing they can walk here with such short legs." The infantilization of indigenous youth across administrative and judicial domains adversely shapes treatment, sponsorship options, and legal options available to indigenous youth.

According to Edwin's specialist, Edwin's sister seemed unwilling to sponsor her younger brother out of concern for her own legal status. His sister's continued failure to comply with the institutional requirements and timeline signaled to the specialist that sponsorship was not viable for Edwin. Instead, she counseled Edwin to accept voluntary departure rather than remain detained until his eighteenth birthday when he would be transferred to an adult immigration detention—"a terribly unhappy place for you," she explained. Edwin's experience of his sister's failure to sponsor him was inconsistent with his understanding of how relatedness functions in everyday life and how siblings express care and responsibility for each other. The restrictions of information only further excluded Edwin by not recognizing the autonomy of his thoughts and his agency to contribute to the sponsorship process. Had he been informed of the risks posed to his siblings in sponsorship, his emotive response might have differed both while detained and following his return to Guatemala.

Taken together, the inflexibility of the bureaucratic process to account for cultural, linguistic, or literacy differences and the underlying racial and class biases of individual workers within a resource-poor environment foster structural barriers that obstruct rather than ensure equitable treatment for indigenous youth. Instead of ensuring quality and consistency, the one-size-fits-all approach to sponsorship creates nearly insurmountable obstacles for indigenous youth to be released expeditiously, to reunify with family members, and to secure legal status. Instead, Guatemalan youth are disproportionately deported.

Assessing Suitability

Throughout the sponsorship process, the facility specialist assesses a sponsor's suitability over the course of several telephone conversations, highlighting both automatic triggers for assessments (e.g., a child is a national of a country "known for trafficking, namely India and China," as commonly cited by ORR supervisors and facility staff) or concerns for the appropriateness or authentic interests of the sponsor. Many ORR criteria are rooted in Western social norms that reflect both a romantic ideal of childhood and the monetization of caregiving—standards often in conflict with the social, cultural, and economic realities of migrant families. At the same time, these standards are often a moving target in which sponsors, children, and advocates alike are unclear of the factors influencing a sponsor's suitability. Often there is no allegation of abuse against the sponsors, but particular risk factors rise to the level of concern for potential abuse or harm to a child and thus result in a home study.

In a small but growing number of sponsorship applications, voluntary agencies subcontracted by ORR conduct these home studies, otherwise known as suitability assessments. I observed requests for a suitability assessment when a father had a criminal conviction; when there were suspicions of domestic violence, alcoholism, or drug abuse in the home; when a mother was HIV positive and thus considered a potential "hazard for the health and safety of the child"; when an uncle sponsored his nephew he had not previously met; when a twenty-three-year-old sought sponsorship of his sixteen-year-old sister; when a mother had seven children in a two-bedroom apartment and her income fell below the national poverty level; when a child had a mental health diagnosis or previous involvement in the juvenile delinquency system; when a child lived in a neighborhood considered "gang infested"; and when a child was hearing impaired. Particularly problematic are the suitability assessments on parents who have a child with a disability. According to ORR, the Trafficking Victims Protection Reauthorization Act of 2008 requires any child who qualifies as having a disability under the American Disability Act to undergo a suitability assessment, even if his or her parent has competently raised that child since birth. The assessment entails a home study over one to two visits, including an FBI criminal background check of the sponsor and all household members over eighteen and interviews with the sponsor and household members. While the voluntary agencies conduct suitability assessments, ranging from forty-five to ninety days, the child remains detained.[8]

Detention facility staff are often reluctant to request a suitability assessment that may prolong a child's detention and would raise the organization's average length-of-stay metric. Because subcontracted organizations rely exclusively on ORR funding to care for unaccompanied children detained in their facilities, it is in their fiscal interests to keep the average length of stay as low as responsibly possible. ORR federal field specialists and facility administrations alike cite this metric as one of the most compelling arguments for increased funding from ORR; suitability assessments increase this factor. Per the Flores Settlement Agreement, ORR is motivated to place children in the least restrictive setting, which is ideally in the community and with family members. However, there is a fundamental disconnect between this mandate, the facility's ability to meet release criteria expeditiously, and ORR's fiscal interests. In a rare moment of vocal discontent, facility directors during a national managers' meeting challenged ORR to reconsider their metric. Given the varying complexity of cases across facilities and triggers for automatic suitability assessments, facility administration pushed back against the uniformity of institutional financial incentives and penalties.

Of the criteria determining suitability both in initial assessments by facility staff and in suitability assessments themselves are factors, such as the consistency between the family reunification application and interviews with the child and the sponsor, income and employment verification, family relationship, and household composition. More subjective elements include the gender composition of the household, authenticity of family ties, child-care arrangements, sleeping quarters, attitude of household members, number of family members in the home, poverty level, and ability of the sponsor or family member to care for the child. While there is no single factor determining a denied placement, the confluence of income, race, and legality in particular shape the social worker's assessment of a child's risk of harm and delinquency.

During a home visit, the social worker walked through the house, noting the two bedrooms and arrangements of beds. "Where will Ricardo sleep?" she inquired of the mother and stepfather, who were hoping to reunify with their twelve-year-old son, who, known to them, had journeyed from El Salvador. Because Ricardo's stepfather had a conviction for drug possession nearly a decade earlier, the suitability assessment was obligatory. "He will sleep there," his mother gestured to the floor between his two stepsisters' twin mattresses. In response to the caseworker's sudden vigorous note taking, the stepfather added, "We will put down a mattress." Depending on a family's socioeconomic status, sharing a bedroom with younger siblings regardless of gender is acceptable in El Salvador. "Poor parents can still be good parents, but you'd never know it around there," lamented a former specialist.

After I observed a home visit by a social worker with Sonia, an aunt petitioning for her nephew Emilio, the caseworker remarked to me, "I don't think she really wants him. She already has three kids and it seems like a burden instead of a genuine concern for a nephew she hardly knows. She is saying 'no' without saying it out loud." Indebted to her younger sister still in Guatemala whom she had not seen in nearly seven years, Sonia did not appear enthusiastic in her desire for Emilio but openly admitted to the caseworker that "I am his only option to remain in the U.S. It is my duty." Institutional conceptions of family assume not only that a family is obliged to provide and care for dependent children but also that those expressions of care are met with a prescribed emotive response. Sonia's articulation of obligation did not coincide with the social worker's expectations for a loving caregiver. Despite meeting criteria for sponsorship, the social worker reluctantly endorsed Emilio's placement.

The forms of screening and evaluation hark back to the turn-of-the century reformers who were instrumental in defining social and behavioral norms for migrant children and parents predicated on upper- and middle-class values. Current tools for the assessment of competency and neglect draw on key concepts established by the child savers, such as cultural norms of obligation and care, child labor, spatialization of child circulation, and financial capacity to parent. In the contemporary domestic child welfare systems, assessments are similarly rooted in historical norms established by the reformers and substantiated by the tutelary complex of social and behavioral scientists through everyday institutional and judicial practices. Child Protective Services responds to a hotline call reporting allegations of abuse or neglect by conducting a preliminary investigation and removing a child from the home only in instances of imminent threat or harm. In the domestic child welfare system, arrangements are often made for the child to remain with a trusted adult or in kinship care until a state court judge determines the long-term care and custody of the child. In the context of immigration detention, what remains distinct from the ways relationships are assessed in the domestic child welfare system is the presumption that the parent is not a viable care provider until proved otherwise. A parent or guardian is presumed unfit until he or she can prove ability and willingness to care for the child and, in some cases, until an outside assessment by a social worker can substantiate the viability of that care arrangement. Throughout the investigation, children are not placed in temporary kinship care but are instead institutionalized and detained until the forty-five- to ninety-day study can be completed.

Western social norms inculcated in the personal beliefs and professional training of social workers are transmitted though assessments of caregiving and caregivers. When working cross-culturally with such a diverse population, the judgments documented in suitability assessments become particularly problematic for migrant children. An examination of a small sample of fifteen suitability assessment reports over three years reveals enduring expectations for conformity rather than consideration of diverging social and cultural norms. The reports routinely recognized the risks unauthorized immigrants face, particularly in states with harsh anti-immigrant policies, and indicated that these risks impeded a sponsor's ability to navigate state bureaucracies necessary for securing services the child may need. As a result, family members, through no fault of their own, were routinely denied custody of their children because the sponsor was presumed ill-equipped to meet the needs of the child.

A sponsor who assumes custody of a child from ORR must sign a Sponsor's Agreement to Conditions of Release form, in which the sponsor assumes responsibility for the child's physical, mental, and financial well-being. The sponsor must agree to ensure that a child attends all immigration proceedings; that a child remains in the United States while the child's case is adjudicated; and that a child report for removal if he or she is ordered to be deported. The sponsor must agree to notify DHS within seventy-two hours if a child flees placement or is threatened by smugglers or traffickers. Furthermore, the sponsor agrees that if he or she does not comply with the agreement, DHS may take custody of the child again. In signing this agreement, the sponsor

Table 3: Release Status of Unaccompanied Children at Time of Survey

Status	Number	Percent
Released to sponsor	14	19.7
Not released	3	4.2
Returned (ordered deported/voluntary departure)	25	35.2
Status changed (accompanied)	4	5.6
Immigration status changed	4	5.6
Transferred facilities	4	5.6
Foster care	5	7.0
Escaped facility	3	4.2
Adult status (aged out)	6	8.5
Adult status (age redetermined)	3	4.2
Total	71	100

assumed taking on surveillances and discipline of the unaccompanied child from ORR and DHS.

As an administrative body rather than a judicial one, ORR maintains the discretion to approve or to deny a child's release; there is no judge assessing a parent or sponsor's suitability or the veracity of claims of abuse or neglect; there is no clear system of appeal of ORR's custody determinations; and children remain in immigration detention throughout the process rather than in foster care or with a trusted adult. While ORR claims that denials of family reunification are never final until a parent's rights have been legally terminated, there are no clear mechanisms of appeal or steps identified to parents who wish to regain custody of their child at an undisclosed point in the future. During my research, in cases where ORR denied a child's release to a parent, ORR identified some measures that would encourage ORR to redetermine a parent's petition for custody. Such measures included a parent moving to a new apartment with more bedrooms; a family moving to a safer neighborhood; having family members (stepparent, elder sibling, uncle) with criminal backgrounds (e.g., driving under the influence) leave the household; enrolling in parenting classes; applying for public aid for U.S.-citizen children; finding a second job to augment income, or leaving a second job to provide greater supervision; identifying a co-sponsor to meet the financial requirements necessary to sponsor a child; and filing a legal petition to reopen pending deportation proceedings against the sponsor. Few of these measures touch substantive concerns for a child's safety and violate the child's right under international law to family unity. Furthermore, no written plan is provided to parents and no local assistance is provided to sponsors to access these services or benefits. While lacking the jurisdiction and funding to mandate these services, ORR maintains the unchecked power to deny a child's release without the protections and rights afforded to children and their families in family court. In other words, although ORR is an administrative body, in all practical matters regarding sponsorship, ORR functions as judge, jury, *and* appellate court. Perhaps most concerning of all is the absence of attention paid to the violence inflicted on children and their families through prolonged detention, multiple transfers, and lengthy, nontransparent assessments. Despite claims to the contrary, the bureaucratization of care fails to consider the long-term emotional and physical harm to children amid claims to ensure their "best interests."

Goz

In most instances, children decipher the sponsorship process from their peers and family members during their weekly twenty-minute phone call. However, the anxieties, disappointments, and resentments they experience during the sponsorship process do not resolve on their release from immigration detention, but linger in their relationships, whether they remain in the United States or are deported to their countries of origin. The profound consequences of an unsuccessful or prolonged sponsorship are not benign, as ORR would suggest. Although the bureaucraticization of care may prevent sponsorship, the children's feelings of confusion, uncertainty, abandonment, or betrayal toward family members who are unable or unwilling to secure their release from immigration detention pervade their social relationships across transnational spaces.

Family reunification specialists and ORR federal field specialists pressured eleven-year-old Goz to divulge the names and address of his parents in New York. Sergio, a fellow detainee, advised Goz to resist, given his father's conviction for driving under the influence two years prior, which might risk his family's deportation to his father's native Nigeria. Goz's parents also advised him to conceal his family history and contact information from the facility caseworkers. In a phone call with the specialist, Goz's father insisted that Goz was a national of the United Kingdom to the vocal disbelief of facility staff, ORR, and ICE. His father produced a British passport secured when Goz was an infant, though State Department forensic evaluations were inconclusive in trying to determine whether the passport was authentic. An ICE officer explained to me, "Nigerians make incredibly accurate false documents—birth certificates, passports, school records. Even with forensic evaluations, we can't always tell." Throughout his detention, Goz consistently maintained his father's British citizenship claim, though he later admitted to me that he did not believe he was a British citizen. "My mother is from Kenya and my father is from Nigeria. I don't ever remember living in England. My father was a student there for a year when I was little, but I have lived in the Bronx since I was two. The Giants are my team. I am an American." Without an individual legal claim to remain in the United States, with his parents unwilling to divulge information in a sponsorship application, and without compelling evidence that Goz was in fact Nigerian, he was deported to England, where he now lives with his paternal grandmother. His parents and his U.S.-citizen sister remain in New York.

After a month in a London suburb with his grandmother, Goz told me over the phone, "It is alright here. My grandmother is helping me to get into school and to feel better about being here. I miss my friends from home a lot. I miss my parents and my sister, but we get to talk on Skype each week, and I e-mail everyday. They say they are going to come visit as soon as school is out." State policies and practices forced Goz to choose between risking his family's residence and livelihood in the United States and his own place in that kinship network. Ultimately, he was forced to restructure his family life. Choosing to protect his family, Goz was removed from the United States, leaving him to maintain familial relationships through virtual communication and intermittent visits. The elasticity of his transnational kinship ties stretched for another six months until Goz's father alone was able to visit him for two weeks. Goz continues to be unable to reunite with his family or visit his mother and sister in New York.

While the state structures kinship in a particular way, youth navigate the state's involvement in caregiving arrangements beyond the confines of detention. In my research with voluntary agencies, I observed the coordination of follow-up services for those released from detention. Follow-up services are provided to less than 3 percent of unaccompanied children nationwide, principally overlapping with those who undergo suitability assessments. In nearly a third of cases with follow-up services, children left their initial sponsors' homes, often seeking out parents whom ORR denied as suitable guardians during the sponsorship process. Once a child departs from his or her approved sponsor's custody, ORR advises the voluntary agency to close the case in order to terminate ORR responsibility to and liability for the child. However, social workers will often scavenge for local services in the child's new locale. Lily, a fifteen-year-old from Ecuador, left her aunt's home in Pennsylvania to live in Tennessee with her mother, who, based on a pending order of deportation, had not been approved for reunification. A social worker remarked, "Lily came here to be with her mom. She said she didn't want to live with her aunt but with her mom. She said this throughout the suitability assessment, but ORR didn't listen. So, why are they surprised she left? I could have told you this even before her aunt picked her up from [the facility]." In the same ways that transnational migrants employ "autonomous family reunification" to preserve family integrity, unaccompanied children may defy ORR placements in an effort to reunite with trusted caregivers whom the state does not recognize as such (Boehm 2008: 798). The illogic of a custodial system that ignores children's rights to information, only minimally consults children in decisions regarding their care and custody, and lacks transparency and oversight defies child welfare best practices and ignores international safeguards. Despite claims to the contrary, the best interests of the child are not well served by detention, institutionalization, and bureaucratic processes that restrict rights and negate the social agency of children.

Relationality and Belonging

For Saul, Jesus, Edwin, Goz, and Lily, immigration law, institutional policies determining family reunification, everyday practices of specialists at the detention facilities, and suitability assessments by voluntary agencies reshape the ways youth conceptualize notions of obligation, care, and relatedness. Saul became a vocal advocate against the state policies that forced him to make a false choice between his citizenship and his mother who was deported to Mexico. Frustrated by what appeared to be multiple instances of abandonment, Jesus returned to Nicaragua and has refused to maintain communication with his mother. Amid false pretenses constructed by a critical absence of information, Edwin severed his relationship with his sister. Goz chose to protect his family by refusing to divulge information about their identity and nationality, leaving him struggling to maintain transnational kinship ties with his parents and sister in the United States while fostering a new caregiving relationship with an unfamiliar grandmother abroad. And Lily endangered her future legality in the United States to reunite with her mother across state lines.

In assigning the legal identity of the "unaccompanied alien child," the state creates a false dichotomy between the state and the migrant family, ignoring migrant children's relationality to their kinship and social networks. Divesting children from their kinship networks and their sociocultural contexts ignores vital aspects of their migratory decisions, patterns of circulation, and everyday living conditions. A child's relationality becomes both critical to the motivation for and the feasibility of migration but also problematic in the ways the state seeks to define and contain migrant youth. Often overlooked, children and families are not immune to these bureaucratic processes and institutional decisions; to the contrary, families are profoundly impacted, forced to make difficult calculations to ensure family integrity, to sustain a family's well-being, and to care for their children. The ways children make meaning of their family's ability to navigate these processes and the implications of institutional value judgments passed on their parents and caregivers pervade for years to come.

Conclusion

I knew from a young age that I was undocumented. As a child, I wanted to visit my grandma in California, but my father had no license to drive us. As a teenager, I wanted to get my first job, but I was not permitted to work. In high school, I wanted to attend college but could not apply for financial aid. Being undocumented, I find myself frustrated, angry, and sad that I don't control my own destiny.

But, today I am tired of being afraid, hiding in my own community. I am not sorry for being in the United States. And I am not ashamed of my parents who came here for me and my future. My dream is to become a scientist and to contribute to conservation efforts locally and globally. There are people who have helped me to see the value in my life and that I can make a contribution to this world. I have learned that I am not alone.

So, today, in the face of so much discrimination, I say: I am undocumented. To those that hate me for the color of my skin or the place of my birth, I say: I am unafraid. To those that dehumanize me and treat me as unworthy, I say: I am unapologetic.

Today, I come out of the shadows to reclaim my destiny. I am undocumented, unafraid, and unapologetic.

—Eulalia, a twenty-year-old DREAMer

Since 2001, the state has invested record levels of human and financial capital to militarize the U.S.-Mexico border. Through institutionalized partnerships with local law enforcement and significant levels of foreign aid to Mexico to thwart thru-migration from Central and South America, the state has expanded the administration of federal immigration law. The normalization of vigilante groups such as the Minute Men alongside the proliferation of highly sophisticated and brutal transnational gangs mark not only the border but also the interior of the United States. As Gilberto Rosas argues, "the borderlands condition, or the coupling of exceptionality and political imaginaries, no longer necessarily remains geographically fixed in the southwestern United States" (2006: 336). Discourses that criminalize migrants and conflate migration with terrorism create the illusion that this moment in history is one of exceptionalism and thus warranting state intervention at a global level. An increasingly organized immigrant rights movement has denounced state policies of detention and deportation under the guise of "national security" as discordant with the realities of contemporary migration and as a willful disregard of human rights. In other words, the borderlands between the United States and Mexico are "thickening" (Rosas 2006). Children are now among the ranks of migrants caught in the crosshairs of the state's wars on drugs, gangs, and terror.

In their signal volume *The Deportation Regime: Sovereignty, Space, and the Freedom of Movement*, Nicholas De Genova and Nathalie Peutz (2010) argue that the deportation of unauthorized migrants "has come to stand in as the apparently singular and presumably natural or proper retribution on the part of state powers to this apparent 'problem'" (1). Framed as a logical response to the threat of unauthorized or "irregular" migrants, they argue, the detention and deportation of migrants masks the excesses of state power inflicted on migrant bodies (1). The individual migrant crossing into national territory without permission poses limited threat to the nation-state yet garners the full force of the state. The fearmongering of pundits, conflations of terrorists and immigrants in public policies, and routinization of surveillance of mundane social life have resulted in the normalization of detention and removal of migrants from national territory, so much that the public has come to expect detention and deportation as reasonable state action in response to the unlawful presence of migrants (De Genova and Peutz 2010).

An integral technology of the deportation regime is an invisible system of immigration detentions that riddle the U.S. landscape. To use journalist Mark Dow's (2004) term from a decade ago, the "American Gulag" has proliferated to include facilities for families and children. In 2011, the modern deportation regime detained 32,800 adults and 1,910 children daily and deported more than 400,000 people in that year alone. Absent comprehensive immigration reform, these rates of detention and deportation are estimated to increase. In this historic expansion of state technologies, William Walters (2002: 266) argues that the "deportation industry" has moved beyond the private sector to a "system that implicates all manner of agents—not just police and immigration officials, but airline executives, pilots, stewards, and other passengers." As I have detailed in this book, no longer does the private sector maintain a monopoly on the "recession-proof industry" of detaining migrants (Dow 2004: 156–57). We must now add social workers, nonprofit staff, and attorneys to this troubling list of actors and institutions intimately involved in the "industry" of deportation.

This book has mapped out the varied "stakeholders" in the detention and deportation of migrant children by entering into invisible and highly restricted spaces of detention facilities for children, border patrol stations, immigration and state courts, and within unauthorized communities. Through sustained multisited ethnography, I dissect the ways the normative character of detention and deportation have entered forms of legal relief available to children, the bureaucratic practices of caregiving in the government and nonprofit sectors, and the ways these policies and practices shape kinship relations beyond the walls of federal facilities for children. Amid the global normalization of the detention and deportation of migrants, there are critical sites of resistance that warrant close examination. Within the labyrinth of government agencies, departments, and nonprofit organizations, removal of children becomes a site of highly contested negotiations between the law enforcement regime, the humanitarian regime, and children and their families.

On closer examination of these everyday negotiations, what emerges are the competing discourses of victimhood and deviance that surround migrant youth and an imperative to analyze the social agency of children with "all the attendant contradictions, tensions, and paradoxes."[1] Straining to recognize children independent of their parents or guardians, the law relies on a vision of agency that seeks to affix responsibility and assign punitive measures for transgressive behaviors to the individual, indistinguishable of difference. In such a framework, an independent, "nonrational" being collides with the law's pursuit of responsibility and complicates the oversimplifications routinized in policies and practices that criminalize adults. The juridical category of the "unaccompanied alien child" forces children into an impossible space: it demands recognition by laws that view children as inherently or biologically incapable of assuming responsibility for their migration decisions and yet simultaneously and indiscriminately accountable for their (il)legality.

In response, advocates embrace an agencyless, individualistic depiction of the migrant child in order to divorce children from responsibility or blame seeking that may subject them to punitive laws. In the humanitarian regime, advocates deemphasize a child's agency for the very reasons law enforcement accentuates it—to constitute the deserving victim or the culpable delinquent. The humanitarian conception of children's agency as existing within a moral dimension only serves to disempower children and negates their essential contributions to global society. Thus, there is an incommensurable tension between the ways the two regimes not only conceptualize agency but also constitute the child.

The discourses of human rights offer a potential alternative to the impasse between these competing regimes by recognizing both children and adults as inherently possessing rights regardless of nationality, political opinion, socioeconomic status, race, ethnicity, gender, sexual orientation, or age. However, the human rights paradigm in relation to children is also fraught. In practice, like agency, rights are recognized in some legal and institutional settings but ignored or forfeited in others. The notion of agency and the recognition of rights shift and mutate as they rub against the various interests and claims running through the law. In many ways, rights and agency have become substitutions for a focus on youths' own conceptions and pursuit of justice.

Within this highly contested landscape, I have traced how children and youth conceptualize, experience, and resist deportability. For adult and child migrants alike, deportability becomes a mode of being—a disciplinary practice that shapes everyday movements, access to rights and services, and sentiments of belonging (De Genova and Peutz 2010: 14). While detained in ORR facilities, children and youth are subsumed by experiences of deportability, ranging from behavioral modification programs to eating practices to educational curriculum to forms of acceptable communication. Even on their release, ORR policies and practices continue to seep into the everyday lives of both children who remain in the United States and those who are deported. The experiences of children in ORR custody reveal the ways the state (de)values and (un)recognizes some kinship relations and how these state policies and practices shape children's notions of relatedness and belonging. In other words, state practices become so pervasive that there are few ways in which youths' lives are not constrained or informed by these institutional modes of being.

While acknowledging the all-encompassing nature of the deportation regime, my research has revealed that there are critical sites in which youth negotiate and contest state power, and thus, in spite of the pervasive belief, youth are not passive recipients of these practices. Youth are active and creative subjects who engage in constant negotiation with the state and its apparatus. Migrant youths evade, resist, and transform the law and institutional practices that attempt to discipline them. Within the quotidian of facilities, their resistance takes shape as youth create knowledge and circulate information among their peers. On their release from facilities, youth reconstitute prohibited kinship relationships and fulfill social, emotional, and financial obligations that tie them to families and transnational communities. Perhaps the most vivid example of this resistance is the vocal civic engagement of DREAMers who have organized politically through rallies, marches, petitions, sit-ins, teach-ins, and civil disobedience, while adeptly enlisting the media to demand justice on behalf of unauthorized migrants in the United States. They have enlisted a culturally mediated vocabulary to divorce the rhetoric of delinquency from one's (il)legality and have reminded the public of the capacity of youth to foster meaningful social change.

The ways children and youth move in and out of various legal and extra-legal spaces complicates these one-dimensional and static depictions of rights and agency under the law. With a more expansive and nuanced understanding, we might radically reconfigure and reconceptualize agency that moves the discussion beyond action, intention, responsibility, and morality to an understanding of how migrant youths shape and are shaped by the law. By simultaneously detailing the state practices that govern children's lives and youths' navigation of this imposition, we might explore what resides within the shadows by the state. This evidence of complexity and agency not only challenges current methods of understanding these youths' lives but also has important implications for both policy and practice.

Deportability in Transnational Spaces

While this book centers on the experiences of migrant youth in the United States, increasingly imperative is the need to extend our gaze to how experiences of deportability permeate transnational spaces. The most prevalent legal trajectory for children and youth in ORR custody is deportation. "Voluntary departure" or "repatriation" is often framed as a form of care—returning a child home to reunite with his or her family. As a discretionary "benefit" to those who have crossed illicitly into the United States, "voluntary departure" for children is not experienced as such. "Deportation, at its point of application, tends to operate as a radically individualizing and thus also atomizing and isolating event, through which the full force of the sovereign power of the state is wielded against an individual life and deployed to circumscribe it" (De Genova and Peutz 2010: 23). While a child's departure from detention implies an end to his narrative, as though his return or reunification signifies success, the effects of deportation on children and their families persist. The violence inflicted on the individual migrant body reverberates into the families and communities to which children and youth are removed. At the most basic level, apprehension and removal of youth may thwart efforts to seek and maintain family reunification, disrupt future employment or educational plans, and limit a youth's ability to support family, escape poverty, and ensure safety.

From my fieldwork with youths deported to El Salvador and Guatemala, I have found that the impact of deportation bleeds into the lives of youth and their families over the long term. Surrounded by rumors of delinquency, failure, and, for girls, allegations of promiscuity and prostitution, deported youths are assumed to have committed a legal transgression or to have succumbed to a moral weakness, such as drinking or taking drugs, thereby warranting their detention. Often ostracized by the community and at times by their own families, youth may experience tremendous anxiety and stigma. In spite of rising numbers of deportees to Central America, there is little distinction made between youths who entered immigration detention due to unlawful presence and youths who are charged with committing a delinquent or criminal act in the United States. In many ways, this reflects those social and legal discourses in the United States that conflate illegality with criminality. Youths often feel tremendous shame and guilt at their failure to arrive in the United States, and several youths reported hiding in their homes for three or four weeks on their return, embarrassed and ashamed by what they viewed as a personal failure. The normalization of state violence inflicted on the migrant child becomes internalized as a personal and sometimes spiritual failure to successfully settle, even if temporarily, in the United States. While many children do not envision migration as a rejection of "home" but rather see it as a pursuit of betterment, forced removal may reframe youths' initial motivations for migration and complicate their belonging within the family and community.

It is not just the physical removal from the United States that marks the deportee as Other in communities of origin. Home communities may associate youths' experiences in the United States as a contamination or a "loss of culture." Little consideration is given to the impact behavioral modification programs, institutional values, and consumption practices have when children deported from ORR facilities rejoin their families. Acquired behaviors, values, and beliefs mark the deportee who has spent some time in the United States as Other or as one who has lost customary beliefs and social practices, making the youth feel "out of place" on return "home." The tentacles of deportability extend beyond the individual's physical removal from the state and grab hold of transnational spaces.

Bridging the Impasse

Given that children compose nearly 20 percent of the world's migratory flows, a research agenda focusing on children and migration is critical (Dobson and Stillwell 2000: 395). Research can help to drive the conversation on the migration of young people and foreground their voices in discussions of laws, policies, and practices. In spite of best intentions, policies are often misguided and provide minimal opportunities for children to voice their opinions, to be heard, and to be understood. However, there are opportunities for federal authorities to learn from the expertise of domestic and international child welfare authorities; for attorneys and social workers to overcome their disciplinary impasse to enhance their shared advocacy on behalf of children; for international authorities and state authorities to become engaged and active participants in the international repatriation of children; and for parents to become essential figures in a federal custodial system that largely disregards their assessments of their children's best interests. The tenuous relationship between research and practice requires investment and transparency from institutions and practitioners and attention, commitment, and analysis from researchers. Well positioned to examine social agency, researchers analyze the social worlds of children beyond the walls of the detention facility and sustain attention to their lifeworlds over time, offering the state the vital contextualization to inform both policy and practice.

Amid a backdrop of state power, scholarship investigates the clashes between agency and structure, attending to difference across culture, gender, ethnicity, and legality (see, e.g., Schwartzman 2001; Amit-Talal and Wulff 1995; Jenks 1996; Rosen 2008). As children circulate locally and transnationally, researchers are well equipped to solicit children's perspectives, so vital to informed, meaningful social and political change. Yet relying on modes of behavioral pathology or on biological and developmental models of childhood is insufficient. Rooted in a universalized and romanticized ideal of childhood, these approaches gloss over the complexity and variation in experiences of migrant children and youth. Instead, a contextualization of the ways children and youth navigate structural constraints and express individual and collective agency is needed; this begins to deconstruct the oversimplifications that underpin the institutional interventions and legal frameworks that shape migrant children's everyday lives. For many children, migration is a vehicle for collective advancement in a globalizing world. In order to penetrate these powerful discourses, research on the agency of children and youth and the differing spaces of childhood allows for a transcendence of the clashing binaries of dependency or independence, natural or pathological, delinquent or victim, child or adult, and positive or negative that are the basis of institutional policies, professional practices, and legal frameworks.

With such a partnership, we may begin to understand how children comprehend and express social agency rather than the ways those in power assign meaning to it. As Eulalia so eloquently articulated in the interlude opening of this chapter, her worldview transcends legal parameters and institutional interventions: "in the face of so much discrimination, I say: I am undocumented. To those that hate me for the color of my skin or the place of my birth, I say: I am unafraid. To those that dehumanize me and treat me as unworthy, I say: I am unapologetic."

ACRONYMS

ACF	Administration for Children and Families
BIA	Bureau of Immigration Appeals
CBP	Customs and Border Protection
CIA	Central Intelligence Agency
CPS	Child Protective Services
CRC	UN Convention on the Rights of the Child
DCFS	Department of Children and Family Services
DHS	U.S. Department of Homeland Security
DHHS/HHS	U.S. Department of Health and Human Services
DOJ	U.S. Department of Justice
DCS	Division Children's Services
EOIR	Executive Office of Immigration Review
FBI	Federal Bureau of Investigation
ICE	U.S. Immigration and Customs Enforcement
ICE ACCESS	ICE Agreements of Cooperation in Communities to Enhance Safety and Security
IJ	Immigration Judges
INA	Immigration and Nationality Act
INS	Immigration and Naturalization Service
IRCA	Immigration Reform and Control Act
NGO	nongovernmental organization
OIG	Office of the Inspector General
ORR	Office of Refugee Resettlement

SIJ	Special Immigrant Juvenile status
SIR	significant incident report
TPS	temporary protected status
UAC	unaccompanied alien child
URM	unaccompanied refugee minor
URNG	Unidad Revolucionaria Nacional Guatemalteca /Guatemalan National Revolutionary Unity
USCIS	U.S. Citizenship and Immigration Services

NOTES

Chapter 1. Children on the Move

1. The highly publicized case of Edgar Chocoy highlights these tragic deficits. At fourteen, Edgar fled the gangs in Guatemala and sought to reunite with his mother who had migrated to the United States years earlier. Following denial of political asylum in the United States and a failed attempt to commit suicide while in detention, he was deported to Guatemala. In less than three weeks, Edgar was murdered by the very gang members who spurred his initial flight (see also Finley 2004a, b; Bhabha 2006).

2. See also Boswell 1988, which provides a historical account of child abandonment in Europe before the establishment of foundling homes in which children circulated between households, relying on the "kindness of strangers" to care for them. The thirteenth and fourteenth centuries introduced institutionalized care for displaced children in hospitals and foundling homes, as a means of responding to the needs of children unattached to families.

3. I do not suggest that children migrate exclusively from the global south to the north.

4. Bhabha and Schmidt found that U.S. Customs and Border Protection (CBP), the agency responsible for monitoring points of entry such as airports and official points of entry on land, does not distinguish children from adults in its statistical records. The U.S. Coast Guard, another initial point of apprehension of many unauthorized migrants, does not track an individual's minor status. Immigration and Customs Enforcement indicates that they apprehended more than 86,000 accompanied and unaccompanied children annually between 2001 and 2005, but makes no distinction between those with adult care providers and those traveling "unaccompanied." Yet the U.S. Department of Justice (DOJ) reports that in fiscal year 2000 alone, the Border Patrol apprehended and repatriated 94,823 Mexican minors crossing the U.S.-Mexico border without adequate legal status (OIG 2001b: 1). The high rate of apprehension of Mexican nationals gestures toward a much larger phenomenon than government statistics reveal. Moving beyond the points of entry, the Executive Office of Immigration Review (EOIR), which adjudicates the cases of asylum seekers, does not track birthdates (Bhabha and Schmidt 2006: 186). The asylum office

indicates that in 2003, there were 500 children as principal asylum applicants. Some children qualify for special visas, including the "nonimmigrant status" for victims of human trafficking (T visa) and the Special Immigrant Juvenile (SIJ) status visa. Thirty-two children were eligible to apply for T visas and only twenty-two were granted T visas in 2002–4; and 521 SIJ visas were approved in 2002 (Bhabha and Schmidt 2006: 35, 195).

5. The most reliable data have come from the ORR, which was mandated to track basic data in Section 462(b)(1)(J) of the 2002 Homeland Security Act.

6. Estimates from Manuel Capellin, director of Casa Alianza Honduras, cited in *La Prensa*, April 3, 2008.

7. See, e.g., Haddal 2007.

8. The detention of families began in 2001 with the Berks Family Residential Facility in Leesport, Pennsylvania and expanded in 2006 to the notorious T. Don Hutto Residential Care Facility in Taylor, Texas run by the Corrections Corporation of America through a subcontract with ICE. The 512-bed facility housed children and their families in a previously-designated medium security prison. In March 2007, the American Civil Liberties Union (ACLU) filed suit against ICE contesting the conditions of children detained in the facility. The ACLU eventually settled the suit and in September 2009 detention of families at Hutto ceased. As of 2011, the facility houses immigrant women. In 2012, the Berks Family Residential Facility remains the only family immigration detention facility, as ICE solicitations for new family facilities have been blocked by efforts led by the ACLU.

9. While Mexican youth may qualify for legal relief when screened effectively, they are classified differently and follow a separate legal trajectory that expedites deportation from the country in contrast to their Central American, African, or Asian counterparts.

10. See also U.S. Department of Homeland Security 2008.

11. ORR has developed several types of facilities that range in the types of services available to children and the level of security. The most common type of facility is a shelter. Shelters are the least restrictive setting, characterized by the largest number of beds, a high staff to child ratio of approximately 1:7, limited excursions outside the facility, and facilities with alarmed windows and doors and with security cameras. Staff-secure facilities have a smaller number of children per facility, a lower staff to child ratio of approximately 1:5, greater security measures throughout the facility, and limited outings for children. Children who have been accused of or charged with a crime are placed in staff-secure facilities. Secure facilities are akin to juvenile jails, often rented bed space in state juvenile facilities. Children placed in secure facilities may have pending charges or previous encounters with law enforcement.

12. I am grateful to an anonymous reviewer for this phrasing.

13. Following disciplinary custom, I use pseudonyms for all children.

14. Most interviews were taped and later transcribed. In the interviews that were not taped, I took copious notes and immediately following, transcribed the content, body language, and impressions in my field notes.

15. From over a decade of work in the human rights and public health fields in Latin America and lusophone Africa, I learned of the complex international and national networks of individuals and institutions involved in the lives of migrants globally. Through this work, I became sensitive to the emergent legal, social, and political sensibilities toward unaccompanied children specifically in the United States. In my research, I draw on this acquired knowledge, leaning on this knowledge to make claims about the care, custody, and legal identity of migrant youth.

16. While my own movement between these spaces alongside research participants allowed for greater insight into how children navigate the complex network of institutions and actors in their home countries and in the United States, many institutional and personal challenges faced by migrant youth are localized. In several interviews, advocates lamented that this study was not conducted nationally, due to the extreme variation between local contexts and the ways federal law and protocols are interpreted at the local level. While this limitation, in many respects, is unavoidable, I hope that the detailed, ethnographic nature of this study will still offer insight into the personal and physical journeys of migrant youth.

17. Since completing my research, I volunteered with the Young Center for Immigrant Children's Rights, a pilot project of the University of Chicago School of Law that provides guardians ad litem to children in immigration proceedings. I served as a Child Advocate for two youths, continue to participate in best interest determination panels, and in 2010–12 worked part-time for the project, serving as guardian ad litem for unaccompanied children with mental health issues. None of the research included in this book comes from my volunteerism or employment. The observations, research, opinions, and errors are exclusively my own. None of the opinions reflected in this book are those of the staff or board of the Young Center.

18. Tape recording and photography were methods enlisted with nondetained children and with children following release.

19. In other words, the law is not a static, top-down means of the state imposing its will on the individual or the community, but a reciprocal exchange between the law structuring life and life structuring law, just as racialized or gendered experiences of the law and institutional interventions shape the specificity of youth experiences (Cammarota 2004; Daly and Maher 1998). Youth also imagine and produce social spaces that are flexible and multiple (Mitchell and Parker 2008: 28). Youth actively and passively assign meaning to the law, which affects not only their social relationships but also the state institutions themselves.

20. 8 U.S.C. § 1101(a)(3) (West 2012). For the legal history of the term, see Johnson 1997. For a useful discussion on the sociolegal history of the term "illegal alien," see Ngai 2003.

21. See Junck 2012: 58, which notes: "State laws, however, generally require that a child be under 18 at the time he or she first is declared a juvenile court dependent. Because courts often do not accept jurisdiction of children 18 or older, some children may not be eligible to apply for SIJS even though they are under 21."

Chapter 2. Criminal Alien or Humanitarian Refugee?

1. The Development, Relief and Education for Alien Minors Act of 2010, S. 3827, 111th Cong. (2010). DREAMers are young migrants have might have benefited from the now stalled Development, Relief and Education of Alien Minors Act.

2. The DHS entered into a settlement agreement in 2008. *Perez-Olano v. Holder*, CV 05-3604 (C.D. Cal. 2010), Settlement Agreement, http://www.uscis.gov/USCIS/ Laws/Legal%20Settlement%20Notices%20and%20Agreements/Perez-Olano%20v %20Holder/Signed_Settlement_Agreement.pdf. Prior to *Perez-Olano v. Holder*, children in actual or constructive federal custody required *specific consent* from DHS/ICE before proceeding into state court for a dependency finding. 8 U.S.C. § 1101 (a)(27)(J) (iii)(I) (West 2012). See *Perez-Olano v. Gonzales*, No. 05-03604 (Federal District Court California, January 8, 2008).

3. 8 U.S.C. § 1357(g) (West 2012). The program, commonly referred to as "287(g)," was established by section 287(g) of the Illegal Immigration Reform and Responsibility Act of 1996. 287(g) authorized federal immigration enforcement to enter written contracts with state local law enforcement to perform aspects of federal immigration law, including the investigation, apprehension, or detention of aliens, under the direction and supervision of the Department of Homeland Security.

4. Administratively created by DHS in 2008, Secure Communities is a program designed to prioritize deportation of criminal aliens by entering into partnerships with local and state law enforcement. Through accessing existing federal and immigration databases, local and state law enforcement can identify "individuals who present the most significant threats to public safety as determined by the severity of their crime, their criminal history, and other factors." Secure Communities, Immigration and Customs Enforcement, http://www.ice.gov/secure_communities. However, the program has come under public criticism for misrepresentation of how DHS prioritizes removal of unauthorized migrants.

5. See, e.g., 8 U.S.C. § 1101(a)(43) (West 2012).

6. Foucault argues that surveillance is both a powerful and an efficient way states might enlist citizens to serve as policing agents in everyday life, rather than relying on hierarchical structures to enforce law. An essential feature of this strategy, power is characterized as "capillary," rather than "centered," and thus able to permeate throughout the most private areas of social life (Foucault 1977: 198; Hoy 1986: 134) Taken together, the Homeland Security Alert System, public announcements calling individuals to report suspicious behavior, and the special registration program are technol-

ogies of social surveillance. Since the events of September 11, 2001, these technologies have expanded. Most notable, Texas governor Rick Perry's Virtual Border Watch—a real-time Internet site where individuals can monitor the U.S.-Mexico border and notify Border Patrol via e-mail of any alleged unlawful crossings. *Virtual Border Watch*, BlueServo, http://www.blueservo.net/index.php?error=nlg.

7. In the massive immigration rallies in Chicago in 2007, conservative news outlets openly criticized immigrants for waving Mexican flags rather than American ones. Instead of recognizing the flag as a symbol of one's ethnic heritage, it was a revelation of one's indisputable allegiance.

8. U.S. District Court, Central District of California, *Jenny Lisette Flores et al. v. Janet Reno, Attorney General of the United States, et al.*, CV 85-4544 (C.D. Cal 1997).

9. *Flores v. Reno* Stipulated Settlement Agreement, No. CV-85-4544 (C.D. Cal., January 17, 1997).

10. Bhabha cites the United Nations Protocol to Prevent, Suppress and Punish Trafficking in Persons, Especially Women and Children, Supplementing the UN Convention Against Transnational Organized Crime, art. 3.

11. While believed to be as old as the United States itself, the popular term "nation of immigrants" originated in 1964 with John Kennedy's book *Nation of Immigrants*. Intimately linked to Cold War politics and the civil rights movement in the United States, Kennedy's project professed a political, social, and historical commitment to cultural pluralism in America. As Ngai (2010) adeptly identifies, however, Kennedy's work failed to include immigrants from Asia and Latin America, instead focusing exclusively on European immigrant history in the United States.

12. See, e.g., Thompson 2003.

13. The other being Somalia.

14. As of spring 2012, ORR funded 70 programs: 37 shelter facilities, 9 staff secure facilities, 6 secure facilities, 3 residential treatment centers, 2 therapeutic staff secure, and 13 foster care programs with a capacity of 2,850 beds. The number increased significantly in 2013 to nearly 26,000 unaccompanied migrant children entering ORR custody.

15. *Plyler v. Doe*, 457 U.S. 202 (1982).

16. The case upheld a previous ruling in which education is not a fundamental right to noncitizens in *San Antonio Independent School District v. Rodriguez*, 411 U.S. 1 (1973). This ruling stands in opposition of Article 28 of the Convention on the Rights of the Child, which states that parties to the convention "recognize the right of the child to education, and with a view to achieving this right . . . they shall . . . make primary education compulsory and available free to all."

Chapter 3. Youth at the Intersection of Family and the State

1. For example, in 1943, the Commonwealth of Massachusetts intervened in the case of a nine-year-old Jehovah's Witness preaching on public streets. The court

determined that the child's caregiver had violated state child labor laws by asking the child to distribute flyers in exchange for contributions. Amid claims that the state's intervention violated the child's right to religious freedom and the caregiver's right to raise the child, the U.S. Supreme Court ruled that the intervention was constitutional (*Prince v. Massachusetts*, 321 U.S. 158 (1944), cited in Lloyd 2006: 237).

2. *In re Gault*, 387 U.S. 1 (1967); in June 1964 fifteen-year-old Gerald Gault was taken into custody after being accused of making lewd telephone calls; finding him to be delinquent, a juvenile court judge ordered him to be committed to the State Industrial School until he reached majority (a period of six years); his parents petitioned the Arizona Supreme Court for a writ of habeas corpus to obtain their son's release; the court referred the case back to the original judge, who dismissed the habeas petition; the Gaults appealed to the Arizona Supreme Court, which agreed that due process should apply to delinquency proceedings, but held that due process requirements were not offended by the proceedings in the Gault case, and affirmed the dismissal of the petition. The case was appealed to the U.S. Supreme Court, which reversed the Arizona decision.

3. See, e.g., *Kent v. United States*, 383 U.S. 541 (1966); and *In re Winship*, 397 U.S. 358 (1970).

4. See, e.g., *Eddings v. Oklahoma*, 455 U.S. 104, 115–16 (1982) in which the court ruled that youth is a mitigating factor in the death sentence of a sixteen-year-old.

5. In January 1996, the National Study of the Incidence of Child Abuse and Neglect of the U.S. Department of Health and Human Services released its initial findings that the rates of child abuse and neglect had doubled between 1986 and 1993. While the official report was not released to the public until late 1996, it heightened awareness of child abuse and significantly shaped policy and legislative efforts on behalf of children (Sedlak and Broadhurst 1996).

6. Adoption Assistance and Child Welfare Act of 1980; Adoption and Safe Families Act of 1997; and Child Abuse Prevention and Treatment Act of 2000 (see, e.g., Lloyd 2006).

7. Legal scholar David Thronson (2002) skillfully traces the ways immigration law both mirrors and buttresses historic approaches to the rights of children, attending specifically to the adverse consequences that impact their experiences with the law.

8. For example, contract law considers a contract voidable based on a child's minor status, and tort law either releases children from any liability at all or affords them flexible liability given their "intelligence, maturity, and experience" (Bien 2004: 830; Bhabha and Scmidt 2006: 46; Nogosek 2000). Under the jurisdiction of the juvenile court, criminal law affords children special procedures with a stated intent of "rehabilitation" instead of punishment, harking back to the reformist's initial intent for assistance rather than punishment for the court in 1899.

9. INA, 8 U.S.C. §1101(a)(27)(J) (2003).

10. For further discussion, see Bhabha 2002.

11. Hamm cites *Gao v. Jenifer*, 185 F. 3d 548 (6th Cir. 1999), which found that "state courts may still exercise jurisdiction over a neglected or abused immigrant child who has been paroled to foster care by the Immigration and Naturalization Service (INS) without necessarily interfering with the federal mandate to regulate immigration" (Hamm 2004: 324). Hamm cites, *In re C.M.K.*, N.W.2d 768 (Minn. Ct. App. 1996), indicating that "once INS had taken the child into custody, the state court had no jurisdiction over that child regardless of need because federal immigration proceedings preempted state proceedings" (Hamm 2004: 324).

12. See *Gao v. Jenifer* (1999).

13. It is important to note that SIJ in state court does not necessarily require termination of parental rights, though it does happen with frequency.

14. A child granted SIJ status could apply for a sibling, but must first become a naturalized U.S. citizen (which requires a five-year waiting period following the child's adjustment of status to a legal permanent resident), and be over twenty-one before applying for the sibling(s) to immigrate to the United States. Currently, there is a backlog of over ten years for sibling petitions of U.S. citizens. Immigration law is very clear that a child granted SIJ status cannot petition for his or her parent(s), stating "no natural parent or prior adoptive parent of any alien provided special immigrant status under this subparagraph shall thereafter, by virtue of such parentage, be accorded any right, privilege, or status under this chapter" (INA, 8 U.S.C, §1101(a)(27)(J)(iii)(II)).

Chapter 4. Forced to Choose

1. "Garifuna" is a singular noun referring to an individual member of the Garinagu (collective), as well as the language and culture. "Garinagu," derives from "Carib" (= *garif*), known as *Karaphuna* in the Garifuna language, and refers to the population. In the late eighteenth century the British deported the Garinagu, an ethnic group of African, Arawak, and Carib ancestry also known as Black Caribs, from the island of St. Vincent to the Caribbean coast of Central America, where shipwrecked and escaped African slaves had intermarried with the indigenous Carib population since the early seventeenth century. See, e.g., Bonner 2001; Gonzalez 1984. The Garinagu in Livingston, located in the Department of Izabal, are geographically isolated from Guatemala City, which is only reachable by boat from Puertos Barrios and then a seven- to eight-hour bus ride to the capital. Facing social and structural discrimination for their African ancestry, the Garinagu as well as the Xinca are also culturally ignored in most post-Civil War national discourses on indigenous rights, commonly framed by Maya-ladino relations (see, e.g., Gorres 2008). Deruba embodied this isolation in his circulation in Guatemala and his experiences in the United States.

2. In summer 2003, I worked in Guatemala City and Panajachel and vacationed in Livingston. Unbeknown to me, Deruba and Isura slept just down the road from my

pension. The violence during that time had noticeably increased in the run-up to the 2003 presidential elections. In the span of twenty-four hours, my colleagues and I had been targets of three attempted robberies—at gunpoint on a crowded public bus during morning rush hour, in a village by two impoverished youths with machetes, and by two drunk police officers who sought to harass as a form of entertainment—experiences new to me in my frequent travels to Guatemala. In Guatemala City we were rushed into a restaurant and scolded by the middle-aged owner: "You are out too late. Don't you know it is not safe?" It was 5:30 p.m. on a Sunday.

3. Due to lack of resources and political will in Guatemala, there are no government institutions or orphanages dedicated to the care of abandoned children. Only a few privately run shelters attempted to respond to the growing population of street children, estimated at 4,500 in Guatemala City alone and 14,500 countrywide, according to local social workers interviewed in 2010.

4. Indeed, gangs have begun to wield AK-47s and other sophisticated weaponry imported from Mexico and the United States. Advocates continue to voice concern about the continuation of such wartime enforcement tactics in dealing with new social problems such as human and drug trafficking, organized crime, and corruption. One's "illicit association" is sufficient justification for detention for the state to detain an individual as a suspected gang member, replacing a legal need for charges of criminal activity (Washington Office on Latin America 2006: 10).

5. A month following Deruba's departure from the Guatemala-Mexico border, the U.S.-owned Genesee & Wyoming, Inc., would halt service along the Chiapas-Mayab railway due to the deterioration of rail lines damaged by Hurricane Mitch in 2005, stranding nearly 7,000 migrants. Mexican authorities deported 350 Central Americans, principally Honduras and Guatemalans, while hundreds continued their journey by foot to Villahermosa, the nearest terminal, nearly 200 miles away.

6. ORR guidelines require children to remain in a particular form of shelter care for a minimum of thirty days without any significant incidents or disruptive behaviors before stepping down to a less-secure shelter or, in practice, for three months before transferring them to federal foster care. The official justification for this length of time is to assess the child for the most appropriate type of program or facility.

7. INA, 8 U.S.C. §1101(a)(27)(J)(ii)(2000). Under the William Wilberforce Trafficking Victims Protection Reauthorization Act of 2008, inclusion of "last habitual residence" has been voided for unaccompanied minors and the language of long-term foster care has been stricken in the federal statute.

8. Despite a presumption of the state as the most trustworthy guardian, or parent of the nation, there have been several high-profile legal cases in which subcontracted federal facilities have systematically verbally, physically, and sexually abused unaccompanied children in their care. Eight youths in the Abraxas Hector Garza Treatment Center outside San Antonio, Texas, and several in the Nixon facility east of San Antonio, children who otherwise had no form of legal relief in the United States, were granted a U visa for being victims of crimes—namely, severe physical and sexual

abuse perpetrated by federally contracted organizations and Texas state police officers. While abdicating direct responsibility, the federal government, as both protector
and violator, granted children legal status based on the abuse they suffered at the hands
of the state.

9. A 2009 decision by the Nebraska Supreme Court marks a potential important
shift in state practices whereby state courts terminated a mother's parental rights over
her two American-born children following her detention on charges of falsely identifying herself to a police officer and deportation to her native Guatemala. The state
court ruled that the woman was not given sufficient notice or access to appeal to the
state court to retain custody. The woman's parental rights under Nebraska state juvenile law came into direct conflict with federal immigration law, which removed her
from national territory, resulting in a severing of her parental relationship to her children. The court claimed that parental custody of children is one of the "oldest of the
fundamental liberty interests recognized by the United States Supreme Court" and
that reinstating the woman's parental rights sought to remedy the ways children are
caught in a "clash of laws, culture and parental rights that occur when parents cross
international boundaries." The court found that the state failed to prove the mother
unfit, instead resisting family reunification because social service workers "thought
the children would be better off staying in the United States" (*In re: Interest of Angelica
L. and Daniel L. (State v. Maria L.)*, No. S-08-919, Nebraska, June 26, 2009). In Illinois,
juvenile courts currently must give notice to parents prior to terminating parental
rights, which translates into the court giving notice to the last known address of the
parent and in two local English-language newspapers, which obviously limits communication for parents living outside Chicago (not to mention internationally) or with
limited English proficiency. The court occasionally, though not consistently, contacts
foreign consulates to assist in locating parents in their country of origin.

Chapter 5. The Shadow State

1. ORR's Division of Unaccompanied Children's Services (DUCS), as it was called
in 2003, was renamed in 2012 to reflect restructuring of ORR programs; it became the
Division of Children's Services (DCS)/Unaccompanied Alien Children's Program.

2. It would seem that because Guantanamo is not physically within the territory
of the United States, but a naval base on the island of Cuba, the conditions are unique.
In many respects Guantanamo Bay is unique in its history of immigration control, as
a staging ground for migrants, reception center, and detention facility. Specifically for
migrant children, Guantanamo Bay held a diverse group of migrants whom the government has brought through formal programs—Operación Pedro Pan (Operation
Peter Pan) from 1960 to1962 and the Mariel boat lift in 1980. Operation Peter Pan was
a government-designed program in which the U.S. Department of State and the CIA,
in conjunction with the Roman Catholic Archdiocese of Miami, facilitated the

evacuation of over 14,000 Cuban children to the United States. The children came from primarily lower-middle-income families who opposed Castro's revolutionary government and who feared their children would be sent to Soviet labor camps. On their arrival in the United States, the archdiocese placed children in group homes and with individual families scattered throughout the United States. On the other hand, Guantanamo became a reception center for returned Marielitos from the 1980 Mariel boatlift in which nearly 125,000 Cubans, many of them male youths, left Cuba. From most accounts, Castro emptied prisons, releasing criminals and homosexuals into the general population of Cubans fleeing the island. The administration of President Jimmy Carter detained many of the individuals and sought to repatriate them to Cuba, though the Cuban government never accepted their return. As a result, many were detained at Guantanamo Bay indefinitely despite having completed their original sentences. It is with this population of youth and young adults that the leadership of the Illinois-based detention facilities for unaccompanied migrant children first began their work.

3. Most notably, ICE ACCESS programs include the Criminal Alien Program (CAP), Immigration Cross Designation 287(g), Secure Communities, and Rapid Removal of Eligible Parolees Accepted for Transfer (Rapid REPAT).

4. The "scientization" of childhood development, particularly in the context of immigrant children, maintains eugenic undertones that remain unarticulated but infiltrate the facilities' discourses on the pathologization of migrant children and the social contexts from which they come.

5. As Sergio and other youths explained, a *pandilla* is a group of peers or friends with whom you develop a strong bond. Contrary to much analysis of *pandillas*, they do not begin as gangs with specific violent tendencies or purposes. While some *pandillas* will coalesce through the group's self-recognition and self-segregation with special handshakes, colors, jackets, T-shirts, or code words, they typically remain groups of (most commonly) young males who spend time together. The transformation to *pandillas* in the more pejorative sense of street gangs is often the result of established gangs folding in smaller *pandillas* as a source of recruitment.

6. Throughout much of Latin America and Spain, under civil law a *notario* has expansive legal powers, including preparation of legal contracts. A *notario* is different from the American notary public whose powers are restricted to administering oaths, taking depositions, and making certified copies.

Chapter 6. Reformulating Kinship Ties

1. Since September 11, 2001, ICE has increasingly conducted workplace raids as an immigration control strategy, charging unauthorized workers with Social Security fraud, a federal criminal charge with immigration consequences of almost certain deportation.

2. ICE increasingly threatened unauthorized migrants with aggravated identity theft, which comes with a mandatory sentence of two years in prison, to force migrants to agree to deportation or face expanded prison sentences. In 2008 ICE accused over 270 workers of identity theft in a raid on a meatpacking plant in Postville, Iowa, which led to pleas for expedited hearings or lesser charges. Following outrage by advocates and legal experts at this pervasive practice, the U.S. Supreme Court ruled in *Flores-Figueroa v. United States*, 556 U.S. 646 (2009) that the government must establish that the person knowingly used identification belonging to another person. While this has not ended the strategy of prosecuting for identity theft, it has certainly curtailed its pervasiveness as a first-line strategy for ICE.

3. See, for example, the case of Guatemalan national Encarnación Bail Romero, apprehended in a workplace raid in 2007 and accused of using false identity documents. She was charged with aggravated identity theft and separated from her young son Carlos, whom she initially entrusted to the care of her relatives and later to other caretakers. During her two years of incarceration, Bail was not permitted visitations with her son. At age two, Carlos came into the care of Melinda and Seth Moser. Although Bail did not grant consent for the Mosers to adopt him, a family court ruled that Bail had abandoned her child and permitted the Mosers to proceed with adoption. On appeal, the Missouri Supreme Court reversed the decision to terminate Bail's parental rights and remanded the case to the lower courts, calling the decision a "travesty." On retrial, in July 2012, the lower courts ruled that it was in the best interests of Carlos to have Bail's parental rights terminated and to be adopted by the Mosers. In 2009, *Flores-Figueroa v. United States* struck down the criminalization of aggravated identity theft because the Supreme Court ruled there must be intent. In effect, Bail was separated from and lost custody of her son for committing a crime that is no longer considered a crime.

4. In June 2011, John Morton, director of ICE, issued a memo (the "Morton Memo") to ICE personnel about how they should exercise prosecutorial discretion—prioritizing the deportation of those subject to removal. In the memo, Morton (2011) details some "positive" factors that should "prompt particular care and consideration." Specifically, he discussed youth who came to the United States as young children. While it remains unclear, senior officials in the Obama administration have said that individuals with strong family and community ties, including same-sex couples, are not priorities for deportation. In 2013, legislative proposals for comprehensive immigration reform deliberately excluded same-sex couples for fear of Republican opposition to national reform.

5. During the period of research in 2006–2009, ORR made only a few exceptions, transferring children to facilities in the northern United States to allow undocumented parents to claim their children.

6. At the insistence of advocates and under threat of lawsuit, more recently ORR has allowed parents to identify another trusted adult to travel to the facility site to

accept temporary custody of the child from ORR or to arrange for a facility staff member to accompany the child at the family's expense to transfer custody.

7. *American Baptist Churches v. Thornburgh*, 760 F. Supp. 796 (N.D. Cal. 1991).

8. At the time of my research, suitability assessments were approximately ninety days. Since 2011, ORR has decreased the duration to forty-five to sixty days with the option to grant extensions on a case-by-case basis.

Conclusion

1. I thank an anonymous reviewer for this phrase.

BIBLIOGRAPHY

Adelman, M., and C. Yalda. 2000. "Seen But Not Heard: The Legal Lives of Young People." *Political and Legal Anthropology Review* 23 (2): 37–58.

Agustin, L. 2003. "Forget Victimization: Granting Agency to Migrants." *Development* 46 (3): 30–36.

Ajemani, A. 2007. *Alone and Ignored: Unaccompanied Alien Children Seeking Asylum in the United States, Canada and Australia*. Unpublished paper.

Amit-Talal, V., and H. Wulff. 1995. *Youth Culture: A Cross National Perspective*. London: Routledge.

Bailyn, B. 1986. *Voyagers to the West: A Passage of the Peopling of America on the Eve of the Revolution*. New York: Knopf.

Bastia, T. 2005. "Child Trafficking or Teenage Migration? Bolivian Migrants in Argentina." *International Migration* 43 (4): 57–89.

Battistella, G., and M. C. G. Conaco. 1998. "The Impact of Labour Migration on Children Left Behind: A Study of Elementary School Children in the Philippines. *Sojourn* 13 (2): 220–41.

Becerra, R., and I. Chi. 1992. "Child Care Preferences Among Low-Income Minority Families." *International Social Work* 35 (1): 35–47.

Bernstein, N., and E. Lichtblau. 2005. "Two Girls Held as U.S. Fears Suicide Bomb." *New York Times*, April 7.

Best, A., ed. 2007. *Representing Youth: Methodological Issues in Youth Studies*. New York: New York University Press.

Best, J. 1990. *Threatened Children: Rhetoric and Concern About Child-Victims*. Chicago: University of Chicago Press.

Bhabha, J. 2002. "Internationalist Gatekeepers? The Tension Between Asylum Advocacy and Human Rights." *Harvard Human Rights Journal* 15: 155–81.

———. 2006. "Not a Sack of Potatoes: Moving and Removing Children Across Borders." *Boston University International Law Journal* 15: 205.

———. 2008. "Independent Children, Inconsistent Adults: Child Litigation and the Legal Framework," Innocenti Discussion Paper 2008-2. Florence: UNICEF Innocenti Research Centre.

Bhabha, J., and S. Schmidt. 2006. *Seeking Asylum Alone: Unaccompanied and Separated Children and Refugee Protection in the U.S.* Cambridge, Mass.: Harvard University Committee on Human Rights Studies. June.

Bien, R. 2004. "Nothing to Declare But Their Childhood: Reforming U.S. Asylum Law to Protect the Rights of Children." *Journal of Law and Policy* 23: 797–842.

Bluebond-Langner, M., and J. Korbin. 2007. "Challenges and Opportunities in the Anthropology of Childhoods: An Introduction to 'Children, Childhoods, and Childhood Studies.'" *American Anthropologist* 109 (2): 241–46.

Boehm, D. 2008. "For My Children": Constructing Family and Navigating the State in the U.S.-Mexico Transnation. *Anthropological Quarterly* 81 (4): 777–802.

———. 2012. *Intimate Migrations: Gender, Family, and Illegality Among Transnational Mexicans.* New York: New York University Press.

Bonner, D. 2001. "Garifuna Children's Language Shame: Ethnic Stereotypes, National Affiliation, and Transnational Immigration as Factors in Language Choice in Southern Belize." *Language in Society* 31 (1): 81–96.

Bortner, M., M. Zatz, and D. Hawkins. 2000. "Race and Transfer: Empirical Research and Social Context." In *The Changing Borders of Juvenile Justice*, ed. J. Fagan and F. Zimring. Chicago: University of Chicago Press. 277–320.

Boswell, J. 1988. *The Kindness of Strangers: The Abandonment of Children in Western Europe from Late Antiquity to the Renaissance.* Chicago: University of Chicago Press.

Bourdieu, P. 1977. *Outline of a Theory of Practice.* Cambridge: Cambridge University Press.

Boyden, J. 1990. "Childhood and the Policy Makers." In *Constructing and Reconstructing Childhood*, ed. J. James and A. Prout. New York: Falmer Press. 184–215.

Boyle, P., K. Halfacree, and V. Robinson. 1998. *Exploring Contemporary Migration.* London: Harlow.

Brettell, C. 2003. *Anthropology and Migration: Essays on Transnationalism, Ethnicity and Identity.* Lanham, Md.: Rowman Altamira.

Calavita, K. 1998. "Immigration, Law, and Marginalization: Notes from Spain." *Law & Society Review* 32: 529–66.

Cammarota, J. 2004. "The Gendered and Racialized Pathways of Latina and Latino Youth: Different Struggles, Different Resistances in the Urban Context." *Anthropology & Education Quarterly* 35 (1): 53–74.

Center for Human Rights and Constitutional Law. 2004. Special Immigrant Juvenile Status Manual. http://immigrantchildren.org/SIJS/.

Cepeda, E. 2007. "Young Activist: Saul Arellano." *Chicago Sun Times*, May 8.

Chavez, L. 2001. *Covering Immigration: Popular Images and the Politics of the Nation.* Berkeley: University of California Press.

Christie, N. 1986. "The Ideal Victim." In *From Crime Policy to Victim Policy*, ed. E. Fattah. New York: St. Martin's. 17–30.

Coe, C. et al., eds. 2011. *Everyday Ruptures: Children, Youth, and Migration in Global Perspective.* Nashville, Tenn.: Vanderbilt University Press.

Cohen, H. 1980. *Equal Rights for Children.* Totowa, N.J.: Littlefield, Adams.

Cohen, S. 1972. *Folk Devils and Moral Panics: The Creation of the Mods and Rockers.* New York: St. Martin's.

Coldrey, B. 1999. "A Place to Which Idle Vagrants May Be Sent: The First Phase of Child Migration During the Seventeenth and Eighteenth Centuries." *Children and Society* 13 (1): 32–47.

Coutin, S. 2000. *Legalizing Moves: Salvadoran Immigrants' Struggle for U.S. Residency.* Ann Arbor: University of Michigan Press.

———. 2005. "Being En Route." *American Anthropologist* 107 (2): 195–206.

———. 2011. "Legal Exclusion and Dislocated Subjectivities." In *The Contested Politics of Mobility: Borderzones and Irregularity,* ed. V. Squire. New York: Routledge. 169–83.

Cunningham, H. 1995. *Children and Childhood in Western Society Since 1500.* London: Longman.

Daly, K., and L. Maher. 1998. *Criminology at the Crossroads: Feminist Readings in Crime and Justice.* New York: Oxford University Press.

Das, V., and P. Reynolds. 2003. "The Child on the Wing: Children Negotiating the Everyday in the Geography of Violence." Paper, Workshop One, Rockefeller Foundation Resident Fellowships in Humanities and Study of Culture Program, Johns Hopkins University, November 15, 2003.

Davin, A. 1990. "When Is a Child Not a Child?" In *Politics of Everyday Life: Continuity and Change in Work and the Family,* ed. H. Corr and L. Jamieson. London: Macmillan. 37–61.

Davis, A. 1999. *The Prison Industrial Complex.* San Francisco: AK Press.

De Genova, N. 2002. "Migrant 'Illegality' and Deportability in Everyday Life." *Annual Review of Anthropology* 31: 419–47.

De Genova, N., and N. Peutz, 2010. *The Deportation Regime: Sovereignty, Space, and the Freedom of Movement.* Durham, N.C.: Duke University Press.

Demleitner, N. 2003. "How Much Do Western Democracies Value Family and Marriage? Immigration Law's Conflicted Answers." *Hofstra Law Review* 32: 273–311.

Dobson, J., and J. Stillwell 2000. "Changing Home, Changing School: Towards a Research Agenda on Child Migration." *Royal Geographical Society* 32 (4): 395–401.

Donato, K. M., D. Gabaccia, J. Holdaway, M. Manalansan, and P. R. Pessar. 2006. "A Glass Half Full? Gender in Migration Studies." *International Migration Review* 40 (1): 3–26.

Donzelot, J. 1979. *The Policing of Families.* New York: Pantheon.

Dow, M. 2004. *American Gulag: Inside U.S. Immigration Prisons.* Berkeley: University of California Press.

Duncan, J. 2002. Joint Testimony Before the Senate Subcommittee on Immigration. 107th Cong., 2nd sess. (testimony of Julianne Duncan, Ph.D), February 28.

Durkheim, E. 1982. *The Rules of the Sociological Method: Selected Texts on Sociology and Its Methods*. New York: Free Press.

Eckenrode, J., E. Rowe, M. Laird, and J. Brathwaite. 1995. "Mobility as a Mediator of the Effects of Child Maltreatment in Academic Performance." *Child Development* 66 (4): 1130–42.

Edelman, P. 2002. "American Government and Politics." In *A Century of Juvenile Justice*, ed. M. K. Rosenheim et al. Chicago: University of Chicago Press. 310–28.

Eloundou-Enyegue, P., and C. Stokes. 2002. "Will Economic Crisis in Africa Weaken Rural-Urban Ties? Insights from Child Fosterage Trends in Cameroon." *Rural Sociology* 67 (2): 278–98.

Ensor, M., and E. Gozdziak, eds. 2010. *Children and Migration: At the Crossroads of Resiliency and Vulnerability*. London: Palgrave Macmillan.

Farson, R. 1974. *Birthrights*. London: Collier Macmillan.

Fass, P. 2005. "Children in Global Migrations." *Journal of Social History* 38 (4): 937–53.

Ferguson, A. 2001. *Bad Boys: Public Schools in the Making of Black Masculinity*. Ann Arbor: University of Michigan Press.

Fineman, M. 1988. "Dominant Discourse, Professional Language, and Legal Change in Child Custody Decisionmaking." *Harvard Law Review* 101 (4): 727–74.

Finley, B. 2004a . "Death of a Deportee: Back in Guatemala, Teen Slain by Gang He Tried to Escape." *Denver Post*, April 5.

———. 2004b. "Deportee's Slaying Spurs Reform Push: Advocates Say Teen's Fear of Gang Unheeded." *Denver Post*, April 8.

Finn, J. 2001. "Text and Turbulence: Representing Adolescence as Pathology in the Human Services." *Childhood* 8 (2): 167–92.

Fisher, C., K. Hoagwood, C. Boyce, T. Duster, D. Frank, T. Grisso, and L. Zayas. 2002. "Research Ethics for Mental Health Science Involving Ethnic Minority Children and Youths." *American Psychologist* 57 (12): 1024–40.

Fix, M., W. Zimmerman, and J. Passel. 2001. *The Integration of Immigrant Families in the United States*. Washington, D.C.: Urban Institute.

Fonseca, C. 1986. "Orphanages, Foundlings, and Foster Mothers: The System of Child Circulation in a Brazilian Squatter Settlement." *Anthropological Quarterly* 59: 15–27.

Foster, G., and J. Williamson. 2000. "A Review of Current Literature on the Impact of HIV/AIDS on Children in Sub-Saharan Africa." *AIDS* 14 (3): S275–84.

Foucault, M. 1977. *Discipline and Punish: The Birth of the Prison*, Trans. Alan Sheridan New York: Vintage, 1979.

———. 1982. "The Subject and the Power." In *Michel Foucault: Beyond Structuralism and Hermeneutics*, ed. H. Dreyfus and P. Rabinow. Brighton: Harvester. 208–26.

———. 1997. "Security, Territory, and Population." In *Michel Foucault, Ethics: Subjectivity and Truth*, ed. P. Rabinow. New York: New Press. 67–71.

Fox, S. 1970. "Juvenile Justice Reform: A Historical Perspective." *Stanford Law Review* 22: 1187–1239.

Freire, P. 1970. *Pedagogy of the Oppressed*. Trans. M. Bergman Ramos. New York: Continuum.

Garcia, M. 2006. *Seeking Refuge: Central American Migration to Mexico, the United States, and Canada*. Berkeley: University of California Press.

Georgopoulos, A. 2005. "Beyond the Reach of Juvenile Justice: The Crisis of Unaccompanied Immigrant Children Detained by the United States." *Law and Inequality* 23: 117–33.

Gingrich, Newt. 2005. "Gangs: A Threat to National Security." *Fox News*, June 29.

Giroux, H. 1998. *Channel Surfing: Racism, the Media and the Destruction of Today's Youth*. New York: Griffin.

———. 2000. *Stealing Innocence: Youth, Corporate Power and the Politics of Culture*. New York: St. Martin's.

Glenn, E. 2002. *Unequal Freedom: How Race and Gender Shaped American Citizenship and Labor*. Cambridge, Mass.: Harvard University Press.

Godoy, A. 2006. *Popular Injustice: Violence, Community and Law in Latin America*. Stanford, Calif.: Stanford University Press.

Goffman, E. 1961. *Asylums: Essays on the Social Situation of Mental Patients and Other Inmates*. New York: Anchor Books.

Gonzalez, N. 1984. "Rethinking the Consanguineal Household and Matrifocality." *Ethnology* 23 (1): 1–12.

Goody, E. 1982. *Parenthood and Social Reproduction*. Cambridge: Cambridge University Press.

Gordon, C. 1991. "Governmental Rationality: An Introduction." In *The Foucault Effect: Studies in Governmentality*, ed. G. Burchell, C. Gordon, and P. Miller. Chicago: University of Chicago Press. 1–51.

Gorres, S. 2008. "The Garinagu and Their Indigenous-Black Identity: Improving Inter-Ethnic Relations by Increasing Awareness of the Complex Reality of Guatemala." Thesis, University of Kansas.

Greulich, W., and S. Pyle. 1959. *Radiographic Atlas of Skeletal Development of the Hand and Wrist*. Stanford, Calif.: Stanford University Press.

Griffiths, A. 2002. "Doing Ethnography: Living Law, Life Histories and Narratives from Botswana." In *Practicing Ethnography in Law: News Dialogues, Enduring Methods*, ed. J. Starr and M. Goodale, New York: Palgrave Macmillan. 160–84.

Grossberg, M. 1985. *Governing the Hearth: Law and the Family in Nineteenth-Century America*. Chapel Hill: University of North Carolina Press.

———. 2002. "Changing Conceptions of Child Welfare in the United States, 1820–1935." In *A Century of Juvenile Justice*, ed. M. Rosenheim et al. Chicago: University of Chicago Press. 3–41.

Haddal, C. 2007. *Unaccompanied Alien Children: Policies and Issues*. Washington, D.C.: Congressional Research Service.

Haefeli, E., and K. Sweeny. 2003. *Captors and Captives: The 1704 French and Indian Raid on Deerfield*. Amherst: University of Massachusetts Press.

Hagan, J. 1994. *Deciding to Be Legal: A Maya Community in Houston*. Philadelphia: Temple University Press.

Haggerty, K. 2004. "Ethics Creep: Governing Social Science Research in the Name of Ethics." *Qualitative Sociology* 27 (4): 391–414.

Hamm, D. 2004. "Special Immigrant Juvenile Status: A Life Jacket for Immigrant Youth." *Journal of Poverty Law and Policy* 38 (5–6): 323–28.

Hannerz, U. 1996. *Transnational Connections: Cultures, People, Places*. London: Routledge.

Hashim, I. 2006. *The Positives and Negatives of Children's Independent Migration*. Brighton: Development Research Centre on Migration, Globalisation and Poverty.

Hecht, T. 1998. *At Home in the Street: Street Children of Northeast Brazil*. Oxford: Oxford University Press.

Henderson, S., R. Taylor, and R. Thomason. 2002. "In Touch: Young People, Communication and Technologies." *Information, Communication and Society* 5 (4): 494–512.

Holt, J. 1974. *Escape from Childhood: The Needs and Rights of Children*. Boston: Dutton.

Honwana, A., and F. de Boeck, eds. 2005. *Makers and Breakers: Children and Youth in Postcolonial Africa*. Oxford: James Currey.

Horton, S. 2008. "Consuming Childhood: 'Lost' and 'Ideal' Childhoods as a Motivation for Migration." *Anthropological Quarterly* 81 (4): 925–43.

Hoy, D. C. 1986. "Power, repression, progress: Foucault, Lukes, and the Frankfurt School." In *Foucault: A Critical Reader*, ed. D. C. Hoy. Oxford: Blackwell Publishing: 123–48.

Inda, J. 2011. "Borderzones of Enforcement: Criminalization, Workplace Raids, and Migrant Counterconducts." In *The Contested Politics of Mobility: Borderzones and Irregularity*, ed. V. Squire. New York: Routledge. 74–90.

Isiugo-Abanihe, U. 1994. "Parenthood in Sub-Saharan Africa: Child Fostering and Its Relationship with Fertility." In *The Onset of Fertility Transition in Sub-Saharan Africa*, ed. T. Locoh and V. Hertrick. Brussels: Derouaux Ordina. 163–74.

James, A., and A. James, 2004. *Constructing Childhood: Theory, Policy and Social Practice*. London: Palgrave Macmillan.

Jans, M. 2004. "Children as Citizens: Towards a Contemporary Notion of Child Participation." *Childhood* 11 (1): 27–44.

Jenks, C. 1996. *Childhood*. London: Routledge.

Jensen, J., and M. Howard. 1998. "Youth Crime, Pubic Policy, and Practice in the Juvenile Justice System: Recent Trends and Needed Reforms." *Social Work* 43 (4): 324–34.

Johnson, K. 1997. "'Aliens' and the U.S. Immigration Laws: The Social and Legal Construction of Nonpersons." *University of Miami Inter-American Law Review* 28: 263–92.

Junck, A. 2012. "Special Immigrant Juvenile Status: Relief for Neglected, Abused, and Abandoned Undocumented Children." *Juvenile and Family Court Journal* 63 (1): 48–62.

Kennedy, J. 1964. *A Nation of Immigrants*. London: Hamish Hamilton.

King, S. 2010. "U.S. Immigration Law and the Traditional Nuclear Conception of Family: Toward a Functional Definition of Family That Protects Children's Fundamental Human Rights." *Columbia Human Rights Law Review* 41 (2): 509–67.

Kinoshita, S., and K. Brady. 2005. *Special Immigrant Juvenile Status for Children Under Juvenile Court Jurisdiction*. San Francisco: Immigrant Legal Resource Center.

Lacey, M. 2011. "Birthright Citizenship Looms as Next Immigration Battle." *New York Times*, January 4.

Leinaweaver, J. 2007. "Choosing to Move: Child Agency on Peru's Margins." *Childhood* 14 (3): 375–92.

———. 2008. *The Circulation of Children: Kinship, Adoption, and Morality in Andean Peru*. Durham, N.C.: Duke University Press.

Leiter, V., J. McDonald, and H. Jacobson. 2006. "Challenges to Children's Independent Citizenship: Immigration, Family and the State." *Childhood* 13 (1): 11–27.

Levine, C., R. Faden, C. Grady, D. Hammerschmidt, L. Eckenwiler, and J. Sugarman. 2004. "The Limitations of 'Vulnerability' as a Protection for Human Research Participants." *American Journal of Bioethics* 4 (3): 44–49.

Liebmann, T. 2006. "Family Court and the Unique Needs of Children and Families Who Lack Immigration Status." *Columbia Journal of Law and Social Problems* 40 (4): 583–604.

Lloyd, A. 2006. "Regulating Consent: Protecting Undocumented Immigrant Children from Their (Evil) Step-Uncle Sam, or How to Ameliorate the Impact of the 1997 Amendments to the SIJ Law." *Boston University Public Interest Law Journal* 15: 237–61.

Madriz, E. 1997. *Nothing Happens to Good Girls: Fear of Crime in Women's Lives*. Berkeley: University of California Press.

Maira, S. 2009. *Missing: Youth, Citizenship, and Empire After 9/11*. Durham, N.C.: Duke University Press.

Males, M. 1999. *Framing Youth: 10 Myths About the Next Generation*. Monroe, Maine: Common Courage Press.

Maples, W. R. 1978. "An Improved Technique Using Dental Histology for Estimation of Adult Age." *Journal of Forensic Science* 23: 764–70.

Marlan, T. 2006. *Racing the Calendar: America's Rule That's Supposed to Save Abused Immigrant Children*. Washington, D.C.: Alicia Patterson Foundation.

Mason, M. 1994. *From Father's Property to Children's Rights: A History of Child Custody*. New York: Columbia University Press.

Massey, D., J. Arango, G. Hugo, A. Kouaouci, A. Pellegrino, and J. E. Taylor. 1993. "Theories of International Migration: A Review and Appraisal." *Population and Development Review* 19 (3): 431–66.

McKendrick, J. 2001. "Coming of Age: Rethinking the Role of Children in Population Studies." *International Journal of Population Geography* 7: 461–72.

Medina, J. 2011. "Arriving as Pregnant Tourists, Leaving with American Babies." *New York Times*, March 28.

Milanich, N. 2004. "The Casa de Huerfanos and Child Circulation in Late-Nineteenth-Century Chile." *Journal of Social History* 38 (2): 311–40.

Minow, M. 1995. "Children's Rights: Where We've Been, and Where We're Going." *Temple Law Review* 68: 1573–84.

Mitchell, K., and W. C. Parker. 2008. "I Pledge Allegiance to . . . Flexible Citizenship and Shifting Scales of Belonging." *Teachers College Record* 110 (4): 775–804.

Moreno, J. 2005. "A Desperate Quest: Latin American Towns Lose Generations of Teens; Passage to the U.S. Is Perilous but Necessary for Boys to Help Their Impoverished Families." *Houston Chronicle*, March 20.

Morton, J. 2011. *Exercising Prosecutorial Discretion Consistent with the Civil Immigration Enforcement Priorities of the Agency for the Apprehension, Detention and Removal of Aliens.* Washington, D.C.: Department of Homeland Security, June 17.

Murray, T. 1996. *The Worth of a Child.* Berkeley: University of California Press.

Nann, R. 1982. *Uprooting and Surviving.* Dordrecht: Reidel.

Neale, B. 2002. "Dialogues with Children: Children, Divorce and Citizenship." *Childhood* 9 (4): 455–75.

Nessel, L. 2005. "Forced to Choose: Torture, Family Reunification, and United States Immigration Policy." *Temple Law Review* (78): 897–948.

———. 2008. "Families at Risk: How Errant Enforcement and Restrictionist Integration Policies Threaten the Immigrant Family in the European Union and the United States." *Hofstra Law Review* 36: 1271–1302.

Ngai, M. 2003. "The Strange Career of the Illegal Alien: Immigration Restriction and Deportation Policy in the United States, 1921–1965." *Law and History Review* 21: 69–108.

———. 2004. *Impossible Subjects: Illegal Aliens and the Making of Modern America.* Princeton, N.J.: Princeton University Press.

———. 2010. "'A Nation of Immigrants': The Cold War and Civil Rights Origins of Illegal Immigration." Occasional Paper 38, School of Social Sciences, Institute for Advanced Study, Princeton, N.J.

Nogosek, K. 2000. "It Takes a World to Raise a Child: A Legal and Public Policy Analysis of American Asylum Legal Standards and Their Impact on Unaccompanied Minor Asylees." *Hamline Law Review* 24: 1–23.

Notermans, C. 2004. "Fosterage and the Politics of Marriage and Kinship in East Cameroon." In *Cross-Cultural Approaches to Adoption,* ed. F. Bowie. London: Routledge. 48–63.

Nugent, C. 2005. "Protecting Unaccompanied and Immigrant Children in the United States." *Human Rights Magazine*, Winter.

OIG (Office of the Inspector General). 2001a. *Unaccompanied Juveniles in INS Custody*. Report I-2001-009. Washington, D.C.

———. 2001b. *Juvenile Repatriation Practices at Border Patrol Sectors on the Southern Border*. Report I-2001-010. Washington, D.C., September.

———. 2008. *Division of Unaccompanied Children's Services: Efforts to Serve Them*. Report OEI-07-06-00290. Washington, D.C.

Olwig, K. 1999. "Narratives of the Children Left Behind: Home and Identity in Globalised Caribbean Families." *Journal of Ethnic and Migration Studies* 25 (2): 267–84.

O'Neil, J. 1997. "Is the Child a Political Subject?" *Childhood* 4 (2): 241–50.

Ong, A. 1999. *Flexible Citizenship: The Cultural Logics of Transnationality*. Durham, N.C.: Duke University Press.

Orellana, M., B. Thorne, A. Chee, and W. Lam. 2001. "Transnational Childhoods: The Participation of Children in Processes of Family Migration." *Social Problems* 48 (4): 572–91.

ORR (Office of Refugee Resettlement). "Unaccompanied Children's Services." http://www.acf.hhs.gov/programs/orr/programs/unaccompanied_alien_children.htm.

Ortner, S. 1984. "Theory in Anthropology Since the Sixties." *Comparative Studies in Society and History* 26 (1): 126–66.

O'Toole, M. 2011. "Analysis: Obama Deportations Raise Immigration Policy Questions." *Reuters*, September 20.

Panter-Brick, C. 2002. "Street Children, Human Rights, and Public Health." *Annual Review of Anthropology* 31: 147–71.

Parreñas, R. 2001. *Servants of Globalization: Women, Migration and Domestic Work*. Stanford, Calif.: Stanford University Press.

Passel, J., and D. Cohn. 2009. *A Portrait of Unauthorized Immigrants in the U.S.* Washington, D.C.: Pew Hispanic Center.

Patrick, M., E. Sheets, and E. Trickel. 1990. *We Are Part of History: The Story of Orphan Trains*. Virginia Beach: Donning.

Pearson, G. 1985. *Hooligan: A History of Respectable Fears*. London: Macmillan.

Platt, A. 1969. *The Child Savers: The Invention of Delinquency*. Chicago: University of Chicago.

Punch, S. 2002. "Research with Children: The Same or Different from Research with Adults?" *Childhood* 9 (3): 321–41.

Ressler, E., N. Boothby, and D. Steinbock. 1988. *Unaccompanied Children: Care and Protection in Wars, Natural Disasters and Refugee Movements*. New York: Oxford University Press.

Rodriguez, C. 1997. *Latin Looks: Images of Latinas and Latinos in the U.S. Media*. Boulder, Colo.: Westview Press.

Rosas, G. 2006. "The Thickening Borderlands Diffused Exceptionality and 'Immigrant' Social Struggles During the 'War on Terror.'" *Cultural Dynamics* 18 (3): 335–49.

Rose, N. 1989. *Governing the Soul: The Shaping of the Private Self.* London: Routledge.

Rosen, D. 2008. "Children's Rights and the International Community." *Anthropology News* 49 (4) (April): 5–6.

Rossi, P. 1980. *Why Families Move.* London: Sage.

Rumbaut, R. 1994. "The Crucible Within: Ethnic Identity, Self-Esteem, and Segmented Assimilation Among Children of Immigrants." *International Migration Review* 28: 748–94.

Sampson, R. 1988. "Local Friendship Ties and Community Attachment in Mass Society: A Multilevel Systematic Model." *American Sociological Review* 53: 766–79.

Sassen, S. 1999. *Guests and Aliens.* New York: New Press.

Schlosser, E. 1998. "The Prison-Industrial Complex." *Atlantic Monthly*, December.

Schneider, D. 1968. *American Kinship: A Cultural Account.* Englewood Cliffs, N.J.: Prentice Hall.

Schultz, J. 1973. "The Cycle of Juvenile Court History." *Crime and Delinquency* 19: 457–76.

Schwartzman, H. 2001. *Children and Anthropology: Perspectives in the 21st Century.* Westport, Conn.: Bergin and Garvey.

Sedlak, A. and D. Broadhurst, 1996. *Third national incidence study of child abuse and neglect: Final report.* US Department of Health and Human Services, Administration for Children and Families, Administration on Children, Youth and Families, National Center on Child Abuse and Neglect.

Seugling, C. 2005. "Toward a Comprehensive Response to the Transnational Migration of Unaccompanied Minors in the United States." *Vanderbilt Journal of Transnational Law* 37: 861–95.

Shook, J. 2005. "Contesting Childhood in the U.S. Justice System: The Transfer of Juveniles to Adult Criminal Court." *Childhood* 12 (4): 461–78.

Simon, J. 1997. "Governing Through Crime." In *The Crime Conundrum: Essays on Criminal Justice*, ed. L. M. Friedman and G. Fisher. Boulder, Colo.: Westview Press. 171–89.

Somers, A., P. Herrera, and L. Rodriguez. 2010. "Constructions of Childhood and Unaccompanied Children in the Immigration System in the United States." *University of California Davis Journal of Juvenile Law and Policy* 14 (2): 311–80.

South, S., and K. Crowder. 1997. "Escaping Distressed Neighborhoods: Individual, Community, and Metropolitan Influences." *American Journal of Sociology* 102: 1040–84.

Spencer, S., and A. Becker. 2010. "ICE Officials Set Quotas to Deport More Illegal Immigrants." *Washington Post*, March 27.

Stephens, S. 1995. *Children and the Politics of Culture.* Princeton, N.J.: Princeton University Press.

Sutton, H. 1988. *Stubborn Children: Controlling Delinquency in the United States, 1640–1981.* Berkeley: University of California Press.

Terrio, S. 2004. "Migration, Displacement, and Violence: Prosecuting Romanian Street Children at the Paris Palace of Justice." *International Migration* 42 (5): 5–31.

———. 2008. "New Barbarians at the Gates of Paris? Prosecuting Undocumented Minors at the Juvenile Court." *Anthropological Quarterly* 81 (4): 873–901.

———. 2009. *Judging Mohammed: Juvenile Delinquency, Immigration and Exclusion at the Paris Palace of Justice.* Stanford, Calif.: Stanford University Press.

Thompson, G. 2003. "Crossing with Strangers: Children at the Border; Littlest Immigrants, Left in the Hands of Smugglers." *New York Times,* November 3.

Thronson, D. 2002. "Kids Will Be Kids? Reconsidering Conceptions of Children's Rights Underlying Immigration Law." *Ohio State Law Journal* 63: 979–1016.

———. 2005. "Of Borders and Best Interests: Examining the Experiences of Undocumented Immigrants in U.S. Family Courts." *Texas Hispanic Journal of Law and Policy* 11: 45–73.

———. 2006. "You Can't Get Here from Here: Toward a More Child-Centered Immigration Law." *Virginia Journal of Social Policy and Law* 14: 58–86.

Tilton, J. 2010. *Dangerous or Endangered? Race and the Politics of Youth in Urban America.* New York: New York University Press.

Tully, C. 2002. "Youth in Motion: Communicative and Mobile; A Commentary from the Perspective of Youth Sociology." *Young* 10 (2): 19–43.

Turner, V. 1967. *The Forest of Symbols.* Ithaca, N.Y.: Cornell University Press.

Turnley, J., and J. Smrcka. 2002. *Terrorist Organization and Criminal Street Gangs: An Argument for an Analogy.* Washington, D.C.: Advanced Concepts Groups.

Tyrrell, N. 2011. "Children's Agency in Family Migration Decision Making in Britain." In *Everyday Ruptures: Children, Youth, and Migration in Global Perspective,* ed. C. Coe et al. Nashville: Vanderbilt University Press. 23–38.

Uehling, G. 2008. "The International Smuggling of Children: Coyotes, Snakeheads and the Politics of Compassion." *Anthropological Quarterly* 81 (4): 833–71.

U.S. Department of Homeland Security. 2008. *One Team, One Mission, Securing Our Homeland: U.S. Department of Homeland Security Strategic Plan—Fiscal Years 2008–2013.* Washington, D.C., March 20.

U.S. Immigration and Customs Enforcement. 2003. *ENDGAME: Office of Detention and Removal Strategic Plan, 2003–2012.* Washington, D.C.: Department of Homeland Security.

——— 2008. "ICE Multifaceted Strategy Leads to Record Enforcement Results: Removals, Criminal Arrests, and Worksite Investigations Soared in Fiscal Year 2008." Press release. Washington, D.C., October 23.

Verhoef, H. 2005. "A Child Has Many Mothers: Views of Child Fostering in Northwestern Cameroon." *Childhood* 2 (3): 369–90.

Waldram, J. 2009. "Challenges of Prison Ethnography." *Anthropology News* 50 (1): 4–5.

Walters, W. 2002. "Deportation, Expulsion, and the International Police of Aliens."
   Citizenship Studies 6 (3): 256–92.
Washington Office on Latin America. 2006. *Youth Gangs in Central America.* Wash-
   ington, D.C.: Washington Office on Latin America.
Women's Commission for Refugee Women and Children. 2002. *Prison Guard or
   Parent? INS Treatment of Unaccompanied Refugee Children.* New York: Women's
   Commission.
Women's Refugee Commission with Orrick Herrington and Sutcliffe, LLP. 2009. *Half-
   way Home: Unaccompanied Children in Immigration Custody.* New York: Wom-
   en's Refugee Commission.
Woodhouse, B. 1992. "'Who Owns the Child?': Meyer and Pierce and the Child as
   Property." *William and Mary Law Review* 33 (4): 995–1122.
Young, L. 2004. "Journeys to the Street: The Complex Migration Geographies of Ugan-
   dan Street Children." *Geoforum* 35 (4): 471–88.
Zelizer, V. 1985. *Pricing the Priceless Child: The Changing Social Value of Children.*
   New York: Basic Books.

INDEX

ACKNOWLEDGMENTS

This book would not have come to fruition without the guidance, support, and enthusiastic encouragement of a number of people. First and foremost, I would like to thank my colleagues and the faculty in the Department of Anthropology at Johns Hopkins University for their intellectual stimulation and extraordinary institutional support. I extend special gratitude to Pamela Reynolds, who, from across the Atlantic, provided insight, guidance, and mentorship. I am indebted to Debbie Poole, Veena Das, Lingxin Hao, and Margaret Keck for their valuable criticisms and suggestions in this evolving project. My deepest appreciation extends to Jane Guyer, Juan Obarrio, and Naveeda Khan for their enthusiasm and support in the initial stages of research. My colleagues Samantha Gottlieb and Abigail Baim-Lance provided positive encouragement and critical engagement, amid their busy family schedules and research agendas; for this, I am so grateful.

Initial stages of research would not have been possible without the support of The Program in Latin American Studies and the Department of Anthropology at Johns Hopkins University, which funded research in Maryland (2006), El Salvador (Summer 2007), and the Texas-Mexico border (Spring to Summer 2007). The Wenner Gren Foundation (2008) and the National Science Foundation Law and Social Science Program (2008–2009) generously supported my research conducted in the Midwest and in Washington, D.C.

This book benefited significantly from comments on Chapters 3, 4, and 5 from participants and co-panelists at the American Anthropological Association (AAA) Childhood and Youth Interest Group meeting in 2011; the AAA 2008 and 2009 Annual Meetings; the Newberry Library Seminar in Latino and Borderland Studies; the Working Group on Childhood and Migration; the Johns Hopkins University Department of Anthropology 2008 Spring Seminar series; and the Johns Hopkins University Program in Latin American Studies Spring 2008 Conference. In particular, I wish to thank Rachel Reynolds and an anonymous reviewer for their comments and critiques on earlier drafts of Chapter 2. Excerpts from Chapter 4 previously appeared in *Transnational Migration, Gender and Rights* from Emerald Press (2012). Selections from Chapter 2 previously appeared in the *Children's Legal Rights Journal* (Spring 2013). I am grateful for their editorial comments and suggestions on the original material and their permission to reprint iterations of the articles here.

My appreciation also to the anonymous reviewers of this manuscript, whose critical and encouraging comments strengthened the structure and clarity of my arguments. Special thanks to Allison Nanni, Jay Heidbrink, Michele Statz, Ragnhild Sollund, Brad Olson, Diane Nititham-Tunney, and Steve Thompson. The writing benefited from the keen eyes of Richard Gottlieb, Hadley Leach, and Alison Anderson. I extend my gratitude to Bert Lockwood, Jr., for his enthusiasm for my work and for including this book in an impressive collection of scholars in the Pennsylvania Studies in Human Rights. Peter Agree of the University of Pennsylvania Press—a patient, responsive, and wise editor.

I am deeply indebted all those who took the time to speak with me and to welcome an unknown researcher into their work and their family lives. I am profoundly thankful for their willingness to share often-painful details of their personal lives, journeys, and struggles with me. To the staff of the federal facilities who graciously hosted me and engaged in lengthy interviews and conversations: thank you. This research would not have been possible with the permission and support of Maureen Dunn, Director of the Division of Children's Services of the Office of Refugee Resettlement (ORR) and the legal guardian of all unaccompanied children in ORR custody. Maria Woltjen, Director of the Young Center for Immigrant Children's Rights, was instrumental in facilitating my access to a rich network of advocates and stakeholders involved in the care and custody of unaccompanied children. All opinion and analysis expressed in this book are exclusively my own, as are the errors.

While conducting research and writing this book, I raised three phenomenal children, whose vigor and enthusiasm for life kept me both energized and focused. I would not have been able to complete the project without the unquestioning flexibility of my mother- and father-in-law, who through tragedy graciously and unconditionally cared for our family. I am always grateful to my parents who, from an early age, taught me to question the human condition. And, to Walter, whose patience, support and humor made all things bearable and enjoyable.